THE LOGIC OF SECURITIES LAW

The book opens with a simple introduction to financial markets; it understands the action and the players of Wall Street by comparing them to the action and the players of Main Street. First, the book explores the definition of a security by its function, the departure from the "buyer beware" environment of corporate law, and the entrance into the "seller disclose" environment of securities law. Second, it shows that the cost of disclosure rules is justified by their capacity to combat irrationalities, fads, and panics. The third part explains how the structure of class actions is designed to improve deterrence. Next it explores the economic harm from insider trading and how the law fights it. In sum, see how all these parts of securities law serve the virtuous cycle from liquidity to accurate prices and more trading and how the Great Recession showed that our securities regulation reacted mostly adequately to the crisis.

Professor Georgakopoulos is the H.R. Woodard Professor of Law at the Robert H. McKinney School of Law, Indiana University. He has researched and published extensively on securities law and related fields. His previous publications include *Principles and Methods of Law and Economics* and a coauthored five-volume treatise *Blumberg on Corporate Groups*.

The Logic of Securities Law

NICHOLAS L. GEORGAKOPOULOS
Indiana University

CAMBRIDGE
UNIVERSITY PRESS

CAMBRIDGE
UNIVERSITY PRESS

University Printing House, Cambridge CB2 8BS, United Kingdom

One Liberty Plaza, 20th Floor, New York, NY 10006, USA

477 Williamstown Road, Port Melbourne, VIC 3207, Australia

4843/24, 2nd Floor, Ansari Road, Daryaganj, Delhi – 110002, India

79 Anson Road, #06–04/06, Singapore 079906

Cambridge University Press is part of the University of Cambridge.

It furthers the University's mission by disseminating knowledge in the pursuit of education, learning, and research at the highest international levels of excellence.

www.cambridge.org
Information on this title: www.cambridge.org/9781107158504
10.1017/9781316665671

First published 2017

A catalogue record for this publication is available from the British Library.

Library of Congress Cataloging-in-Publication Data
Names: Georgakopoulos, Nicholas Leonidas, author.
Title: The logic of securities law / Nicholas Georgakopoulos.
Description: Cambridge [UK] ; New York : Cambridge University Press, 2017. | Includes bibliographical references and index.
Identifiers: LCCN 2017011614 | ISBN 9781107158504 (hardback)
Subjects: LCSH: Securities – United States. | Corporations – Finance – Law and legislation – United States. | Disclosure of information – Law and legislation – United States. | Class actions (Civil procedure) – United States. | Securities fraud – United States. | Insider trading in securities – Law and legislation – United States. | BISAC: LAW / Banking.
Classification: LCC KF1439 .G46 2017 | DDC 346.73/0666–dc23
LC record available at https://lccn.loc.gov/2017011614

ISBN 978-1-107-15850-4 Hardback

To Lee and Dimitri.

Contents

Figures and Tables

Figures

Tables

Foreword

Nicholas L. Georgakopoulos is much more than just a professor of law at Indiana University. He is an economist and an expert on finance and the financial markets, and he has written extensively on the application of economics to a variety of fields of law not limited to the laws regulating the financial markets. But this has been the primary focus of his current research and has resulted in this important, as well as thoroughly up-to-date, book on the regulation of securities trading.

Naturally, there is much discussion in this book of the crash of 2008 and its aftermath – the aftershocks continue to be felt. But the focus is broader. Indeed, Professor Georgakopoulos's focus is on the perennial controversies in the securities field, such as insider trading; the breadth of the book's scope makes the book a treatise on the law and economics of securities markets.

Insider trading had long been deplored and even punished when the pioneer "law and economics" law professor Henry Manne began to defend it in the 1960s. His defense did not result in a change in the law, but it started a lively debate to which Professor Georgakopoulos in this book (and in a precursor article that the Securities and Exchange Commission used to persuade the Supreme Court to maintain the prohibition) makes the important contribution of demonstrating that insider trading is indeed a harmful practice. "Insider trading" means trading on information concealed from the public and therefore unavailable to securities traders who are among (or are fed confidential information from) the insiders of firms. Knowing that trading on inside information is going on discourages securities trading by investors lacking such information by subjecting them to competition from traders who have superior knowledge of forthcoming changes in the values of securities. But this is a crude summary of the nuanced analysis in this book; Professor Georgakopoulos shows that not all insider trading harms the securities markets.

Interestingly, this book does not treat insider trading as a practice remote from other practices that are harmful to efficient markets, such as concealment of information from prospective traders; the book endorses rules requiring disclosure by participants in the securities market of information necessary for efficient trading and likewise rules punishing fraud, which is widespread in investment markets, as it is elsewhere. Professor Georgakopoulos rejects what he calls the "free-market objection to regulation. In the eyes of the inflexible free-market proponent, private parties would perfectly foresee the ills that regulation seeks to prevent and would make the least costly arrangements to avoid those ills. The inflexibility and the distorted incentives that regulation creates would never arise." As he shows, this is not true.

What really unifies this book is that, as Professor Georgakopoulos shows, ultimately securities regulation is all and only about information – about allaying, notably, "traders' fear of manipulated prices." Many securities investors, left to their own devices, as it were, would make investment decisions without obtaining readily available information to guide those decisions; many would seek no information at all, but trade on pure hunch or even pure gamble. Others would yield to irrational instinct to buy when securities prices are rising and sell when they are falling, even though prices often rise bubble-like before a crash (making it risky to buy when prices are rising, especially when they are rising fast and steep) and fall to bargain levels (making purchases likely to produce significant gains). Whether the issue is disclosure rules, fraud, insider trading, or "irrational exuberance" (buying in an expanding bubble), the focus of regulation remains, as it should, on maximizing the amount of truthful information in securities trading. As Professor Georgakopoulos points out, "Misrepresentations about financial goods tend to influence price more, last longer, attract wider (potentially global) attention, be more frequent, and be more costly to uncover than misrepresentations about real goods" (with, I would add, some notable exceptions, such as drugs).

The financial crisis centrally involved securities, such as the mortgage-backed securities that, when the real estate market plummeted, wreaked such havoc. And so the final section of this book "looks for anticrisis features in the law of securities regulation." Professor Georgakopoulos does not find many and is not at all enamored of Dodd-Frank and other measures to prevent a similar financial collapse in the future. He sees the crisis of 2008 as primarily a psychological phenomenon, what I would call an example of the tendency to keep buying as prices rise, and he sees the government as complicit in the crisis largely because of its sharing the market's sentiments and engaging in procyclic regulation that is too lax during the bubble (the euphoria period) and too strict after the crisis. He perhaps might have said more about what appears to have been the exceedingly lax regulation of the Wall Street securities firms (and not only Lehman Brothers) by the Securities and Exchange Commission, but he makes an intriguing proposal for moving toward countercyclic regulation. Throughout the book, his discussion of the crisis is lucid, interesting, and informative.

Richard A. Posner

Acknowledgments

This book would have been impossible without the encouragement and guidance of Reinier Kraakman not only during my doctoral dissertation, a quarter-century ago, but also in reaction to this project. Special thanks go to Richard Posner for his comments and the generous Foreword. The help of my editor at Cambridge University Press, John Berger, was priceless. Parts of this book have appeared as articles, one in a peer-edited journal and the rest in student-edited journals, and the referees of the former and the student editors of the latter, despite their namelessness, deserve thanks, as do my colleagues who commented on those drafts and their conference presentations. I also thank Ina Melengoglou, Claudia Breger, Dan Cole, Amitai Aviram, Don Langevoort, and Eric Gerding.

The text received enormous help from Susan D. DeMaine of the Indiana University R. H. McKinney School of Law Library, who patiently suffered through several obscure iterations. The graphics had the benefit of much feedback from Ina Melengoglou.

This book is a rewriting of a series of my articles: Introduction and Part V of *Financial Armageddon Routs Law Again*, 14 U.C. DAVIS BUS. L.J. 1–49 (2013); Part I of *The Ralston-Landreth-Gustavson Harmony: A Security!*, 41 CAP. L. REV. 553–602 (2013); Part II of *Why Should Disclosure Rules Subsidize Informed Traders?*, 16 INT. REV. L. & ECON. 417–31 (1996); Part III of *Frauds, Markets, and Fraud-on-the-Market: The Tortured Transition of Justifiable Reliance from Common Law Deceit to Securities Fraud*, 49 MIAMI L.REV. 671–730 (1995); and Part IV of *Insider Trading as a Transactional Cost: A Market Microstructure Justification and Optimization of Insider Trading Regulation*, 26 CONN. L. REV. 1–51 (1993).

1

Introduction

Real Markets and Financial Markets

This book deals with the regulation of securities markets, but some readers may have little understanding of these markets. This chapter offers a quick (and optional) introduction to the world of financial markets with a focus on stock markets. The first section looks at some striking differences between real and financial markets and introduces the concept of the bid-ask spread, which is important for understanding securities pricing. The second section introduces stock markets, their basic structure, their cast of characters, and their treatment by the media. Finally, the third section discusses the interdependence between the real sector of the economy and the financial sector.

A. DIFFERENCES BETWEEN FINANCIAL AND REAL MARKETS

Paradigmatic markets for real goods are farmers' markets, retail malls, grocery stores, and retail neighborhoods. Real markets focus on satisfying consumers' desires by matching goods with individuals. Financial markets are about money rather than goods. Investors or savers place their money in investments that they hope will safely store it for some duration and produce interest (in the case of loans) or dividends and price appreciation (in the case of stocks and the aggregation of stocks into *mutual funds* or *variable life insurance* and *annuities*).[1] Investors often move their money between investments and then liquidate when they need to finance major expenditures or retirement. Financial intermediaries such as banks and brokerage houses help move the money from the investors to its users, usually the business firms that borrow or issue securities, and between investments.

[1] Mutual funds aggregate the investments of many investors and hold a portfolio of securities that is professionally managed. Life insurance and annuities are investments that also have a mild insurance function. They are investments due to the lack of uncertainty about the insured event: all those whose life is insured will die. Their mild insurance function cancels the timing of that event for each insured. Life and annuity that are variable adjust the payout to the policyholders depending on the performance of stock market indices or mutual funds. Conceptually, one can envision variable life insurance as having the insurance company place a fraction of the insured's funds in those investments and, upon the insured event, having the company pay the beneficiaries from the proceeds of their sale.

Significant distinctions between financial and real markets appear in the variety of goods and markets, the centrality of seller identity, the ratio of sellers to buyers, and the way dealers set their prices: the *bid-ask spread*. Let us consider each of these in turn.

i. Variety of Goods and Markets

In markets for real goods, the variety of types of goods is so large as to be nearly infinite. Department stores, for example, offer an encyclopedic selection of goods, from furniture to clothes, fragrances, and appliances. Grocery stores offer wines, meats, flowers, stationery, plus health and pharmacy products. Furthermore, sellers are legion. Indeed, in the age of eBay and Craigslist, anyone can sell almost anything. Markets for real goods are virtually everywhere, as stores in urban neighborhoods and small rural villages demonstrate.

An unusual nonfinancial asset, real estate, is worth a digression because it has played a central role in at least two crises, the Savings and Loan (S&L) crisis of the early 1990s and the much graver 2008 crisis – and probably also the Great Depression and several others (crises are the topic of Chapter 21). Real estate is a real good because its users put it to nonfinancial use. Homeowners, for example, use it for housing, businesses for facilities, and farmers to make agricultural products. Real estate, however, is unusual among real goods because land tends not to deteriorate with time. Therefore, it has investment value,[2] and lenders trust it to an unusual degree as collateral. No lender would make a 15-year car loan, but 15-year home loans are routine. Moreover, the social importance of housing has produced significant government involvement in home financing. This involvement in the United States mostly facilitates the bundling of many mortgage loans into funds or pools. Investors or lenders can buy fractions of these funds and have much lower risk than they would if they bought or made loans to individual homeowners. This is the *securitization* of mortgage loans.[3]

In stark contrast to the virtually infinite types of real goods and the ubiquity of their markets, financial goods tend to be traded in few markets and have few categories or types. It is important to realize that this is a difference in the number of the types of goods rather than of the goods themselves. Consider the relatively small ratio of types of cars to types of real goods, which must be in the hundreds (e.g., try to count each of eBay's categories of goods). Compare that to the much larger ratio of the number of stocks of different businesses, which number several thousands, to types of financial goods, which are only a handful. The difference in those ratios is striking and influences the introduction to finance. Learning what corporate stock is, for

[2] This does not make real estate into a financial good because its real use is significant. Many durable goods have a financial component. Car buyers, for example, may take into account which cars retain more value.

[3] See Adam J. Levitin & Tara Twomey, *Mortgage Servicing*, 28 YALE J. ON REG. 1–90, 13 (2011).

example, happens once and differs from learning about a specific corporation's stock, the same way that learning what a car is differs from learning the features of a specific car. Furthermore, rarely does learning the features of a type or genus of a real good – such as a car – pose difficulties. In contrast, learning both the basic types of financial goods – what a stock is and what a bond is, for example – and the features of specific types – individual stocks or bonds – tends not to be intuitive. When learning about a field of real goods, the participants tend to already have a basic understanding of those goods. For example, someone learning about car racing likely already knows what a car is. This may not be true in finance. Newcomers may lack even a basic understanding of the artificial and recent universe of finance.[4]

Before the introduction of means for individuals to invest as members of a group, financial markets traded only two types of securities, *stocks* and *bonds* – namely, fractions of business ownership and slices of loans to businesses, governments, and municipalities. In the United States during the late nineteenth and early twentieth centuries,[5] financial intermediaries gradually introduced more complex instruments, starting with aggregations of stocks or bonds into closed-end funds, (open-ended) mutual funds, or exchange-traded funds,[6] eventually reaching *derivatives*: contractual arrangements the value of which depends on (i.e., derives from) one or more *underlying*, more basic goods such as stocks or bonds.[7] Moreover, financial markets are centralized and therefore few in number. Typically, each developed country has a single major stock market. The United States, with both the New York Stock Exchange (NYSE) and the NASDAQ Stock Market (NASDAQ), is an exception. A further round of centralization has occurred with the merger of stock exchanges into even larger groups of exchanges.

4 The problem of the lack of knowledge in financial markets is not limited to unsophisticated investors. Buyers of real products know the use they derive from them because the buyers tend to use the products, read the books, or sit on the chairs that they buy. This has the stabilizing effect of limiting price increases and drops. By contrast, buyers of financial products tend merely to seek reselling them. Thus false beliefs about financial goods can be self-perpetuating and destabilizing, underscoring the need for information, as discussed at length in Chapters 9 to 11.

5 Edwin J. Perkins, Wall Street to Main Street: Charles Merrill and Middle-Class Investors 224–27 (Cambridge University Press, 1999); Jerry W. Markham, A Financial History of the United States 137–40 (M.E. Sharpe, 2002). See also A Brief History of the Mutual Fund, Investopedia, available at www.investopedia.com/articles/mutualfund/05/mfhistory.asp (accessed February 15, 2017).

6 Closed-end funds trade like stocks: they have a fixed number of outstanding shares that investors trade as a stock. Open-ended mutual funds have the flexibility to accept new capital and to redeem investors' shares, which they do at the end of each trading day. Exchange-traded funds trade throughout the day, with the issuer likely buying/redeeming and selling/issuing shares.

7 Some derivatives are options, financial futures, and swaps; understanding them is not necessary here. Options are rights to buy or sell the underlying good. Financial futures are contracts that simulate purchases or sales of the underlying good, such as a stock, index, or interest rate, at the value it will have at a future time. Swaps are the exchange between the parties of, usually a stream of, obligations denominated in different underlying goods.

The laws regulating these markets also specialize. Banking law, insurance law, and securities law are governed by separate statutes and, at least in the United States, different regulators.[8] Because this book focuses on securities law, we can leave behind financial goods subject to banking and insurance regulation.[9] Within securities law, the financing of businesses is the central activity that ties the financial system to the real economy; therefore, the focus is on stocks and bonds, ignoring funds and derivatives.

ii. Seller Identity and Credit

In nonfinancial goods, the identity of the seller or producer often does not matter. The irrelevance of the seller's identity is so common that it is part of contract law doctrine that, for example, states that a promisee may not refuse performance by someone other than the promisor.[10] Parties often contract for goods defined in generic terms – T-shirts or tomatoes, for example (granted, of a specific quality). For many real goods, the buyer has no interest in the identity or personal attributes of the seller or the producer. The appeal of a T-shirt or a tomato lies mostly in its features rather than its maker. Obviously, exceptions exist. Provenance is important in the art market or in high-end fashion, but features that are unrelated to provenance still dominate. Most consumers would not willingly buy a product that they did not enjoy simply because of its impressive provenance. Granted, the identity of the manufacturer is also important for some durable goods, especially complex ones like cars or appliances, but often not for less complex ones. Most buyers of ping-pong tables, countertops, and other simple durable goods place little importance on provenance.

By contrast, in financial goods, the identity and creditworthiness of the issuer are vital to the product's appeal. Ownership stakes (stocks) in well-run corporations are very different from stocks of companies with dubious prospects. Loans to (bonds of) safe corporations are very different from bonds of risky or failing enterprises.

8 Financial regulation in the United States has produced a multiplicity of regulators. Some countries have much simpler regulatory systems, with the commentary usually dividing them into single-peak systems, which have a single top financial regulator, and twin-peak systems, which have two, often one for capital adequacy and consumer protection and one for central banking. See, generally, Eric J. Pan, *Understanding Financial Regulation*, 2012 UTAH L. REV. (1897). The legislative reaction to the great recession, however, has been to move authority from independent agencies to the more political finance ministries; see generally Stavros Gadinis, *From Independence to Politics in Financial Regulation*, 101 CAL. L. REV. 327 (2013).

9 The financial goods that banks offer are bank accounts and certificates of deposit. Life insurance companies offer variable annuity and variable life insurance policies.

10 A contracting party can refuse performance by someone other than the counterparty in specific circumstances. 29 WILLISTON ON CONTRACTS § 74:27 (4th ed. 1990) ("Contractual duties are … not delegable if they involve the personal qualities or skills of the obligor, in the absence of consent by the obligee" or "unless prohibited by statute, public policy or the terms of the contract" [citations omitted]).

So central is the identity of the issuer in financial goods that the notion of buying a share of stock or a bond of an unnamed corporation is strange. Rather, because retail investors cannot monitor issuers (effectively, study the provenance of stocks), they often invest via mutual funds or other professionally managed pools.

iii. Seller and Buyer Mix

In markets for real goods, most businesses only sell items to the public rather than both buy from the public and sell to it. Few are the stores for used electronic games, used CDs, used books, and antiques. Those merchants are not merely sellers, but rather *dealers* because they both sell and buy significant amounts of their merchandise. As consumers of real goods, we interact mostly with sellers. Furthermore, the final sellers that consumers meet may conceal many more. Looking behind a good can take us to the manufacturer who assembled the item, a cascading sequence of component sellers and more manufacturers, and the producers of the raw materials. Sellers dominate real markets.

In financial markets, the most visible participants sell and buy about equally. The stock markets, bond markets, and brokerage houses (the principal intermediaries) cater equally to investors when they are buyers as when they are sellers. The trading between investors is so active as to dwarf the other fundamental role of financial markets, which is to provide capital to corporate issuers. This bifurcation of the transactions where the sellers are the issuers and those where the sellers are subsequent buyers produces the misleading terms *primary* markets, where issuers sell securities to investors, and *secondary* markets, where investors exchange securities with other investors. The misleading nature of the terms *primary* and *secondary* markets is that they suggest different locations, but this tends not to be true. The NYSE and the NASDAQ are markets for both types of transactions. The terminology would be clearer if it focused on the transactions rather than the markets. The transactions have a different function, and their regulation is very different depending on whether the transactions are primary (issuers selling to investors) or secondary (trades between investors).

iv. Bid-Ask Spreads

The term *bid-ask spread* comes from financial markets, but it applies to real markets as well. It originates from the practice of calling the price at which a dealer is willing to buy a security the "bid" price and the price at which the dealer is willing to sell the same security the "ask" price. Bid-ask spreads are important for understanding the behavior of the players in financial markets. Therefore, recognizing how small financial bid-ask spreads are compared to real ones is important.

The relatively few dealers who operate in markets for real goods exhibit a large difference between their bid and their ask. Used bookstores that ask \$2 to \$6 for used paperbacks might bid only $0.25 to buy such paperbacks. Music stores that sell used CDs for about $8 rarely bid more than $2 to buy them. As a percentage of the ask price, these bid-ask spreads exceed 75%. The spreads on used cars can be several thousand dollars. They are not quite so large in percentage terms as those on books and CDs, but they can still easily exceed 20% of price.[11]

Financial bid-ask spreads are hair thin by comparison. Stocks can have bid-ask spreads of a few cents or even just one cent.[12] The giant mutual fund firm Vanguard posts the average bid-ask spread for its exchange-traded funds, which reaches as low as 1 cent and 0.02% of price.[13]

The causes of the vast difference between the bid-ask spreads in real and financial markets are many and not fully understood.[14] Primary causes include the expense of handling tangible goods, the cost of their storage, the risk that natural events may deteriorate their condition, the lower degree of trading activity, and the risk that a delay in reselling may expose the dealer to unforeseen adverse price movements. Dealers in financial goods do not have to spend anything on handling or storing their goods because nowadays they are intangible – electronic entries rather than the old paper certificates of stock ownership. The dealers do bear some risk that price may

11 The price a used car dealer is willing to pay for a used car may be thousands of dollars lower than the price the dealer asks for the same car. For example, in April 2013, the KELLEY BLUE BOOK reported the price to sell to a dealer a 2010 Ford Mustang coupe in excellent condition as $12,584. The amount that CarMax.com asked for the cheapest one it had on sale was $15,998, which is a low estimate because its condition may not be excellent. As a percentage of the ask price, this bid-ask spread of more than $3,000 is much smaller than that of used books or CDs, but it is still more than 21%.

12 For example, on the morning of May 8, 2013, Goldman, Pfizer, Home Depot, Merck, Ford, Citigroup, Microsoft, Google, and Apple had an average spread of 0.04%:

Symbol	GS	PFE	HD	MRK	F	C	MSFT	GOOG	AAPL
Bid	$150.13	$28.91	$75.38	$45.35	$14.20	$48.66	$32.90	$863.96	$462.85
Ask	$150.17	$28.92	$75.39	$45.36	$14.21	$48.67	$32.91	$864.97	$463.01
Spread	0.03%	0.03%	0.01%	0.02%	0.07%	0.02%	0.03%	0.12%	0.03%

A statistical study under a previous trading technology estimated the bid-ask spreads in 1998 at around 1% for the NYSE and 1.46% for the NASDAQ. See Hendrik Bessrminder, *Issues in Assessing Trade Execution Costs*, 6 J. FIN. MARKETS. 233, table 2 (2003) (estimating the half-spread on the NYSE as 0.486% and on the NASDAQ as 0.739%).

13 Average Bid/Ask Spread, Vanguard, available at https://advisors.vanguard.com/VGApp/iip/site/advisor/investments/bidaskspread (accessed February 15, 2017).

14 While the research into the components of the bid-ask spread in finance is enormous, the bid-ask spread of real goods is almost ignored. A search for bid-ask spreads in a publication's abstract in the Econlit database of ProQuest on June 7, 2013, produced hundreds of hits (895 articles and 12 books). Only one appears to address nonfinancial goods. Not surprisingly, that study discovers a component of the bid-ask spread that does not exist in financial markets, one related to the probability that eligible buyers and sellers meet. See Brian W. Buckles, *Liquidity Dynamics in Commercial Real Estate*, 14 J. REAL EST. PORTFOLIO MGMT. 307 (October 2008).

move *against* them,[15] but two phenomena mitigate this risk. First, the fast pace of securities trading means that dealers can unwind their positions and shorten their exposure to such a risk. Second, financial markets let dealers *hedge* – neutralize – their risk by taking positions in other securities that can cancel out the risk the dealers want to avoid.[16] Traders finding themselves with too much of a stock, for example, can trade in futures or options to cancel that position out. A car dealer with too many SUVs may not have a way to mitigate the risk of a drop in demand for SUVs.[17]

The small size of bid-ask spreads in financial markets is both a cause and a consequence of the vast volume of trading that occurs in these markets.[18] The narrow bid-ask spread facilitates the trading of financial goods, and the intense trading activity enables market makers to cover their costs with a narrow spread. The physical nature of tangible goods prevents markets for real goods from accelerating to the trading intensity of financial markets. Trading one's car on a weekly basis would be a hassle, but many investors hold stocks or bonds for less than a week.[19]

In sum, markets for real goods are characterized by an enormous variety of types of goods offered at many markets, the usual irrelevance of the seller's identity, the fact that they consist mostly of sellers, and substantial bid-ask spreads. By comparison, in financial markets, the types of goods are no more than

15 A price movement *against* a trader is one that produces loss for the trader. Thus, if a market maker has bought heavily in a security, a movement against the market maker is a drop in the price. Vice versa, if the market maker has sold, it would be a rise in price.

16 *Hedging* means engaging in transactions that neutralize risk; to avoid confusion, note that we will soon also encounter the misleadingly named "hedge funds," which do not cancel out risk but rather take risk to provide their investors with higher returns. The failure of Lehman Brothers revealed a stark example of good hedging. When it entered bankruptcy on September 15, 2008, Lehman had open trades in interest-rate swaps corresponding to $9 trillion of underlying loans, but Lehman's exposure was hedged. Its clearinghouse was able to apply Lehman's hedges and liquidate the entire portfolio without taking any loss. The clearinghouse returned the majority of Lehman's security deposit to the bankruptcy estate. Julia Lees Allen, *Note, Derivatives Clearinghouses and Systemic Risk: A Bankruptcy and Dodd-Frank Analysis*, 64 STAN. L. REV. 1079 at 1090 (2012) (describing that the clearinghouse only had to use 35% of Lehman's margin in liquidating Lehman's $9 trillion of swaps). See also Douglas G. Baird & Edward R. Morrison, *Dodd-Frank for Bankruptcy Lawyers*, 19 AM. BANKR. INST. L. REV. 287 (2011) at 312–14 (discussing the Lehman experience liquidating within two weeks 80% of the more than 1.5 million transactions it had when entering bankruptcy).

17 For example, careful car dealers who find their stock disproportionately populated by SUVs might be able to mitigate a downturn in SUV demand that is caused by the rise of gas prices by buying gas futures. This would not protect, however, from a downturn in SUV demand for other reasons, such as rollover scares or fashion changes.

18 For example, the average *daily* trading volume on the NYSE between January 3, 2017 and January 31, 2017, was over $45 billion. New York Stock Exchange, *Daily NYSE Group Volume in NYSE Listed*, available at www.nyxdata.com (archived at https://perma.cc/PYR3-DENJ) (accessed February 15, 2017).

19 Indeed, the phenomenon of day trading involves systematic buying and selling in a single day. See, e.g., Justin Kuepper, *Day Trading Strategies for Beginners*, INVESTOPEDIA, June 25, 2011, available at www.investopedia.com/articles/trading/06/daytradingretail.asp.

a handful, the markets are few, the identity of the issuer is crucial, dealers rather than sellers predominate, and bid-ask spreads are hair thin. The difference between a farmers' market and an electronics store is minuscule compared to their difference from financial markets. Let us take a closer look at the structure of the financial markets central to this book: stock markets.

B. THE STRUCTURE OF STOCK MARKETS

To gain a basic understanding of stock markets, consider three aspects: their basic operation with a focus on the example of the NYSE, the cast of characters that populate them, and finally, the type of media attention they draw.

i. Basic Function

Stock markets stand between investors as both sellers and buyers but also between corporations as issuers of stocks or bonds and investors as buyers. Technology has changed the trading mechanics dramatically, from handwritten agreements to telegraphic transmissions and finally to today's automated trading. Figure 1.1 illustrates this transition. While the NYSE is now part of a group of stock markets and has international and domestic competition that erodes its dominance, it remains the most active by trading volume[20] and the largest by capitalization.[21]

Consistent with the earlier observation that new types of financial goods are not introduced frequently, stocks only appeared and started changing hands in the seventeenth century (most of human history knew no trading of financial goods; to the extent that debt was transferrable, trading debt preceded the trading of stocks).[22] The "Buttonwood Agreement" that gave birth to the NYSE was signed more than a century later, in May 1792.[23]

The central features of the modern NYSE trading environment are the kiosks that house the "designated market makers" (previously "specialists") to whom the NYSE

20 The latest available annual trading volume of over $11 trillion in 2004 makes the NYSE twice as active as London, almost three times as Tokyo, about seven times as Frankfurt, and about 30% more active than the NASDAQ. See *Global Comparison of Annualized Value of Trading*, NYSE FACTBOOK HISTORICAL STATISTICS, available at http://www.nyxdata.com/nysedata/asp/factbook/viewer_edition.asp?mode=table&key=2215&category=14 (archived at https://perma.cc/J92R-EWTJ; accessed February 15, 2017).

21 The NYSE had almost twice the capitalization of the NASDAQ in 2014, $16.6 trillion to $8.5 trillion. See www.diffen.com/difference/NASDAQ_vs_NYSE (accessed February 15, 2017. The largest capitalizations, in data from the World Federation of Exchanges for December 2016 start with the NYSE at $19.5 trillion, NASDAQ at $7.8, followed by Japan at $5, Shanghai, China, at $4, London at $3.5, Euronext at $3.5, Shenzhen, China at $3.2, and Hong Kong at $3.2. Data from World Federation of Exchanges, www.world-exchanges.org.

22 See, e.g., Andrew Beattie, *The Birth of Stock Exchanges*, INVESTOPEDIA (February 26, 2009), available at www.investopedia.com/articles/07/stock-exchange-history.asp.

23 Jerry W. Markham, A FINANCIAL HISTORY OF THE UNITED STATES at 139 (M.E. Sharpe, 2002).

FIGURE 1.1 From trading under the buttonwood tree to the floor of the NYSE before and after electronic trading.

assigns the privilege and obligation of "making the market."[24] *To make the market* for a security effectively means to stand ready to buy or sell the security if a trader cannot find a counterparty. Each designated market maker is the only official market maker responsible for a handful of stocks on the NYSE. Other exchanges use different trading mechanisms. On the NASDAQ, for example, a security may have multiple market makers.[25] Exchanges need not organize around market makers. In exchanges without market makers, traders must find counterparties for their transactions.

The profit of the market maker comes from having the bid lower than the ask. At turbulent times when prices change fast, the market maker is exposed to the risk of buying before a drop in the price or selling before a rise. Not surprisingly, the stock market may suspend trading in response to major releases of information during trading hours until traders have had the opportunity to digest the new information.[26]

24 The NYSE rules define designated market makers as those approved by the exchange (NYSE Rule 2(i)). NYSE Rule 104.10 adds detail to the role of the market maker, including an obligation to "maintain . . . a fair and orderly market" by "engag[ing] . . . in dealings for his or her own account when lack of price continuity, lack of depth, or disparity between supply and demand exists" that translates into requiring the market maker to post a bid if no public buy orders exist and an ask if no public sell orders exist.

25 See, e.g., Eugene Kandel and Leslie M. Marx, *NASDAQ Market Structure and Trade Patterns*, 45 J. FIN. ECON. 61–89 *passim* (1997).

26 See, e.g., NYSE Rule 123D (establishing the procedure for halting trading pursuant to a warning by the listed corporation about impending information), available at rules.NYSE.com (accessed February 15, 2017). Notable opinions about securities fraud that we will discuss involve a suspension of trading when the fraud comes to light. See, e.g., *Dirks v. SEC*, 463 US 646, 650 (1983) ("[The information Dirks brought to light] led the New York Stock Exchange to halt trading on March 27 [1973 in the stock of Equity Funding of America].")

Retail investors do not have direct access to stock markets. Rather, they interact with the market through financial intermediaries such as brokerage houses, mutual fund companies, or banks. Financial firms, by contrast, often have direct access to the exchange so that they can trade for their customers or on their own account.[27]

Recall also that stock markets function as both primary and secondary markets.[28] The distinction between primary and secondary financial market transactions is important from two perspectives. First, the regulation of issuances is vastly different from the regulation of subsequent trades. Second, the primary markets play an important economic function: issuances perform the capital-allocation function of the markets by moving funds from investors to businesses. Secondary trades have a merely indirect capital-allocative function.[29] Nonetheless, secondary markets are essential to make purchases in primary markets appealing by offering a venue for subsequent sales. Investments that cannot be sold are pointless.

ii. The Cast of Characters

Understanding the flurry of activity in stock markets requires knowing what roles their main participants play. While market makers stand at the center of stock market activity, the traders who swarm around them divide according to various categorizations.

From the perspective of finance scholarship, traders divide into three groups according to motivation: life-cycle or uninformed investors, rational speculators or informed traders, and fad chasers and irrational or noise traders.[30] Of these, life-cycle investors are the least active. They are the millions of passive investors who store value in direct stock ownership, mutual funds, and variable annuity or life insurance policies. Many may not even realize that they have become traders by merely participating in their workplace retirement fund, where a small fraction of every paycheck becomes a small purchase of a mutual fund. These are life-cycle investors because their trading patterns follow their life cycle. They buy during their earning years and sell when retiring or undertaking other major expenses. Rational speculators or informed traders are those who tend to be active and let proper valuation methods drive their trading. Fad chasers and irrational or noise traders are those who trade on information that is not truly relevant or try to ride waves of sentiment or

27 See, e.g., Larry A. Bear & Rita Maldonado-Bear, *The Securities Industry and the Law*, 26 J. BANKING & FINANCE 1867–88 *passim* (2002).

28 See Section A.iii.

29 However, the allocative effect of secondary securities markets can be quite important. For example, firms can use their securities as currency to acquire other firms.

30 See, e.g., Nicholas L. Georgakopoulos, *The Statistics of Legal Infrastructures*, 8 AMER. L. & ECON. REV. 62–78 *passim* (2006) (reviewing the literature). See, e.g., J. Bradford DeLong, *The Survival of Noise Traders in Financial Markets*, 64 J. Business 1 (1991).

spurious correlation. Financial markets may be unusual in being an environment where the coexistence of sophisticated and unsophisticated players may produce instability.[31]

A different categorization of market participants – one that divides financial professionals by their traditional specializations – helps decode business news. These roles tend to be loosely defined by the business press and may change over time. Financial professionals in brokerage firms act as (1) *underwriters* when they bring new issues to the market, (2) *brokers* or *dealers* when they facilitate their customers' trades, (3) *speculators* when they trade in their own account betting on market moves (what is nowadays called "proprietary trading"), (4) *hedgers* when they use market transactions to hedge risk for themselves or their clients,[32] and (5) *arbitrageurs* when they observe a discrepancy in pricing that allows them to make trades that cancel out, take advantage of the error, and tend to correct it by buying the cheap and selling the dear of two equivalent types of goods.

The financial markets host a plethora of other players. Financial institutions, sovereign wealth funds, and the wealthy (by being categorized by Securities and Exchange Commission rules as "accredited investors") can avoid the restrictions on mutual funds by investing in less regulated alternative investment vehicles, such as hedge funds or private equity funds.[33] The tradeoff is that these investors also forego the protections that mutual fund regulation provides. In the chase for higher returns, accredited investors may find themselves exposed to the likes of Bernie Madoff, who defrauded his accredited investors out of about $50 billion.[34]

[31] A concern is that in financial markets, rational people will try to predict the actions of the irrational speculators and thus move prices in unsound ways, a subject of Chapter 10. By contrast, rational motorists tend to help irrational motorists (and vice versa) in the context of traffic congestions because they follow different routes (the rational motorists divert traffic to the uncongested routes, which may risk congestion if all drivers were rational). A third alternative is markets with reputation importance, where either group will dominate. See, generally, John Haltiwanger and Michael Waldman. *Rational Expectations and the Limits of Rationality: An Analysis of Heterogeneity*, 75 AM. ECON. REV. 326 (1985).

[32] See the example of effective hedging that Lehman's bankruptcy revealed, note 16.

[33] Variations in alternative investment vehicles take names that further specify their activity. Some tend to require that investors commit capital for a minimum period, as do *private equity funds, leveraged buyout funds, venture capital funds, angel funds, mezzanine funds*, or the even more colorfully named *vulture funds* that invest in securities of troubled corporations or countries. This leaves *hedge funds* as the investment vehicles that usually provide the expectation of exit at will, akin to mutual funds. Hedge funds further divide according to their primary trading objective into, e.g., *absolute return funds, index arbitrage funds, foreign exchange funds, option trading funds*, or *long-short funds*. This is not vocabulary that the reader needs to know; just avoid being confused by it.

The vocabulary of stock markets gets knottier. The financial press and financial marketing give names, often misleading ones, to other aspects as well. These include trading strategies (e.g., *dollar-cost-averaging* or *portfolio insurance*) or patterns of prices (e.g., *head-and-shoulders*, from the vague shape that it creates in the chart of the stock price, or *support* and *resistance levels*).

[34] Complaint, *SEC v. Madoff*, No. 08-10791, (SDNY December 11, 2008), available at www.sec.gov/litigation/complaints/2008/comp-madoff121108.pdf (accessed February 15, 2017).

Among the cast of market professionals are entities that try to innovate and in the process siphon some activity away from traditional players. *Discount brokers*, for example, compete by omitting some of the services traditional *full-service* brokerage houses provide. *Alternative trading systems*, some of which are called "dark pools" due to the anonymity they provide, compete with the exchanges by offering different trading technologies or environments.[35]

Concluding the list of private entities that are active in the stock markets are the nonfinancial business corporations themselves acting as acquirers or targets of acquisitions. Acquirers can be categorized by function into financial and strategic ones. *Financial acquirers* are motivated by a price they perceive as attractive. *Strategic acquirers* seek to expand or restructure their businesses through acquisitions or mergers and thereby realize commercial gains, for example, from synergies, from applying advantages they may have, or from reaping economies of scope or scale. The market and, to a lesser extent, the courts react differently to strategic acquirers than they do to financial acquirers. Listed corporations also create market activity by dividing themselves. They can *spin off* components of themselves to their shareholders. Understanding these ways in which issuers influence the market is important.

Key for this book is the regulatory environment of stock markets. Besides being subject to federal (and state) securities statutes, stock markets are also subject to rules from two layers of lesser authorities: administrative agencies and the exchanges themselves as *self-regulatory organizations*.

The primary agency that regulates stock markets is the Securities and Exchange Commission (SEC), but the Commodity Futures Trading Commission (CFTC) also has a role.[36] Like other administrative agencies, these act as legislators when they have statutorily delegated authority to enact rules, as enforcers, and as initial adjudicators of regulatory violations.[37]

Securities laws call the exchanges "self-regulatory organizations" because the laws share the interest of the exchanges in having good internal rules and enforcing them. The exchanges are supervised in their self-regulation by the SEC and the CFTC.

35 See, e.g., SEC Rule 301, 17 CFR § 242.301 (2009) (requirements for alternative trading systems); Jasmin Sethi, *Another Role for Securities Regulation: Expanding Investor Opportunity*, 16 FORDHAM *J. CORP. & FIN. L.* 783, 807 (2011) (discussing alternative trading systems and dark pools and their differences on information dissemination).

36 When commodity futures were only about nonfinancial commodities, mostly grains and meats, the two regulators had clearly separate jurisdictions, and that of the CFTC did not touch financial markets. The development and the enormous activity of financial futures, contracts about interest rates, stock market indices, exchange rates, and the like created a regulatory overlap which only became deeper as derivatives became more prevalent. The Dodd-Frank Act established a separation, assigning to the SEC regulation of derivatives based on specific securities and to the CFTC the regulation of derivatives based on interest rates and indices. Dodd-Frank Wall Street Reform and Consumer Protection Act, Title VII, Pub. L. No. 111-203, 124 Stat. 1376 (codified as amended in scattered sections of 7 USC and 15 USC).

37 See Richard J. Pierce, Jr. ADMINISTRATIVE LAW (2d ed.) (2012), at 1–6.

For example, the SEC has used its authority to require exchanges to move from pricing in fractions to pricing in cents.[38]

While all these actors create the storm of activity that buffets the financial markets, the fourth estate – the press and mass media – reports on this activity and, in so doing, colors and influences it.

iii. Mass Media and Stock News

The daily flow of financial information tends to ignore the stock markets' structural issues and focuses on which stocks to buy and sell. The focus of the media on trends and prices can be frustrating for those new to finance because such stories may not have meaningful information about events and changes in the markets. It is analogous to reporting on a war by giving weapon advice or bullet counts instead of explaining troop movements, battle outcomes, and their strategic importance. Lively stories about secondary aspects of financial markets or specific corporations receive comparable or greater attention than important phenomena.[39]

Moreover, when the media focus on prices and trends, they confuse the novice because they may rely on spurious approaches to valuation. Granted, the media may not ignore proper approaches to valuation, but those do not make for sensational headlines. Proper approaches to valuation focus on firms' profits (called "earnings").[40] The *capitalization* (of earnings) method is the cruder of the proper valuations (not to be confused with *market capitalization*, the sum of the value of all shares of the stock of a corporation). It assumes that the future will be analogous to the past. First, the capitalization method examines similar stocks to derive the average ratio of the price of these stocks to their per-share earnings: their *price-to-earnings ratio* or *P/E ratio*. Then, assuming that the stock under consideration has

[38] See SEC, Order Directing the Exchanges and the National Association of Securities Dealers, Inc., to Submit A Phase-in Plan to Implement Decimal Pricing in Equity Securities and Options, Release No. 34-42914 (June 8, 2000), available at www.sec.gov/rules/other/34-42914.htm (accessed February 15, 2017) (on decimalization); Order Approving Proposed Rule Change by the NASD Relating to Limit Order Protection and Nasdaq, Exchange Act Release No. 35,571, 60 Fed. Reg. 27,997, (May 22, 1995) (requiring market makers to respect the priority of customer limit orders).

[39] For example, on June 15, 2013, the two arguably most important stories were indications of concerns over inflation or raised interest rates and a World Bank report that excessive fiscal restraint hampered US growth. Comparing the top business/finance news on Google, Yahoo, and Bing and in the Wall Street Journal and the New York Times, however, reveals that none of these news venues carried both stories in their top five. Three of these venues carried one of the two stories in their top five. Instead, greater prominence was given to stories about specific entities (Boeing, Chrysler, and Groupon, the insolvency of Detroit, Lululemon) and markets (Boston parking space cost, coal, and nuclear energy).

[40] Through the Center for Computer Assisted Legal Instruction (CALI at cali.org), I have published a lesson on basic valuation and one on advanced valuation. See N. Georgakopoulos, *Valuation: Basic Skills*, available at www.cali.org/lesson/755; and *The Capital Asset Pricing Model*, available at www.cali.org/lesson/756 (accessed February 15, 2017).

earnings, it finds the price that would produce the same ratio. The *discounting* (of cash flows) method is the more refined approach to valuation. It discounts to the present the value of the stock's future earnings. Finance theory has contributed further sophistication with the capital asset pricing model that Chapter 5 discusses in detail.[41]

The metrics that correspond to these methods (earnings per share, P/E ratio, growth estimates, and beta) do not appear on front pages if at all. The barrage of news about stocks revels in trends and other shapes that fluctuations of price leave on charts, the feelings perceived among traders or in the retail marketplace, and spurious correlations such as those of royal weddings and sports to stock market behavior. While psychology can influence pricing significantly, the topic of Chapter 10, the focus on it by the news media is grossly misleading.

By focusing on specific stocks and industries, the media fail to deliver news on the impact of the financial system on the overall economy. Thus the shortcomings of the media lead to the next topic: the interdependence between financial and real markets.

C. THE INTERDEPENDENCE OF THE REAL WITH THE FINANCIAL SECTOR

In a stylized but accurate simplification, the real sector of the economy is where people work to earn and spend to satisfy their needs. The financial sector is where they invest their savings for interest or for dividends and capital gains. From the perspective of a business, the real sector is where it hires and sells goods or services. The financial sector is where the business obtains financing for its operations and pays for that financing by providing either interest and debt repayment or dividends and capital gains.

Figure 1.2 illustrates this interdependence of the financial and real sectors of the economy. The outer, thicker loop corresponds to the real sector. The arrows pointing from the people to the city and back represent flows of money. From the perspective of individuals, people provide employment to the real sector to earn wages and spend part of what they earn again in the real sector on the goods and services that they desire as consumers. From the perspective of the businesses as producers, the corresponding activities are the payroll spent for human resources and the production and sale of goods and services.

[41] See generally John Lintner, *The Valuation of Risk Assets and the Selection of Risky Investments in Stock Portfolios and Capital Budgets*, 47 REV. ECON. & STAT. 13 (1965); Harry Markowitz, *Portfolio Selection*, J. FIN. 77 (1952); William F. Sharpe, *Capital Asset Prices: A Theory of Market Equilibrium Under Conditions of Risk*, 19 J. FINANCE 425 (1964). For a less technical explanation, see generally Nicholas L. Georgakopoulos, PRINCIPLES AND METHODS OF LAW AND ECONOMICS: BASIC TOOLS FOR NORMATIVE REASONING 197–224 (2005); Nicholas L. Georgakopoulos, *The Capital Asset Pricing Model*, CALI lesson at Cali.org.

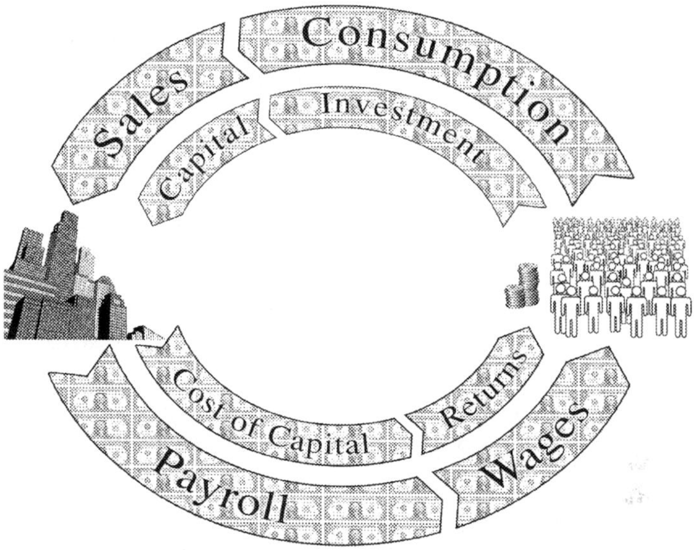

FIGURE 1.2 The interdependence of the real and the financial sectors.

The inner loop of the figure illustrates the financial sector. Again, the arrows pointing from the individuals' savings to the city and back represent the flows of money, but now the money is capital invested and returned. Individuals (now seen as investors) invest the funds that they do not spend to receive the returns that the investments will produce, be they interest, dividends, or capital gains. From the perspective of the firms (now seen as borrowers or as issuers of securities), they obtain capital and pay for its use (the cost of capital).

The trap that financial crises pose for the real economy is already visible. If the financial sector is in shambles, with many banks failing, for example, then the businesses of the real sector have trouble financing their operations and meeting their payroll expenses. Individuals, in turn, do not receive wages and cannot spend. The reduction of spending has a feedback effect that aggravates the crisis. When demand for goods and services declines, businesses reduce their production and their expenses, including their spending on labor, further depressing individuals' incomes and their capacity to spend. The regulation of financial markets cannot afford to ignore this risk; as the Great Depression and the rise of Nazism – to the extent that they were consequences of financial calamities – demonstrated, the consequences can be devastating.[42]

[42] See, e.g., Jeanne Mirer & Marjorie Cohn, *Lost in the Debt Ceiling Debate: The Legal Duty to Create Jobs*, 68 NAT'L LAW. GUILD REV. 116, 118 (2011) ("for the short time between the end of the war and the beginning of the Cold War, there was an international consensus that one of the causes of the Second World War was the failure of governments to address the major unemployment crisis in the late '20s and early '30s, and that massive worldwide unemployment led to the rise of fascism and Nazism").

Even before reaching the issue of financial crises, the interdependence of the real and the financial sectors demonstrates the need for effective securities regulation. A regulatory structure that facilitates investment translates into lower cost of capital for businesses. When the cost of inputs drops, as it does when the cost of capital drops, then businesses can produce and sell their goods or services more cheaply, increasing the purchasing power of individuals and families. Good securities regulation is a vital component of a legal system that enables the market better to fulfill consumers' desires.

This book demonstrates that the components of the law of securities regulation support a virtuous cycle, illustrated in Chapter 20. Reducing the cost of trading leads to greater liquidity in the market, the ability to trade faster, moving prices less against the trader. Greater liquidity leads to more accurate prices, which reduce the risk of trading and thus reduce the cost of trading, completing the cycle. Securities laws reduce the costs of trading, deepen liquidity, and aim to increase price accuracy. Securities law fits the virtuous cycle and helps it. We cannot interpret securities law without understanding the virtuous cycle and how the different parts of securities law are synergistic with the virtuous cycle.

PART I

Definition of a Security

When to Leave Buyer Beware for Seller Disclose

2

Toward Defining a Security

The theme of this book is the logic of securities law, the idea that securities regulation consistently pursues some basic synergistic goals that form a virtuous cycle, a sequence of feedback effects that improve securities markets – lowering the costs of trading, which leads to liquidity, which begets accurate prices, which reduces the cost of trading. The cycle itself is the subject of Chapter 20. This first part of the book builds toward the virtuous cycle by identifying its location. To talk about a body of law – a collection of rules, an area of jurisprudence – we need to first define it and draw its boundaries. In the case of securities law, the challenge of defining this area of law is identical to the task of defining a security, its subject. This does not make it easier, however.

One way to establish a shared understanding of what a security is would be to turn to the statutory definition, but this approach poses two problems. First, it begs the question of why to so construct the definition – why should the law define a security the way it does? Moreover, in the case of securities regulation, the statutory definition of "a security" is meaningless. As we will see, the various securities statutes offer a list of terms rather than a principled definition. As if this were not enough, the defined subject is part of that list: the statutory definition can be shortened to "any[thing] known as a 'security.'"[1] Of all the weak foundations on which to build a statutory scheme of regulation, this may be the weakest from the perspective of logic yet one of the most durable in terms of functionality.

This vacuous statutory definition of "a security" calls for us to apply the principle that law is driven by its consequences. The chapters that follow will show that the consequences that drive the definition of a security are the buyer's access to information and control.

The consequentialist method used here matches the rest of the book. We will try to derive first principles from the consequences of the operation of markets and laws. The difference between the market for, say, eBay shares (and securities generally) and the market for, say, tomatoes (and nonfinancial goods generally) drives their

[1] Section 2(a)(1) of the Securities Act of 1933 (1933 Act), 15 USC 77b (2017).

regulation. Transactions that are not about securities fall by default to contract law. Contract law follows the principle of "buyer beware." In the regime of buyer beware, buyers bear the risk that the purchased item is appropriate for their purpose. Tomato buyers must decide if the offered tomato serves their purpose. For example, a buyer might prefer unripe tomatoes for storage, ripe ones for immediate consumption, or overripe ones as projectiles for artistic or political criticism. Buyer beware corresponds to the idea that sellers may offer tomatoes of any kind and may stay silent about their features, not knowing their ultimate use. Securities are different. Securities law follows a reverse principle, call it "seller disclose" (this principle also appears in some other regulated areas, such as the lemon laws for the car market,[2] which we can ignore). The issuing corporation bears the burden of disclosing all the risks that may befall investors at pain of being liable for rescission. All buyers use eBay shares the same way, to store wealth for hoped appreciation and later sale (something mentioned in Chapter 1 and into which we will dive deeper in Chapter 4 – on the function of the definition of a security – and Chapter 5 – on the differences of the pricing mechanisms of securities from real goods). The issuer of eBay shares knows what the buyers will do with the shares and bears the burden of disclosing their features as investments, namely, their risks. Undisclosed risks allow buyers to rescind.

A different approach to regulating securities markets would have the regulator filter securities for their adequacy or merit as investments. Very few legal systems choose this path, the United States does not either, and this book does not seek to upend this equilibrium. Nevertheless, note that some recent evidence points to some success of merit regulation.[3]

Chapter 3 discusses the case law of the definition of a security. Chapter 4 analyzes the case law to find the definition's functional role. Chapter 5 presents finance theory and finds its analysis harmonious with legal analysis. Chapter 6 explores a departure from this harmony and its implicit reinstatement by *Gustafson*. Chapter 7 argues that the resulting regime is surprisingly effective.

[2] See, e.g., Magnuson-Moss Warranty Act, Pub. L. No. 93–637, 88 Stat. 2183 (1974) (codified at 15 USC §§ 2301–12).

[3] A study of the vitality of stock markets in numerous countries identifies Hong Kong as an outlier with an exceptionally vital stock market; Hong Kong is also one of the very few jurisdictions that use merit regulation of securities. See Howell E. Jackson & Mark J. Roe, *Public and Private Enforcement of Securities Laws: Resource-Based Evidence*, 93 *J. Fin. Econ.* 207–38 (2009).

3

The Vacuous Definition of a Security

Whether something is a security has enormous importance in theory and practice. For the theory toward which this book leads – that the fundamental aspects of securities law facilitate the virtuous cycle from low trading costs to liquidity and accurate prices, which lower trading costs – the definition of a security is important because only securities law is subject to this virtuous cycle. As a practical matter, identifying something as a security causes a dramatic change in its legal environment.

Under securities law, the buyer has the right to rescind the purchase if the seller has failed to disclose all the material attributes of the security,[1] sellers and those facilitating the sale are subject to expansive liability for false statements,[2] and issuers of securities are subject to obligations to disclose,[3] restraints on trading,[4] and heightened antifraud liability.[5] Ordinary contract law, by contrast, follows the principle of "buyer beware."[6] Barring special regulation such as lemon laws,[7]

1 See, e.g., § 12 of the Securities Act of 1933 (1933 Act), 15 USC § 77l (2017) ("Any person who – (1) offers or sells a security in violation of section 5, or (2) offers or sells a security . . . by means of a prospectus or oral communication, which . . . omits to state a material fact . . . shall be liable.").

2 See, e.g., § 11 of the 1933 Act, 15 USC § 77k (2011) ("In case any part of the registration statement . . . omitted to state a material fact . . . any person acquiring such security . . . may . . . sue – (1) every person who signed the registration statement; (2) every person who was a director of . . . the issuer . . . (4) every accountant, engineer, or appraiser . . . who has . . . prepared or certified any part of the registration statement, or . . . any report or valuation which is used in . . . the registration statement . . . (5) every underwriter.").

3 See, e.g., § 13 of the Securities Exchange Act of 1934 (1934 Act), 15 USC § 78m (2017) ("(a) Every issuer . . . shall file with the [SEC] . . . – (1) such information and documents . . . as the [SEC] shall require . . . (2) such annual reports . . . as the [SEC] may prescribe.").

4 See, e.g., rule 13d-1, 17 CFR § 240.13d-1, which requires any person who acquires "directly or indirectly the beneficial ownership of any equity security" of particular classes to file certain information with the Securities and Exchange Commission (SEC).

5 See, e.g., rule 10b-5, 17 CFR § 240.10b-5; rule 14e-3, 17 CFR § 240.14e-3.

6 See, e.g., 28 Corbin on Contracts §28:35.

7 See, e.g., Magnuson-Moss Warranty Act, Pub. L. No. 93-637, 88 Stat. 2183 (1974) (codified at 15 USC §§ 2301–12).

neither sellers nor intermediaries have obligations to speak.[8] Buyers obtain the right to rescind contracts in very limited circumstances.[9] Liability in deceit is much more difficult to establish.[10]

The statutory definition of a security is frustratingly circular (including "any[thing] known as a 'security'"), vague (including "investment contract"), and long (spanning more than 130 words, for example, in the federal definition in the Securities Act of 1933).[11]

In interpreting the federal definition of a security, the US Supreme Court has focused on "investment contract" and has visited the issue in numerous opinions.[12]

8 See RESTATEMENT (SECOND) OF CONTRACTS § 161 cmt.a ("Non-disclosure without concealment is equivalent to a misrepresentation only in special situations. A party making a contract is not expected to tell all that he knows to the other party, even if he knows that the other party lacks knowledge on some aspects of the transaction. His nondisclosure, as such, has no legal effect except in the situations enumerated in this Section.").

9 See I FARNSWORTH ON CONTRACTS §§4.11–15 (2004) (discussing the requirements for rescission based on misrepresentation: must be fraudulent or material, promisee must have relied on the assertion, the reliance must have been justified, and the contract must not have been "ratified.").

10 RESTATEMENT (SECOND) OF TORTS § 551, cmt.a ("Unless he is under some one of the duties of disclosure stated in Subsection (2), one party to a business transaction is not liable to the other for harm caused by his failure to disclose to the other facts of which he knows the other is ignorant and which he further knows the other, if he knew of them, would regard as material in determining his course of action in the transaction in question.").

11 Section 2(a)(1) of the 1933 Act, 15 USC 77b (2017), defines a security:

> The term "security" means any note, stock, treasury stock, security future, bond, debenture, evidence of indebtedness, certificate of interest or participation in any profit-sharing agreement, collateral-trust certificate, preorganization certificate or subscription, transferable share, *investment contract*, voting-trust certificate, certificate of deposit for a security, fractional undivided interest in oil, gas, or other mineral rights, any put, call, straddle, option, or privilege on any security, certificate of deposit, or group or index of securities (including any interest therein or based on the value thereof), or any put, call, straddle, option, or privilege entered into on a national securities exchange relating to foreign currency, or, in general, *any* interest or instrument commonly *known as a "security"*, or any certificate of interest or participation in, temporary or interim certificate for, receipt for, guarantee of, or warrant or right to subscribe to or purchase, any of the foregoing [emphasis added].

12 The Supreme Court's jurisprudence on the definition of a security includes *Securities & Exchange Commission v. W.J. Howey Co.*, 328 US 293 (1946) (land sale with service contract making it a fractional participation in citrus grove is a security); *United Housing Found., Inc. v. Forman*, 421 US 837 (1975) (shares entitling buyers to apartments in coop condominium are not securities); *International Bhd. of Teamsters, Chauffeurs, Warehousemen & Helpers of Am. v. Daniel*, 439 US 551 (1979) (employee's participation in noncontributory, compulsory pension plan is not a security); *SEC v. Variable Annuity Life Ins. Co.*, 359 US 65 (1959) (variable annuity is a security despite insurance exemption); *SEC v. United Benefit Life Ins. Co.*, 387 US 202 (1967) (flexible variable annuity is a security despite insurance exemption); *Tcherepnin v. Knight*, 389 US 332 (1967) (withdrawable capital share in Savings & Loan Association is a security); *Marine Bank v. Weaver*, 455 US 551 (1982) (certificate of deposit is not a security); *SEC v. C. M. Joiner Leasing Corp.*, 320 US 344 (1943) (fractional participation in oil leases is a security); *Reves v. Ernst & Young*, 494 US 56 (1990) (notes issued by Farmers Cooperative are securities); *Landreth Timber Co. v. Landreth*, 471 US 681 (1985) (stock of closely held corporation is a security), *Gould v. Ruefenacht*, 471 US 701 (1985) (same); *SEC v. Edwards*, 540 US 389 (2004) (sale and leaseback of payphones could be a security despite that it offered a fixed return).

The opinions bracketing the issue with the greatest generality are *Howey*[13] and *Forman*.[14] Buyers of land in *Howey* were held to be buyers of securities; buyers of shares in *Forman* were held to be buyers of land.

A. THE INVESTMENT CONTRACT FOUNDATION: *HOWEY* AND *FORMAN*

In *Howey*, the sellers of the alleged securities entered into two transactions with each buyer, a land sale and a service contract.[15] The land sale transferred to the buyer a segment of a citrus grove. The service contract gave the seller the exclusive right to cultivate and harvest the citrus grove, commingling the fruit with that of the rest of the grove, while the buyer received a monetary return based on the buyer's fractional interest in the greater grove. The sellers claimed that they sold land; the buyers argued that they bought securities.

Focusing on the definition of a security as an investment contract, the Supreme Court interpreted it to mean "a contract, transaction or scheme whereby a person invests his money in a common enterprise and is led to expect profits solely from the efforts of [others]."[16] Did *Howey* buyers invest with the expectation of profits from the effort of others, or did they buy land? The Court concluded the former. The *Howey* buyers bought securities.

In *Forman*, the buyers acquired shares in a condominium cooperative and signed a lease for a specific unit.[17] Each share purchase entitled the buyer to a specific unit along with fractional ownership of some aspects of the building complex.[18] The buyers received the benefit of reduced rent due to the income from leases of common areas.[19]

The United States Court of Appeals for the Second Circuit (Second Circuit) saw *Forman* buyers as akin to *Howey* buyers.[20] Although the sellers in *Forman* claimed that the buyers purchased the right to live in an apartment, the object of the transaction was shares. Furthermore, the buyers *did* have financial consequences from a common enterprise: the rent collected by the association from leasing the common spaces. The Supreme Court, however, ignored the form of the transaction – a purchase of shares – and held that the *Forman* buyers did not receive securities. Although monetary consequences from a common enterprise did flow to

13 *SEC v. W.J. Howey Co.*, 328 US 293 (1946).

14 *United Housing Found., Inc. v. Forman*, 421 US 837 (1975).

15 *Howey*, 328 US at 295.

16 *Id.* at 298–9. The "solely" component of this definition proved too easy to circumvent. Would merely making the investor a full partner prevent the application of the *Howey* test? The courts have functionally replaced the word "solely" with "mostly." Also, a transaction that is formally and substantively not an investment may become a security if it has the risk of starting an enterprise, according to the *risk capital* test, per *Silver Hills Country Club v. Sobieski*, 55 Cal.2d 811, 361 P.2d 906, 12 Cal. Rptr. 186 (1961) (buyers of golf club memberships, ordinarily not securities, due to the startup nature and risk of the club, did buy securities).

17 *Forman*, 421 US at 842.

18 *Id.* at 855–6.

19 *Id.*

20 *Forman v. Community Services, Inc.*, 500 F.2d 1246 (1974).

both the *Howey* and *Forman* buyers, an "expectation of profit" was the motivation of only the *Howey* buyers.[21]

The two cases set a foundation of elevating substance over form in the definition of a security. Labels are not dispositive. Neither creating a hidden investment relationship using ordinary transactions nor using the form of a security in a transaction that is manifestly not about the security will trick the courts in following the appearance instead of the substance of the transaction. However, the *Howey* test has a defect that remains uncorrected.

B. HOW MOTIVATIONS UNRAVEL THE DEFINITION

The Supreme Court distinguished *Forman* from *Howey* based on the buyers' motivations. This focus on motivations can mislead. The Court did not interpret the facts de novo to learn what the actual motivation of the buyers was. Rather, the Court drew a legal conclusion that imputed a motivation to the buyers. The Court concluded that, as a matter of law, the *Forman* buyers' motivation was different from that of the *Howey* buyers.

The Court does not identify which facts lead to one imputation versus the other. The essence of the security definition should be identification of the facts that lead to the different imputations of motive. Despite the acceptance of *Howey* in practice, the definition is unclear at best. On closer examination, the investment contract definition does not guide courts in identifying which buyers are motivated by a desire to invest in a common enterprise with the expectation of profit mostly from the effort of others.

In sum, defining a security as an investment contract makes little progress from the vacuous statutory definition. The definition of a security is still a cipher. Chapter 4 tries to interpret the investment contract definition from a consequentialist perspective.

21 *Forman*, 421 US at 857.

4

The Function of Investment Contract

Ideally, the "investment contract" definition of a security would be driven by its consequences. The chief consequence is the switch from the "buyer beware" regime of contract law to the "seller disclose" of securities law. If the definition is about consequences, then the facts that lead courts to impute the motivation to "invest in a common enterprise with the expectation of profit mostly from the effort of others" should relate to the purpose of the switch in legal regimes. These facts should relate to the propriety of the buyer beware legal environment for *Forman*-like buyers and its impropriety for *Howey*-like buyers. A closer examination of motivations reveals the salient factors.

Compare the motivations of an ordinary buyer of land to those of the buyers in *Howey*. An ordinary buyer of land tends to care about unique features of the object of the transaction, such as the land's location, accessibility, the composition of the soil, access to water, or the health of its trees. The *Howey* arrangement, however, rendered moot each individual buyer's evaluation of his land. Rather, the sole motivation for the purchase was receiving a fraction of the profits of the greater citrus grove, the common enterprise. Each buyer assessed the financial appeal of the collective project rather than the suitability of specific tracts of land to that individual's preferences.

Crucially, each buyer of land is typically able to determine the appeal of a piece of land for that buyer's own use: the buyer can evaluate the land's features to comport with that buyer's own satisfaction. By contrast, the buyer of a fractional interest in a collective project like the *Howey* citrus grove cannot assess it by merely evaluating the offered land. The common enterprise changes the size and nature of the buyer's analysis.

Compared to an ordinary land sale, what a *Howey* buyer should inspect changes, first, in size. Since the buyer's return depends on the aggregate harvest, the buyer needs to draw conclusions about aspects of the common enterprise. The buyer's return depends on the health and productivity of trees that are not on the buyer's land. The *Howey*-like buyer has to inspect the entire grove instead of only the offered land.

Second, the common enterprise changes the nature of the buyer's future involvement. Whereas the buyer of one acre of land needs to determine the buyer's own ability to manage that land, *Howey*-like buyers have to determine the abilities and prospects of those administering the entire grove. In a true land sale, the buyer's efforts will determine the land's productivity, but the *Howey*-like buyer's own efforts will have no effect on the management of the common enterprise.

Whereas buyers of land tend to inspect the offered land and bear the risk of their own administration, buyers of fractional participation in common enterprises tend to have difficulty assessing the greater enterprise and have no control of its management. The regulatory environment of buyer beware is adequate for true land sales because it puts the risk on the shoulders of the buyer, who must inspect and will administer the property. For sales of fractional participation in a collective project like that of *Howey*, the buyer beware regime is *not* adequate because each buyer cannot appropriately inspect and will not have the control necessary to administer the common enterprise.

Unlike the *Howey* buyers, the motivation of the *Forman* buyers was the desire to obtain low-income housing. The buyers sought to characterize the transaction as the purchase of a security in order to avoid subsequent rent increases as undisclosed material risks. The sellers argued that the transaction, in substance, did not involve a security despite taking the form of a purchase of shares. The Supreme Court agreed, reversing the Second Circuit. The Second Circuit, focusing on money – the rent reduction that tenants enjoyed from participation in the returns from commercial activities in the building such as coin-operated laundry machines – had concluded that the transactions involved securities.

Because the *Forman* buyers sought apartments rather than investment returns, the linked shares produced a transaction different from that of the *Howey* buyers. The difference in the size and nature of the buyer's assessment is evident.

In contrast to *Howey* buyers, *Forman* buyers cared about which apartment corresponded to their purchase. *Howey* buyers, rather than caring about the quality of their land's trees, cared about those of the greater grove from which they would receive their return. *Forman* buyers, however, would live in their apartments and have preferences for aspects such as silence, accessibility, and view. *Forman* buyers had no need to assess apartments other than the one in which they intended to live.[1]

Also in contrast to *Howey* buyers, *Forman* buyers will have control of their apartments. A *Howey* buyer's returns depended on the management of the common enterprise, on which the *Howey* buyer had no influence. The appeal of a *Forman* buyer's apartment – such as cleanliness, decor, maintenance, and equipment –

[1] The financial future of *Forman* buyers, however, did depend on a common enterprise run by others. The success of the common aspects of the enterprise in *Forman* would influence the financial appeal of the transaction for the buyers by influencing the rent. Nevertheless, those common aspects were not the buyers' primary motivation and were not sufficient to render the transaction a security.

depended on his or her efforts. The *Forman* buyer had no need to assess another's management.

These contrasts justify the distinction of *Howey* from *Forman* on the basis of problems that the buyer beware legal environment posed for *Howey* buyers. The *Howey* buyer had two problems with the contract. First, the buyer could not access the trees beyond the offered acre – the greater enterprise – in order to evaluate it at the time of the transaction. The quality of the offered acre was irrelevant because every acre entitled its owner to the same fractional proceeds from the enterprise. By contrast, a *Forman* buyer who visited an offered apartment hardly needed any information about features of the rest of the complex in order to decide whether that apartment was satisfactory.

Second, the lack of control of a *Howey* buyer meant that the buyer's skills and efforts would have no consequence for the future success of the object of the transaction. The future of the grove depended on the skills and efforts of the grove's management. By contrast, the skills and efforts of a *Forman* buyer would directly influence the appeal of his or her home. The next sections analyze these two differences.

A. EVALUATION DIFFICULTY AT TIME OF OFFER

The evaluation difficulty that accompanies the purchase of securities is a product mainly of control, transaction practice, and collective action problems. A *Howey* buyer considering the purchase of one acre does not have control to access and evaluate the entire grove, but the lack of access is not a product of lack of control alone. Buyers of nonsecurities also lack control over the object of the transaction until the transaction is consummated. However, transactional practice and the parties' bargaining power tend to result in buyers of nonsecurities inspecting the offered item to their satisfaction. Transactional practice and bargaining power in the sale of securities are such that buyers cannot access the common enterprise.

The collective action problem is a result of the fractional nature of the purchase. If a buyer were purchasing the entire grove, he or she would decide how much to spend on an appraisal in view of receiving the entire value. Since a *Howey* buyer obtains only a fraction of the grove, he or she has a much reduced incentive to appraise the entire grove. The lone *Howey* buyer cannot force other buyers to share any appraisal expenses.

This difficulty of evaluation is cured by switching from the regime of buyer beware to that of securities law – seller disclose. The seller has access to the information and knows that the buyer is interested in nothing but investment returns and their risk. Therefore, the seller is in a position to make a full disclosure (in contrast to the seller of a nonfinancial good such as a tomato, who does not necessarily know the buyer's intended use).

The seller disclose regime is also appropriate in light of the frictions and costs of trading and organizing. In a world with no costs of trading or organizing, all the *Howey* buyers would act in concert, share the appraisal expenses, and exercise control. Reality makes this prohibitively costly, justifying the rule that the seller must disclose.

B. LACK OF FUTURE CONTROL

The problem posed by a lack of future control relates to the measures that the buyer can take if the purchase does not work as planned. If conditions deteriorate, an owner who controls a good can attempt to change its use. If the old use is no longer ideal, the good may attain more value in a new use. However, a buyer of a security will have no control over management of the enterprise. Thus, if the management will not change its mission, the holder of the enterprise's securities will suffer the consequence of lower value with no remedy.[2]

The allocation of responsibility for maintaining optimal use of the property, that is, control, dictates the allocation of legal responsibility. In the sale of a nonsecurity, the buyer will control the good and will have responsibility for changing the good's use. Thus buyer beware is appropriate. In the sale of a security, the seller maintains control, and seller disclose is appropriate. The economic function of the changed legal regime becomes apparent if we consider a quick change in circumstances. In the wake of a securities transaction, if the management does not adapt to the new circumstances, buyers will exercise the rescission remedy that securities law gives them. As a result, the harm will return to the seller, giving the seller full incentive to prevent the harm in the first place. The seller disclose regime ensures that the incentive to optimize the enterprise's use stays with the seller, who has the control to do so.

C. SELLER DISCLOSE AND BUYER BEWARE

In sum, the selection between the buyer beware and the seller disclose regimes places the risk on the party who has access to information and who will determine the ultimate success of the enterprise. Securities buyers have neither access to the greater enterprise nor control over its future. Subjecting them to the buyer beware regime does not make sense. The consequences justify the selection of legal regime, validating and aligning with the investment contract definition of a security.

[2] State law governs the claims of shareholders for mistreatment; see *Santa Fe Ind., Inc. v. Green*, 430 US 462 (1977) (Shareholders could not use federal securities law to pursue remedies for being mistreated but were confined to their state remedies.). State laws treat informed and disinterested decisions by the directors of the corporation as immune under the doctrine of the business judgment rule; see, e.g., David Rosenberg, *Galactic Stupidity and the Business Judgment Rule*, 32 J. CORP. L. 301 (2006–7); David Rosenberg, *Supplying the Adverb: The Future of Corporate Risk-Taking and the Business Judgment Rule*, 6 BERKELEY BUS. L.J. 216 (2009).

5

Pricing Mechanisms

Although the courts focus on "investment contract" to define a security, economic theory reveals the difference between securities and other (real) goods through an analysis that focuses on the forces of supply and demand in producing the prices of goods. The economic approach, like that of the courts, turns on buyers' motivations, but it does so in different ways. This chapter will show that economic theory treats goods prone to subjective valuation, and hence sloping supply and demand curves, differently from goods prone to the objective valuation of the capital asset pricing model (CAPM), which produces horizontal supply and demand curves.

One of the primary contributions, revolutions even, of finance theory is the development of a pricing theory for "capital assets" – the CAPM. This contribution received the Nobel Prize in Economics in 1990.[1] In brief, the CAPM calculates the return that investors require from a stock based on the stock's undiversifiable risk. For the purpose of securities laws, the CAPM separates securities from goods that are subject to the conventional pricing mechanism of sloping supply and demand curves. After reviewing the two pricing mechanisms, supply-demand, and the CAPM, this chapter compares the economic distinction between securities and real goods to the legal definition of a security and finds them consistent.

Readers who only seek a summary description of the CAPM can skip the details of its foundations and go directly to the section entitled, "Pricing Undiversifiable Risk." Readers familiar with the CAPM can skip to the concluding section entitled, "Goods Subject to Each Pricing Mechanism."

A. SUPPLY-DEMAND

Conventional economic theory posits that supply and demand establish the prices of goods. This theory begins with a few background assumptions: (1) that sellers know how much producing additional units of a good would cost them, (2) that buyers

[1] Nobel Prize in Economics 1990 Press Release (October 16, 1990), available at www.nobelprize.org /nobel_prizes/economics/laureates/1990/press.html (accessed February 15, 2017).

know how much benefit they would derive from using additional units of a good, and (3) that both buyers and sellers are subject to diminishing returns, meaning that producing and using additional units becomes costlier, reducing the gains from trade. The diminishing nature of returns suggests that if sellers made significantly fewer units, the good would be cheaper for the sellers to produce and give greater benefits to buyers. The opposite is also true: if sellers made significantly more units, their production costs would go up, and the good would become less useful to buyers.

This setting of supply and demand produces the economic ideal of "equilibrium." If either too few or too many of the good come to the market, some buyers and sellers will regret their decisions. The equilibrium of supply and demand occurs when the price of the good induces sellers to supply the same number of goods as buyers want to consume. In that equilibrium, no sellers and no buyers regret their decisions.

Consider handcrafted goods that are either perishable or costly to store, for example, woven baskets. Basket weavers have limited time and alternative uses for their time. They can produce some reasonable number of baskets, but producing more becomes increasingly costly. Buyers of baskets have a strong need for the first few baskets for carrying their things, but buying more baskets quickly becomes wasteful. The pricing theory of supply and demand tells us that the market price of baskets produces an equilibrium. Weavers weave as many baskets as buyers want because of pricing.

If weavers wove too few, buyers would create a shortage in the market. Those who derive great value from baskets would ask for more and would pay high prices for them. This would prompt more weavers to make more baskets.

If weavers wove too many baskets, buyers would not buy them all. The market would experience a glut. The perishability of the good would come into play as the sellers react to the glut. "Perishability" means that sellers cannot wait out a glut by storing their unsold stock. If baskets were completely perishable (meaning that they would eventually become worthless), then weavers would cut prices dramatically to attract the buyers who derive low benefits from baskets. Eventually, sellers will accept virtually any price. The surprisingly low price means that some sellers would regret their actions. The weavers who have the highest costs or the most profitable alternatives would prefer not to have woven as many baskets.

The appeal of this traditional theory of pricing is that the lack of an equilibrium tends not to persist. Those who regret their past conduct change it until an equilibrium occurs. This economic explanation of the pricing of real goods rests on diminishing returns and subjective valuations – each buyer or seller has different benefits and costs. Contrast this with the objective nature of stock pricing. All investors and traders have the same valuation as long as they anticipate the same future.

B. THE CAPITAL ASSET PRICING MODEL

Finance offers a different mechanism for the pricing of stock – the CAPM. The CAPM does not deny supply and demand, but rather it predicts the price that supply and demand will produce. In a parallel step, modern finance also probes the limits of the CAPM theory with a body of empirical scholarship known as the "efficient capital markets hypothesis."[2]

The CAPM (pronounced "cap-EM") is a massive intellectual tower with foundations in probability theory and statistics. Oversimplified, the CAPM makes two giant steps. From the history of the prices of each stock, the statistical method of regression calculates the undiversifiable risk about which investors must and do care. From that measure of risk, the CAPM determines the appropriate rate of return that investors ought to expect from each stock. Because the CAPM determines the appropriate return for each risk, the CAPM also prices each stock using the return that the stock's risk dictates.

To understand the CAPM, one must understand several profound concepts from statistics and finance:

1. Risk and measuring risk through average deviation or standard deviation;
2. Diversification and how it reduces risk;
3. That the reduction of risk through diversification has a limit when applied to stocks due to the common influence of the economy on all businesses;
4. The beta that the regression method produces is the statistical measure of each stock's tendency to change with the stock index (which, in turn, reflects the economy's predicted behavior); and
5. How these four foundations combine into the CAPM, which calculates expected return depending on the risk that investors cannot diversify away.

i. Risk

Simply stated, "risk" is uncertainty about the outcomes of future events. We manage risk by understanding the nature of the uncertainty in question. To wit, multiple uncertainties may have the same range of outcomes and the same average outcome yet still be different in terms of risk. Take the uncertainty of gambling on fair, 50–50, double-or-nothing coin tosses. Placing one's entire purse on a single coin toss is a much riskier proposition than dividing the purse into two or more equal bets on different coin tosses. The range of outcomes is the same. The range starts from losing everything and extends to doubling one's purse. The average outcome is the same. While some bettors may lose all their money and some may double it, in aggregate, bettors will tend to win about as much as they bet because they will tend to win about half the tosses.

[2] See note 19.

Yet some bettors can plan their future finances while others cannot. Take bettors who place their entire purse on a single coin toss. They have a 50% probability of losing everything. They cannot rationally expect to use the purse funds to meet any financial obligations they have. In contrast, bettors who split the purse into many smaller bets will be able to plan significant expenditures out of the purse money and meet them with near certainty. They expose their purses to different risk despite the same range and average.

For the purpose of understanding the CAPM, risk is best measured by "dispersion" according to the "probability theory" branch of mathematics. Measures of dispersion seek to convey how much the actual outcomes will tend to differ from a metric of the central tendency of the outcomes, such as the average or the median.

Measures of dispersion come in various flavors. Standard deviation is the most famous but also the least pleasant. Its fame derives from its mathematical properties, which allow easy manipulation in equations. It is unpleasant because it relies on square roots, making it void of any intuitive appeal. Average (absolute) deviation and median (absolute) deviation are more intuitive. Average (absolute) deviation answers the question, what is the average distance from the average? Not surprisingly, median (absolute) deviation answers the question, what is the median distance from the median? (Both measure the distance in absolute terms, dropping negative signs.) Fortunately, the choice of a measure of dispersion makes little difference in understanding the CAPM. This allows us to aim for some intuitive appeal and use average deviation.

The coin tossing example can illustrate average deviation. Suppose that the purse is $1,000. Gambling the entire purse on a single toss would lead to a 50% probability of winning $2,000 and a 50% probability of a loss with winnings of zero. The average outcome is $1,000.[3] Average deviation is also $1,000.[4]

Splitting the purse into two and betting $500 on each of two coin tosses changes the average deviation but neither the range (which stays $0 to $2,000) nor the average outcome (which stays $1,000). To win $2,000, both tosses must be wins. The first is a win with 50% probability (half the time), and then the second must also be a win. Two wins happen half the time of half the time (0.5 times 0.5), that is, with 25% probability. Similarly, winning $0 occurs with 25% probability. The remaining 50% of the time, the outcome is either a win followed by a loss or a loss followed by a win, for an outcome of $1,000 with 50% probability.

Betting on two tosses instead of just one makes average deviation much smaller. Now the average deviation is $500: an absolute difference of 1,000 (from $1,000 up to $2,000) with 25% probability plus an absolute difference of 0 [from the outcome of

[3] Calculation of the average is the sum of the products of the probability of each outcome by that outcome. In this case, 0.5 times $2,000 plus 0.5 times 0 sums up to $1,000.

[4] There is 50% probability that the absolute difference is 1,000 (from the +1,000 difference between the average of $1,000 and the outcome of $2,000) plus a 50% probability again of 1,000 (from the −1,000 difference between the average of $1,000 and the outcome of 0).

$1,000 to the average of $1,000] with 50% probability) plus another absolute difference of 1,000 (from $1,000 to $0) with 25% probability.

The change in average deviation corresponds to an important change in the uncertainty. When taking the second bet on the second coin toss, half the time the bettor walks away with the average. The remaining half the time the bettor ends up with a difference of $1,000 from the average. In the bet on the single coin toss, the bettor is certain to always end up $1,000 away from the average.

In sum, measures of dispersion such as average deviation are appropriate measures of risk because they explain the difference between uncertainties despite the fact that the uncertainties may have the same ranges and the same averages.[5] In the example of the $1,000 purse, the individual's ability to plan a future expense of, say, $300 out of that purse is vastly different depending on the number of tosses. With a sufficiently small dispersion, the individual can commit to the expense. Someone who wants to plan with great certainty will stay several multiples of this measure away from any uncertainty that may foil plans. The "six sigma" quality control principle, for example, advocates staying six standard deviations away.[6]

Understanding that measures of dispersion, such as average deviation, measure risk is important because it helps clarify how diversification can reduce risk. When applied to stocks, however, diversification reduces risk only to a limit below which risk cannot fall. Understanding this failure of diversification is necessary to understand the CAPM.

ii. Diversification

To diversify, a bettor must reduce the amount exposed to each risk while increasing the number of risks. The gambler who splits the $1,000 purse into two bets of $500 each is diversifying and does even more so by splitting it into ten gambles of $100 each. The entrepreneur who sells $1 million stake in a new business and invests $10,000 in each of 100 different corporate stocks is also diversifying. The total amount at risk remains the same, but the aggregate risk drops.

Two phenomena cause this drop in risk. First, diversification makes extreme outcomes less likely. For extreme outcomes to occur, all the different independent

[5] More statistical measures may explain even more, but dispersion is enough for understanding the CAPM. Additional statistics may allow differentiation between risks that have both the same average outcomes and the same average deviations. One should not make the mistake of thinking that the range of the uncertain outcome is the most important for (preventing) planning. The importance of range is undermined by the fact that most continuous distributions have infinite range. Since any plan can be foiled by a sufficiently major adversity, the best measure of what prevents planning is a measure of the likely size of the adversity, in other words, the likely deviation from the expectation, which is what dispersion measures convey.

[6] Thomas Pysdek & Paul A. Keller, Six Sigma Handbook 292 (3d ed. 2009); Rajesh Jugulum & Philip Samuel, Design for Lean Six Sigma: A Holistic Approach to Design and Innovation 43 (2008).

risks must produce the same outcome (all wins or all losses). This becomes increasingly unlikely as diversification increases. Second, diversification increases the number of central outcomes. The operation of diversification was visible in the preceding example, the split of the $1,000 purse into two bets of $500. To further illustrate the effect of diversification, let us split the purse into 10 bets of $100 each.

When our bettor splits the purse into 10 bets of $100, the range of outcomes remains $0 to $2,000, but the diversification further reduces the probability of extreme outcomes. Winning or losing all 10 tosses happens with probability less than 1 in 100,000.[7] Similarly, besides being a terrible outcome, winning only one toss is also extraordinarily unlikely, as is losing only one toss. Simultaneously, the diversification produces additional outcomes near the average of $1,000. The diversified bettor may end up merely $100 away from the average (with $900 or $1,100) or merely $200 away from the average (with $800 or $1,200). By producing more outcomes near the average, diversification increases the probability of ending near the average. Both the reduction of the probability of extremes and the accumulation of probable outcomes near the average combine to reduce risk.

The reduction in average deviation confirms the reduction of risk. Moving from betting the entire purse of $1,000 on one toss to betting it on two tosses reduces average deviation from $1,000 to $500. Betting it on 10 tosses reduces average deviation to $246. Betting it on one hundred $10 tosses reduces average deviation to just under $80, and betting it in a thousand $1 tosses reduces it to $25. If there is no lower limit on the size of the gamble, diversification can reduce dispersion below any given positive number.[8]

To compare diversification in independent gambles to that in stocks, we switch from absolute numbers to percentages and generalize the example by transforming average deviation to a fraction of the purse. Betting the entire purse on a single toss produces average deviation equal to the amount of the purse, 100%. Splitting the purse into two tosses reduces average deviation to 50%, whereas dividing it over 10 tosses brings average deviation to 24.6%. One hundred tosses reduce it to 8%, one thousand to 2.5%. Unfortunately, diversification in stocks cannot bring deviation that low.

iii. Limitation of Diversification in Stocks

Stocks do not behave like coin tosses. The experience with diversification in the stock market is sharply different. Research has shown that diversification does not

7 The bettor wins the first toss half the time. The bettor wins both the first two tosses half the time of half the time. The bettor wins all 10 tosses half the time of half the time repeated ten times, or 0.5 raised to the tenth power, namely, once in 1,024 times, or with 0.00097% probability.

8 While the formula for average deviation frustrates the manipulation necessary to solve for the desired average deviation, this is easy for standard deviation. The standard deviation s for the number n of independent 50–50 gambles in which a purse of dollars p is divided simplifies to $s = p\sqrt{1/n}$, which, solved for n, gives the number of tosses that produce the desired standard deviation s, namely, $n = (p/s)^2$.

reduce deviation below a floor near 20%.[9] Diversifying over the 500 stocks of the Standard & Poor's (S&P) 500 Index or diversifying over thousands of stocks reaches the same stumbling block. The investor still carries substantial uncertainty.

Despite not behaving as nicely as diversification among coin tosses, diversification in stocks still has a very significant effect. A diversified portfolio does have much less risk than an undiversified one. The puzzle is why diversifying risk among stocks has a limit.

Finance theory solved this puzzle by realizing that risks for stocks divide into two categories: risks about specific businesses and risks about the entire economic system that influence all businesses. The former, known as "firm-specific," "idiosyncratic," or "unsystematic" risks, include the health of senior executives, the success of products and innovations of each business and it competitors, and accidents to the business's productive resources. Examples of the latter, known as "market-wide," "non-idiosyncratic," or "systematic" risks, include wars, social unrest, and economic crises.

Diversification among stocks only operates on firm-specific risk. It has no effect on market-wide risk. When an investor diversifies over many stocks, the good luck of some firms as to firm-specific risks will tend to cancel out the bad luck of others. This diversification, however, does not help the investor avoid the consequences of general recessions and panics. Those will hurt the prospects of all firms and have a full impact on investors, however diversified.

iv. Measuring Undiversifiable Risk

After realizing that the market-wide risk that reflects the overall economy's fluctuations is not diversifiable, the CAPM takes the next best precaution, which is to measure how sensitive each stock is to this risk. Ideally, finance would do this by computing the sensitivity of each stock to changes in the economy. Several metrics of the economy's performance exist, such as the gross domestic product, productivity, and inflation. These, however, are neither accurately nor immediately observable. Because changes in the economy are difficult to observe accurately and in due time, finance finds a substitute that is sensitive to changes in the economy and measurable. It then calculates the sensitivity of the changes of a stock's price in relation to the changes of the substitute. Financial practice uses a broad stock index as the substitute gauge, usually the S&P 500 Index.[10]

[9] E. J. Elton & M. J. Gruber, *Risk Reduction and Portfolio Size: An Analytic Solution*, 50 *J. Bus.* 415–37 (1977) (diversification decreases standard deviation in portfolios to no less than 19.2%); Richard Brealey & Stewart Myers, Principles of Corporate Finance 119–35 (2d ed. 1984).

[10] The S&P 500 is an index that aggregates the prices of the stock of 500 large publicly traded corporations, adjusting for the capitalization of each firm, so that large firms have proportionally more weight than small ones. See Standard & Poor's 500 Guide (2012); S&P Indices: S&P 500, available at us.spindices.com/indices/equity/sp-500 (accessed February 15, 2017).

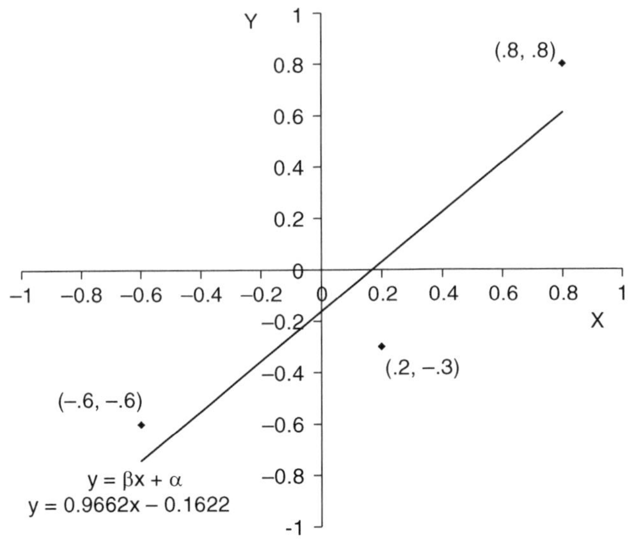

FIGURE 5.1 Cartesian plane and trend line.

Measuring how sensitive each stock is to the index is an application of the linear regression statistical method. Linear regression derives the equation that draws the line closest to a set of points on the Cartesian plane – a trend line.

Figure 5.1 offers an example of three points and the trend line that linear regression produces. Two axes provide the coordinates that identify points on the plane, the horizontal axis (x-axis) and the vertical axis (y-axis). The CAPM places the performance of the index on the horizontal axis (x) and the performance of the stock on the vertical axis (y). Each point corresponds to a pair of numbers, that point's coordinates, conventionally in parentheses with the horizontal or x-coordinate first (x, y). The figure shows three points (0.8, 0.8), (0.2, −0.3), and (−0.6, −0.6). In the context of the CAPM, these points correspond to three time periods, one when the index rose 0.8 while the stock also rose 0.8, one when the index rose 0.2 while the stock dropped 0.3, and one when they both dropped 0.6. Linear regression calculates the coefficients of an equation that draws the straight line nearest to those points. The equation calculates the y that corresponds to each x by using a coefficient (β, or beta) multiplied by x plus another coefficient (α, or alpha). The equation is $y = \beta x + \alpha$. In Figure 5.1, linear regression produces the equation $y = 0.9662x - 0.1622$. In the CAPM, the x corresponds to the index and the y to the stock.

The CAPM holds that the beta coefficient captures the tendency of the stock to change with the economy (the CAPM ignores the other coefficient, alpha, mostly because in a diversified portfolio the alphas should cancel out). Rather than coin a new name for this measure, finance refers to it as "beta." Beta is the tendency of each stock to change with changes of the index. A beta of 1, for example, means that

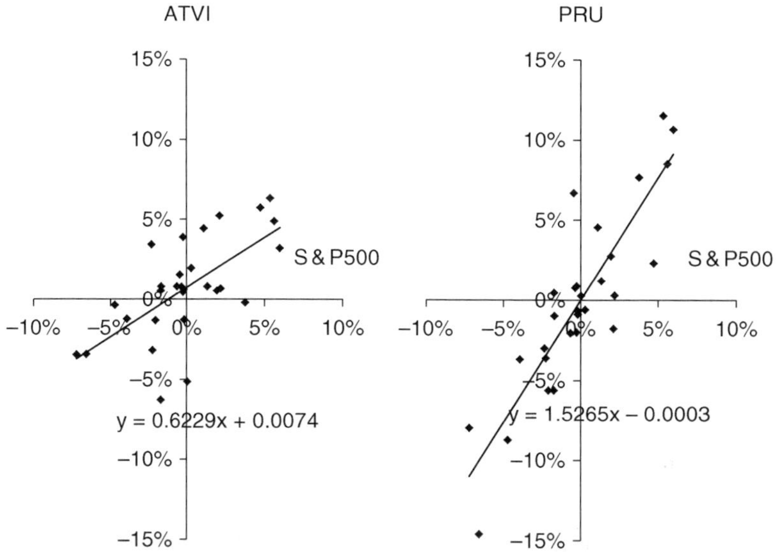

FIGURE 5.2 Price changes of stocks against index.

the stock tends to change as much as the index, a beta of 0.5 indicates the tendency to change half as much, and a beta of 2 twice as much.

Figure 5.2 illustrates calculation of the beta of two stocks. On the left is a graph of the weekly prices of Activision Blizzard, Inc. (the producer of electronic games with stock symbol ATVI) against the S&P 500 Index. These are the prices for the 30 weeks ending October 28, 2011.[11] For comparison, Prudential Financial, Inc. (stock symbol PRU) appears on the right. Linear regression produces the trend lines.[12] Activision Blizzard has a beta of about 0.6, which means that it tends to change about 0.6 times as much as the index, whereas Prudential Financial has a beta of about 1.5 and tends to change about 1.5 times as much as the index.

We know that a diversified portfolio minimizes idiosyncratic risk but remains exposed to the uncertainties of the entire economy. However, a diversified portfolio of stocks that are like Activision Blizzard in their sensitivity to the economy's surprises would tend to change less (about half as much as the index) than a diversified portfolio of stocks similar to Prudential Financial (one-and-a-half times as much as the index). Both portfolios have diversified away idiosyncratic risk but produce a different exposure to market risk. How should the returns of those two portfolios differ? As the Section v explains, the CAPM answers this question by calculating the return that corresponds to each beta.

11 The spreadsheet is available at my site, www.nicholasgeorgakopoulos.org, under this book's title on the publications page.

12 For Activision Blizzard, linear regression produces the equation $y = 0.6229x + 0.0074$, and for Prudential, $y = 1.5265x - 0.0003$.

v. Pricing Undiversifiable Risk

The components of the CAPM mesh together to calculate the necessary return that corresponds to each beta, which measures how each stock or portfolio exposes its holder to the undiversifiable risk of overall economic performance. Comparing two portfolios, the one with the larger beta is more sensitive to overall economic performance, carries more risk, and therefore is less appealing unless it offers a sufficiently higher return to compensate for the greater risk. Analogously, the portfolio with the lower beta becomes appealing at a lower expected return.

The CAPM anchors its analysis on two rates of return – that of the market and that of safe lending. The "market return" is the expected return of the entire stock market, such as the expected return of the S&P 500 Index. Finance theory considers the safe lending or risk-free (rate of) return to be the one offered by short-term government obligations such as Treasury securities. The market's return, however, must compensate for risk. It must be higher than the risk-free return. The difference by which the market return exceeds the risk-free return is the "market premium."

The risk-free return is important as a lower bound. Even utterly safe portfolios, invested in Treasury securities, earn a positive return (even if nowadays negligible). Any risk should push returns higher. The amount of additional return corresponding to each risk should be analogous to the additional return that the market offers. Risk less than that of the market should require a return between the risk-free return and that of the market. More precisely, a risk that is a known fraction of the market risk should offer a return that exceeds the risk-free rate by the same fraction of the market premium.

A stock portfolio exposing its holder to half the market risk ought to command more than merely half the return of the entire market. All portfolios are entitled to the risk-free return and, beyond that, according to their beta, a corresponding fraction of the market premium. Thus a portfolio that exposes its holder to half the market risk should give a return equal to the sum of the risk-free return plus half the market premium.

The same analysis applies to portfolios with risks greater than that of the market. Consider a portfolio with a beta of 1.5. It must earn the risk-free return plus one and one half times the market premium. The CAPM shows that every asset with a known beta has an expected return equal to the sum of the risk-free return plus beta times the market premium.[13]

The CAPM is not merely a logical construct. If prices deviate from the pricing that the CAPM indicates, opportunities for riskless profit – "arbitrage opportunities" – arise. When a diversified portfolio with a given beta offers a different expected return than that indicated by the CAPM, traders can construct synthetic portfolios and capture the arbitrage opportunities. Understanding the arbitrage that

[13] Formally, the CAPM is $R_\beta = R_f + \beta(R_m - R_f)$, where R_β is the expected return of the asset with a beta equal to β, R_f is the risk-free return, and R_m is the expected market return.

forces prices to comply with the CAPM explains the connection of the CAPM to supply-demand.

An example of the arbitrage opportunity requires detail on rates of return. Suppose that the risk-free return is 1% and the expected market return is 11%, making the market premium 10%. The CAPM indicates that a portfolio with a beta of 0.5 should have an expected return of the risk-free 1% plus half the market premium, namely, an expected return of 6% (1% + 5%). Similarly, the CAPM indicates that a portfolio with a beta of 1.5 should have an expected return of the risk- free 1% plus one and a half times the market premium, namely, an expected return of 16% (1% + 15%). To observe the arbitrage opportunities, consider four diversified portfolios, a pair at each beta, one with a return lower than the CAPM and one with a higher one: (1) a beta of 0.5 and return of 4%, (2) a beta of 0.5 and return of 8%, (3) a beta of 1.5 and return of 14%, and (4) a beta of 1.5 and return of 18%. The existence of any one of these portfolios gives rise to an arbitrage opportunity.

Traders capture the arbitrage opportunities by synthesizing portfolios with the betas that they need to take opposing positions that cancel out risk. Traders synthesize betas by combining (risk-free) lending or borrowing with investing a fraction of their target funds in the portfolio or in the market index. Thus an investor who wants a beta of 0.5 can invest half the portfolio in the index and half in the risk-free security. This synthetic portfolio will produce the CAPM-predicted return for a beta of 0.5 because half the money will earn the expected market return (which is the risk-free return plus the market premium) and the other half of the money will earn only the risk-free return. The synthetic portfolio also has the risk of a beta of 0.5. If a surprisingly good or bad event moves the index, the synthetic portfolio will experience half that movement, just as would a portfolio with an actual beta of 0.5.

Portfolios with betas greater than 1 can either be synthesized using borrowing, or they can serve as the basis for synthesizing the market portfolio by combining them with risk-free lending. A synthetic portfolio with a beta of 1.5 results from borrowing an amount equal to half the portfolio and investing the entire proceeds, one and a half times the portfolio amount, in the market index.[14] However, the actual beta 1.5 portfolio can also help synthesize a beta 1 portfolio. The synthetic beta 1 portfolio has two-thirds of its funds in the portfolio with an actual beta of 1.5 and the remaining one-third in the risk-free security.

Start with the portfolio with a beta of 0.5 and expected return of 4%. The CAPM assigns this portfolio a return of the risk-free rate of 1% plus half the market premium of 10% for a total of 6%. The portfolio offers too low a return at its current price, and

[14] This portfolio will offer a return equal to 1.5 times the market return, namely, 1.5 times the risk-free return plus 1.5 times the market premium. When repaying the borrowed funds, the portfolio will owe interest computed (hopefully at near the risk-free rate) on half the portfolio amount (hopefully near 0.5 times the risk-free return). Surprises to the market have the expected 150% impact on this portfolio. In a period when the market has some deviation from its expected return, the synthetic portfolio will have 1.5 times the market's deviation.

the CAPM would assign it a lower price. Traders can take advantage of its high price by selling it (perhaps selling it short) and using the market portfolio to synthesize a portfolio with a beta of 0.5. To synthesize a beta of 0.5, traders place half the portfolio's amount in the market index and lend the other half at the risk-free rate. The resulting portfolio would react to risk like a portfolio with a beta of 0.5 but would have a higher return than 4%.[15] After arbitraging by buying the cheap asset, in this case the synthetic portfolio, and selling the dear asset, in this case the actual beta 0.5 portfolio, the trader will enjoy a risk-free expected return of 2%.[16]

Consider next the portfolio with beta of 1.5 and expected return of 18%. The CAPM assigns this portfolio a return of the risk-free rate of 1% plus 1.5 times the market premium of 10% for a total of 16%. The portfolio offers too high a return at its current price, and the CAPM would assign it a higher price. Traders can take advantage of its low price and use it to synthesize a beta 1 portfolio while selling (again, perhaps selling short) the actual beta 1 portfolio. To synthesize a beta of 1, with two-thirds of the portfolio the trader would buy the beta 1.5 portfolio and lend the remaining one-third at the risk-free return. The resulting portfolio would behave as a beta 1 portfolio but would have a higher return.[17] After arbitraging by buying the cheap asset, in this case the synthetic portfolio, and selling the dear asset, in this case the market, the trader will enjoy a risk-free expected return of ⅔ %.[18]

The other two cases follow the same process. The case of a beta of 1.5 and return of 14% creates a portfolio that is too dear, and the arbitrageur will sell it and buy the cheap synthetic equivalent. The case of a beta of 0.5 and return of 6% indicates a portfolio that is too cheap, and the arbitrageur will buy it and sell the dear synthetic equivalent.

15 For example, if the trader's portfolio were $300,000, then the trader would place $150,000 in the beta 1 portfolio that has an expected return of 11% and $150,000 in the risk-free asset for a return of 1%. The entire portfolio has a return of 6% (instead of the 4% of the actual beta 0.5 portfolio). If the market deviates by any percentage from its expected return, the expected deviation of the synthetic beta 0.5 portfolio would be the half that deviation. If, for example, the market were to deviate by 10%, the actual beta 0.5 portfolio would tend to deviate by 5% and the synthetic beta 0.5 portfolio would also deviate by 5%.

16 The synthetic portfolio has an expected return of 6%, and the trader earns that. The actual beta 0.5 portfolio has an expected return of 4%, and the trader sold it and therefore has given it up or owes it. This 2% difference matches the size of the error.

17 For example, if the trader's portfolio were $300,000, then the trader would place $200,000 in the beta 1.5 portfolio that has an expected return of 17% and $100,000 in the risk-free asset for a return of 1%. The entire portfolio has a return of 11⅔% (instead of the 11% of the actual market). If the market deviates by any percentage from its expected return, the expected deviation of the synthetic beta 1 portfolio would be the same. If, for example, the market were to deviate by 10%, the actual beta 1.5 portfolio would tend to deviate by 15%, but the synthetic portfolio would only experience two-thirds of that.

18 The synthetic portfolio has an expected return of 11⅔%, and the trader earns that. The actual market portfolio has an expected return of 11%, and the trader sold it and therefore has given it up or owes it. The difference does not match the 2% size of the error because the arbitrage did not occur at the mispriced beta but at the lower market beta. If the trader could borrow at the riskless rate, then the trader could synthesize the 1.5 beta by borrowing and investing 150% in the market index.

The arbitrageur's buying and selling connect the CAPM to supply and demand. The trading activity predicted by the CAPM pushes prices in the direction that validates the CAPM. The CAPM predicts the buying of assets that it deems cheap and the selling of ones that it deems dear. Effectively, the CAPM predicts trading, that is, supply or demand, for falsely priced assets.

The empirical evidence, mostly under the heading of the "efficient capital markets hypothesis," supports the CAPM but imperfectly. The clearest support is the evidence that returns follow betas, a phenomenon predating formulation of the CAPM. Researchers retroactively calculated the beta of every stock and segmented the market in a handful of portfolios sorted by beta. The returns of the portfolios complied with the CAPM with minor discrepancies.[19] The lowest-beta portfolio had the lowest return, and the portfolio with the highest beta enjoyed the highest return. Moreover, as the CAPM predicts, changes of beta altered returns less than proportionately. A portfolio with a beta of 0.5 enjoyed a return greater than half the return of the portfolio with a beta of 1.

C. GOODS SUBJECT TO EACH PRICING MECHANISM

An understanding of the pricing mechanisms allows us to express the principles separating goods into two groups: those with prices that stem from the CAPM and those with prices that stem from supply and demand. Supply and demand apply to all goods. The CAPM applies to goods that perform only the financial function of carrying value through time.

Financial goods can exceed the valuation assigned by the CAPM if they offer additional value.[20] Examples of such values may be synergies for buyers of control and artistic value for collectors. Consider a corporation that is the target of an acquisition motivated by synergies. Before the acquisition, the CAPM uses the target's expected income to produce its price. The acquirer, however, realizes additional value from the target because the synergies make both the target and the acquirer more productive. The acquirer can offer a price greater than that

[19] The main discrepancy is that the portfolios' returns appear to hinge from a rate higher than the risk-free rate. See discussion and citations to evidence collected by Eugene F. Fama & Kenneth R. French, *The Capital Asset Pricing Model: Theory and Evidence*, 18 J. ECON. PERSP. 25, 32 (2004). However, since the essence of the CAPM would require that the risk-free return and the market return be equal after inflation and taxes, some imperfections and discrepancies between the model and reality are unavoidable, mostly because different investors face different tax rates.

[20] However, nonfinancial goods, particularly durable ones, may also perform some financial functions. Jewelry and art, for example, have value as apparel or decoration and also for resale. Their financial value, however, does not stem from expected future income they may produce. Some nonfinancial goods may derive their financial value from their potential contribution to economic production. A house's yard, for example, may derive part of its value from its potential use as farmland, and the CAPM would apply to the valuation of farmland. The consumer's value of using it as a yard likely exceeds the financial valuation.

indicated by the CAPM. Similarly, old railroad stocks have zero value according to the CAPM, but a collector will offer more than this.

These examples escape the pricing of the CAPM because arbitrage cannot hold their prices low. Sellers cannot synthesize them to the buyers' satisfaction because the buyers seek more than a return for a given beta risk. The buyer of control seeks the operating synergies. The buyer of collectible stock certificates seeks the collector value.

Thus the CAPM appears to govern the value of goods that serve only the function of storing value through time. This is necessary if the holder of the good is to be willing to exchange it for a synthetic substitute with equal beta. Goods that serve additional functions escape from the CAPM and become subject to supply and demand.

The economists' separation of goods into those subject to (sloping) supply and demand from those subject to the CAPM is closer to the legal separation of securities from nonsecurities than at first appears. As we saw in Chapter 4, the function of the definition of a security is the separation of goods that are primarily subject to the buyer's inspection and future control from those that buyers tend not to inspect or control. The focus on inspection matches the subjective valuation of supply and demand versus the objective valuation of the CAPM. The focus on control aligns with active use of real goods versus the passive investment in securities. Noting this agreement of the economic and legal understandings of securities, we can turn to a jurisprudential moment where they appear to have deviated.

6

From the Sale-of-Business Doctrine to *Gustafson*

The legal definition of a security – a presumed intent to invest in a common enterprise with an expectation of profits mostly from the effort of others – and its analysis as an investment with neither access to information nor control are consistent with the economic understanding of a security as a passive investment. The courts, however, have followed a tortured path in applying this analysis to sales of controlling blocks of shares and to private transactions generally. According to the "sale-of-business doctrine," sales of controlling blocks of shares were not sales of securities; therefore, the buyer had neither the rescission remedy nor other securities law protections. Then, in 1985, the US Supreme Court overturned the sale-of-business doctrine with *Landreth* and *Ruefenacht*,[1] giving buyers of control the right to rescind remedy and other securities law protections. A few years later, in a move of legal whiplash, the Court in *Gustafson* granted a reprieve from the remedies of securities law to a seller of a controlling block of shares.[2] This reprieve was both broader and narrower than that of the sale-of-business doctrine. It exempted all private transactions from the rescission remedy of securities law, but buyers retained all other securities law protections.

Chapters 3 through 5 walked through three analyses: (1) the legal definition of a security, which focuses on presumed intent to participate in a "common enterprise" without control ("[mostly] from the effort of others"), (2) the definition's function, which relates it to lack of current access to information and lack of future control, and (3) the economic analysis, which implies passive investment. Harmony among these analyses would be the happy conclusion had the Supreme Court not muddied the waters when it rejected the sale-of-business doctrine. The Court eventually reharmonized the law but only implicitly and partly with *Gustafson*.

According to the sale-of-business doctrine, the sale of the shares forming the controlling block of a business was not the sale of a security despite the fact that it

1 *Landreth Timber Co. v. Landreth*, 471 US 681 (May 28, 1985); *Gould v. Ruefenacht*, 471 US 701 (May 28, 1985).

2 *Gustafson v. Alloyd Co., Inc.*, 513 US 561 (1995).

took the form of a sale of shares. The circuits that adopted this doctrine relied on the distinction between *Forman* and *Howey*.[3] In essence, the sale-of-business doctrine promoted substance over form. The form of a sale of a controlling block as stock is as misleading as was in *Forman* the acquisition of shares that controlled an apartment. The buyers obtain control. Therefore, they do not fulfill the *Howey* definition of a security: they neither invest in a common enterprise nor seek profit from the effort of others. Obtaining control is also antithetical to the function of the *Howey* test because a buyer of control tends to have the negotiating power to examine the entire enterprise and will control it. Buying control also fails the economic understanding of a security as a passive investment because the acquirer can change the administration of the target and can extract synergies or perquisites.

Despite that the sale-of-business doctrine promotes substance over form and adheres to the analysis of *Howey* and *Forman*, the Supreme Court repudiated it in two opinions issued on the same day.[4] The *Landreth/Ruefenacht* pair of opinions rejected applicability of *Forman* and the sale-of-business doctrine rather summarily: because stock in sales of control has the usual features of stock – mostly by including votes and dividends – *Forman* does not apply.[5] The sale-of-business doctrine was rejected because it had the capacity to lead to vagueness and inconsistencies. The vagueness arises from the lack of a specific percentage that constitutes sale of control. The inconsistencies come from the fact that a single transaction can either disperse or create control.

The Supreme Court's choice to abolish the sale-of-business doctrine underlines its concern with vagueness and inconsistencies, as the *Landreth* and *Ruefenacht* facts illustrate. In *Landreth*, 100% of the stock of a lumber mill was acquired by a syndicate of passive investors.[6] *Ruefenacht*, however, featured a buyer of only 50% who expected to be involved in the running of the business.[7] Not only did the "from the effort of others" element of the definition seem to apply in the transaction for the 100% ownership but not in that for the 50% ownership, but control was also unclear

[3] See, e.g., *Frederiksen v. Poloway*, 637 F.2d 1147 (7th Cir.), cert. denied, 451 US 1017, 101 S.Ct. 3006, 69 L.Ed.2d 389 (1981) ("Not all transactions which involve 'stock' are necessarily covered by the securities laws. Rather, the test for coverage, in general, is whether the purchaser is placing money in the hands of another who will control the funds and the business decisions. If, however, the purchaser is assuming control of the critical decisions of the corporation, then the transaction is not considered to involve securities."). See also *Sutter v. Groen*, 687 F.2d 197, 202 (7th Cir. 1982); *Canfield v. Rapp & Son, Inc.*, 654 F.2d 459, 465 (7th Cir. 1981); *Frederiksen v. Poloway*, 637 F.2d 1147, 1151–2 (7th Cir. 1981); *Christy v. Cambron*, 710 F.2d 669, 672 (10th Cir. 1983); *Chandler v. Kew, Inc.*, 691 F.2d 443, 444 (10th Cir. 1977); *King v. Winkler*, 673 F.2d 342, 345 (11th Cir. 1982).

[4] *Landreth Timber Co. v. Landreth*, 471 US 681 (May 28, 1985); *Gould v. Ruefenacht*, 471 US 701 (May 28, 1985).

[5] See text accompanying notes 17–19 (the *Forman* stock did not grant its holders voting power proportional to the number of shares held because voting in the association was by apartment; the stock would not bring any dividends; rather the leasing of common areas benefited financially the occupants by reducing the common expenses).

[6] *Landreth*, 471 US at 683–4, 695–6.

[7] *Ruefenacht*, 471 US at 702–3.

in both. The sellers had 100% control before both transactions. In *Landreth*, the purchase dispersed control. In *Ruefenacht*, the purchase split control between two 50% shareholders, leaving neither one with absolute control.

The Supreme Court corrected the error of the 1985 rejection of the sale-of-business doctrine with *Gustafson*.[8] On its face, *Gustafson* merely held that "prospectus" means a disclosure document used in a public offering. Since private offerings do not use one, buyers in private offerings do not have the rescission remedy of securities law against sellers who make a misleading statement "through a prospectus."[9] Section A introduces the registration process, which is necessary to understand the potential magnitude of *Gustafson*. Section B then underscores the revolutionary approach of *Gustafson*, but Section C recognizes that the dangers *Gustafson* could have caused did not materialize.

A. REGISTRATION PROCESS PRIMER

An appreciation of the changes wrought by *Gustafson* requires an understanding of the Securities Act of 1933 (the 1933 Act). The 1933 Act establishes the process for registering with the Securities and Exchange Commission (SEC) that any corporation must follow when issuing securities to the public.

The heart of the 1933 Act is Section 5, which determines the registration process.[10] Section 5 turns on three events: filing, effectiveness, and free writing. Filing occurs on the date that the registration statement is filed with the SEC. Effectiveness occurs when the SEC declares the filing to be effective. Free writing for each investor starts the moment that a complete and effective registration statement is transmitted to that investor. Free writing is the Holy Grail of the registration process. After this, the issuer is much less constrained and can even send glossy puffery.

The two most restrictive prohibitions of Section 5 are against offers and prospectuses. Their restrictiveness flows from the breadth of the corresponding definitions in Section 2. "Offer" is defined as "every attempt or offer to dispose of, or solicitation of an offer to buy."[11] To appreciate the breadth of this definition, contrast it with contract law's definition of offer as a proposition that can be accepted.[12] Merely presenting an item in appealing circumstances is an offer under securities law, whereas under contract law it is at most a solicitation of an offer. "Prospectus" is defined as "any . . . communication . . . which offers any security for sale or confirms the sale of any security."[13] Contrast this with the plain

8 *Gustafson v. Alloyd Co., Inc.*, 513 US 561 (1995). 9 *Gustafson*, 513 US at 580–2.
10 Section 5 of the 1933 Act, 15 USC § 77f (2017).
11 Section 2(a)(3) of the 1933 Act, 15 USC § 77b(a)(1) (2017).
12 Farnsworth on Contracts § 3.10 (2011).
13 Section 2(a)(10) of the 1933 Act, 15 USC §77b(a)(10) (2017).

understanding of a prospectus as an explanatory manual or guide. Letters soliciting offers and sales contracts would be prospectuses under securities law but not under a "plain English" definition.

In addition to prohibiting offers and the transmission of prospectuses, Section 5 also prohibits sales and the delivery of securities. By deploying these prohibitions at different times, Section 5 shapes the registration process. Through the prohibition of Section 5(c), issuers[14] cannot make offers before filing.[15] Through the prohibition of Section 5(a)(1), issuers cannot make sales before effectiveness.[16] Through the prohibition of Section 5(b)(1), issuers cannot transmit most prospectuses before free writing.[17] Through the prohibition of Section 5(b)(2), issuers cannot deliver securities before free writing.[18]

The definitions of Section 2 interact with Section 5 by design. For example, despite the prohibition against offers, Section 2 creates an exception for offers in the context of negotiations between underwriters and the issuer so as to enable the creation of the underwriting syndicate, the group of brokerage houses that will sell the new security to their customers.[19]

The definition of prospectuses in Section 2(a)(10) is especially interactive with Section 5. Although Section 5 prohibits the transmission of prospectuses (any selling communication per Section 2[a][10]), Section 2(a)(10)(b) exempts some communications from the definition so that very limited advertising can occur.[20] The definition of the prospectus by Section 2(a)(10) also creates free writing, the goal of the registration process. Section 2(a)(10)(a) creates free writing by stating that after the transmission of a fully compliant and effective registration statement,

14 Technically, the prohibitions apply to issuers, underwriters, and dealers. The text uses issuers for expository convenience.

15 Section 5(c) of the 1933 Act, 15 USC § 77e(c) (2017) ("It shall be unlawful … to offer … unless a registration statement has been filed.").

16 Section 5(a)(1) of the 1933 Act, 15 USC § 77e(a)(1) (2017) ("Unless a registration statement is in effect, it shall be unlawful … to sell.").

17 Section 5(b)(1) of the 1933 Act, 15 USC § 77e(b)(1) (2017) ("It shall be unlawful … to transmit any prospectus … unless … " as it interacts with the exception of Section 2[a][10][b] to the definition of a prospectus: "a … communication … after the effective date … shall not be deemed a prospectus if a [complete] prospectus … was sent or given.").

18 Section 5(b)(2) of the 1933 Act, 15 USC § 77e(b)(2) (2017) ("It shall be unlawful … to carry … any security … for delivery after sale unless accompanied or preceded by a [complete] prospectus" 18.).

19 Section 2(a)(3) of the 1933 Act, 15 USC § 77b(a)(3) (2017) ("The terms defined in this paragraph … shall not include preliminary negotiations or agreements between an issuer … and any underwriter or among underwriters.").

20 Section 2(a)(10)(b) of the 1933 Act, 15 USC § 77b(a)(10)(b) (2017) ("[E]xcept that … (b) a notice, circular, advertisement, letter, or communication in respect of a security shall not be deemed to be a prospectus if it states from whom a written prospectus meeting the requirements of section 10 may be obtained and, in addition, does no more than identify the security, state the price thereof, state by whom orders will be executed, and contain such other information as the Commission, by rules or regulations deemed necessary or appropriate in the public interest and for the protection of investors, and subject to such terms and conditions as may be prescribed therein, may permit.").

no communication is a prospectus.[21] This contrasts with *Gustafson*'s (mis)understanding of a prospectus as a document used in public offerings.[22]

The final step in understanding the registration process is Section 10. Unlike the definitional role that *Gustafson* gives it, Section 10(a) of the 1933 Act outlines the information required in the prospectus (by reference to schedules appended to the act).[23] The registration process is enforced mostly through Sections 11 and 12. Section 11 imposes liability on the issuer, the underwriters, experts, and others for misstatements in the registration statement.[24] Section 12 gives buyers the rescission remedy against sellers who made a misleading statement or omission through "a prospectus or oral communication."[25] This rescission of a private sale under Section 12 is what the *Gustafson* plaintiffs sought but did not get. The sale-of-

[21] Section 2(a)(10)(a) of the 1933 Act, 15 USC § 77b(a)(10)(1) (2017) ("[E]xcept that (a) a communication sent or given after the effective date of the registration statement (other than a prospectus permitted under subsection (b) of section 10) shall not be deemed a prospectus if it is proved that prior to or at the same time with such communication a written prospectus meeting the requirements of subsection (a) of section 10 at the time of such communication was sent or given to the person to whom the communication was made.").

[22] *Gustafson*, 513 US at 574 ("The relevant phrase in the definitional part of the statute must be read in its entirety, a reading which yields the interpretation that the term 'prospectus' refers to a document soliciting the public to acquire securities. We find that definition controlling.").

[23] Section 10 of the 1933 Act, 15 USC § 77j (2017) ("(a) Except to the extent otherwise permitted or required pursuant to this subsection or subsections (c), (d), or (e) – (1) a prospectus relating to a security other than a security issued by a foreign government or political subdivision thereof, shall contain the information contained in the registration statement, but it need not include the documents referred to in paragraphs (28) to (32), inclusive, of Schedule A; (2) a prospectus relating to a security issued by a foreign government or political subdivision thereof shall contain the information contained in the registration statement, but it need not include the documents referred to in paragraphs (13) and (14) of Schedule B"; Section 10(b) enables preliminary prospectuses that can be used before free writing: "In addition to the prospectus permitted or required in subsection (a), the Commission shall by rules or regulations deemed necessary or appropriate in the public interest or for the protection of investors permit the use of a prospectus for the purposes of subsection (b)(1) of section 5 which omits in part or summarizes information in the prospectus specified in subsection (a).").

[24] Section 11 of the 1933 Act, 15 USC § 77k (2017) ("In case any part of the registration statement, when such part became effective, contained an untrue statement of a material fact or omitted to state a material fact required to be stated therein or necessary to make the statements therein not misleading, any person acquiring such security (unless it is proved that at the time of such acquisition he knew of such untruth or omission) may, either at law or in equity, in any court of competent jurisdiction, sue – (1) every person who signed the registration statement; (2) every person who was a director of (or person performing similar functions) or partner in the issuer at the time of the filing of the part of the registration statement with respect to which his liability is asserted; (3) every person who, with his consent, is named in the registration statement as being or about to become a director, person performing similar functions, or partner; (4) every accountant, engineer, or appraiser, or any person whose profession gives authority to a statement made by him, who has with his consent been named as having prepared or certified any part of the registration statement, or as having prepared or certified any report or valuation which is used in connection with the registration statement, with respect to the statement in such registration statement, report, or valuation, which purports to have been prepared or certified by him; (5) every underwriter with respect to such security.").

[25] Section 12 of the 1933 Act, 15 USC § 77l (2017) ("Any person who – (1) offers or sells a security in violation of section 5, or (2) offers or sells a security (whether or not exempted by the provisions of

business doctrine would similarly have denied them rescission. Yet, by rejecting the sale-of-business doctrine, rescission is what *Landreth* and *Ruefenacht* granted to their plaintiffs. The timeline thus is that the sale-of-business doctrine initially denied rescission, then *Landreth* and *Ruefenacht* allowed rescission, and finally, the current regime of *Gustafson* again denies rescission.

Two illustrations, a public offering and a private one, show how, before *Gustafson*, Section 10 was not used as a definitional section in illegal offerings of securities. Observe in the first illustration how a public offering with no filing violates every prohibition of Section 5. In the second illustration, follow buyers in a private transaction like that of *Gustafson*. Before *Gustafson*, buyers in a private offering containing a material misrepresentation or omission would obtain the rescission remedy of Section 12 even if the transaction was oral.

An issuer who sells securities to the public without filing violates Section 5 in every way.

- When the issuer makes its offer, the issuer violates the prohibition of Section 5(c) against offers before filing.
- Even if the issuer files a registration statement, when the issuer sends any materials or draft contracts to potential buyers, the issuer violates the prohibition of Section 5(b)(1) against the transmission of prospectuses (defined in Section 2[a][10] to include "any . . . communication . . . which offers any security for sale").[26]
- When the issuer executes the sales contract, the issuer violates the prohibition of Section 5(a)(1) against sales before effectiveness.
- If the issuer delivers the securities, the issuer violates the prohibition of Section 5(a)(2) against deliveries.

Before *Gustafson*, Section 10 provided no definitions relevant to this transaction, whereas after *Gustafson*, it may.

section 3, other than paragraphs (2) and (14) of subsection (a) of said section), by the use of any means or instruments of transportation or communication in interstate commerce or of the mails, by means of a prospectus or oral communication, which includes an untrue statement of a material fact or omits to state a material fact necessary in order to make the statements, in the light of the circumstances under which they were made, not misleading (the purchaser not knowing of such untruth or omission), and who shall not sustain the burden of proof that he did not know, and in the exercise of reasonable care could not have known, of such untruth or omission, shall be liable, subject to subsection (b), to the person purchasing such security from him, who may sue either at law or in equity in any court of competent jurisdiction, to recover the consideration paid for such security with interest thereon.").

26 The sending of materials and draft contracts also violates the prohibition against offers. That prohibition, however, ends with the filing, when the prohibition on the transmission of prospectuses begins. Thus, technically, if the issuer does not file a registration statement at all, the issuer only violates Section 5(c) (prohibiting offers) and Section 5(a) (prohibiting sales and deliveries before effectiveness). As the registration process is sufficiently complex, the text does not focus on the initiation of the prohibition against prospectuses at the time of the filing.

An issuer making a private sale before *Gustafson* entered into an exempt transaction. According to Section 4, "[t]he provisions of section 5 shall not apply to ... (2) transactions ... not involving any public offering."[27] Since the items sold are securities, however, Section 12 still applied and granted the buyer rescission against "(a) [a]ny person who ... (2) offers or sells a security ... by means of a prospectus or oral communication ... which ... omits to state a material fact." Even if the private transaction was not in writing (to avoid the prospectus-based violation of Section 12), the oral communication was enough to trigger Section 12's rescission remedy. Again, Section 10 provides no definition, but after *Gustafson*, it does.

Before *Landreth* and *Ruefenacht*, then, rescission would not apply to transactions about control because the sale-of-business doctrine made Section 12 inapplicable (but rescission applied to all other private transactions and all public offerings). After *Landreth* and *Reufenecht* discarded the sale-of-business doctrine, all sales were subject to the rescission remedy. Now, after *Gustafson*, no private sale is subject to the rescission remedy (but public offerings are).[28]

B. GUSTAFSON AS EARTHQUAKE

The *Gustafson* majority departed from this conventional reading of the securities laws in four ways. First, the *Gustafson* majority read Section 12 to apply only to misrepresentations in a prospectus.[29] Before *Gustafson*, Section 12(b) applied to sales though "a prospectus or oral communication."[30] Second, the *Gustafson* Court construed Section 10 as attempting to define the prospectus.[31] Before *Gustafson*, Section 2(a)(10) defined the prospectus.[32] Third, because the *Gustafson* majority found no definition in Section 10 but only references to the registration statement used in public offerings, the majority took the license to

[27] 15 USC § 77d (2017).

[28] See, e.g., Natasha S. Guinan, *Nearly A Decade Later: Revisiting Gustafson and the Status of Section 12(A)(2) Liability in the Courts – Creative Judicial Developments and a Proposal for Reform*, 72 FORDHAM L. REV. 1053 (2004) ("In 1995 the Supreme Court determined in *Gustafson v. Alloyd Co.* that rescissionary liability under the 1933 Federal Securities Act ... no longer applied to private or aftermarket securities transactions, but only to public securities transactions"; footnotes omitted). See also, generally, notes 37 and 38.

[29] See *Gustafson*, 513 US at 578 ("The intent of Congress and the design of the statute require that § 12(2) liability be limited to public offerings.").

[30] See text accompanying notes 25–7.

[31] See *Gustafson*, 513 US at 574 ("To be sure, [section 10] defines a prospectus as, *inter alia*, a 'communication, written or by radio or television, which offers any security for sale or confirms the sale of any security.'"); *id.* at 589 (Thomas, J., dissenting) ("The majority transforms § 10 into the tail that wags the 1933 Act dog."); *id.* at 597 (Ginsburg, J., dissenting) ("The Court then proceeds backward; it reads into the literally and logically prior definition section, § 2(10), the meaning 'prospectus' has in § 10.").

[32] See text accompanying note 19–22.

interpret "prospectus" as a document used in a public offering.[33] Before *Gustafson*, only Section 2(a)(10) defined prospectus.[34] Fourth, the Court concluded that the buyer did not have the rescission remedy because no prospectus was used.[35] Before *Gustafson*, the sale contract would have been a prospectus with material omissions that would have triggered rescission under Section 12.[36]

The unanimous condemnation of *Gustafson* by the academy[37] and the bar[38] is unsurprising. The reasoning of *Gustafson* had the capacity to upend the application of the securities laws. Consider sales of securities without any filing. Under *Gustafson*'s reasoning, the sales could have been held to violate neither Section 5 nor Section 12 due to the absence of a prospectus. Consider public sales by oral communication. *Gustafson*'s reasoning could easily lead to the conclusion that sellers could avoid rescission, again due to the absence of a prospectus. Even more perniciously, *Gustafson*'s implicit disregard for the statutory language and structure could have become a license to make arbitrary conclusions about securities law. *Gustafson* was an earthquake that could have left securities regulation in shambles.

C. NO RUBBLE AFTER *GUSTAFSON*

Anything but a narrow interpretation of *Gustafson* could have spelled the demise of the 1933 Act. Fortunately, courts did not embrace its expansiveness. Rather, courts restricted *Gustafson*, applying it only to private transactions. Public offerings, written or oral, are still subject to Section 5 and the registration process. For public offerings, selling communications transmitted before free writing can violate Section 5 as illegal prospectuses because, despite *Gustafson*, prospectuses in public offerings are still defined by Section 2(a)(10). Private transactions, however, are subject to *Gustafson*'s understanding of prospectus as a public offering document, which contradicts and precludes the definition of prospectus according to Section 2(a)(10) as "any . . . communication . . . which offers . . . any security."

33 See *Gustafson*, 513 US at 574 ("[T]he term 'prospectus' refers to a document soliciting the public to acquire securities.").

34 See text accompanying notes 11–13.

35 See *Gustafson*, 513 US at 584 ("In sum, the word 'prospectus' is a term of art referring to a document that describes a public offering of securities by an issuer or controlling shareholder. The contract of sale, and its recitations, were not held out to the public and were not a prospectus as the term is used in the 1933 Act. The judgment of the Court of Appeals is reversed.").

36 See text accompanying notes 25–7.

37 See, e.g., Stephen M. Bainbridge, *Securities Act Section 12(2) after the* Gustafson *Debacle*, 50 Bus. Law 1230 (1995); Janet E. Kerr, *Ralston Redux: Determining which Section 3 Offerings Are Public under Section 12(2) after* Gustafson, 50 SMU L. Rev. 175 (1996–7); Michael J. Kaufman, *Mending the Weathered Jurisdictional Fences in the Supreme Court's Securities Fraud Decisions*, 49 SMU L. Rev. 159 (1996). See also Guinan, *Nearly a Decade Later*, 64.

38 See, e.g., Edward Brodsky, *Assessing the Impact of Corporate and Securities Litigation*, N.Y. L.J., March 13, 1996, at 29; Margaret A. Bancroft, *Responding to* Gustafson*: Company Registration and a New Negligence Standard*, 9 Insights, July 1995, at 14.

The consequences of *Gustafson* have been limited. Transactional practice did not change. The only change that *Gustafson* wrought is the elimination of rescission in private sales. Therefore, despite the negative reception of *Gustafson*, we cannot attribute to it broader consequences such as the subprime lending crisis of 2007–8. Rather, *Gustafson*'s repeal of the rescission remedy is appropriate given that *Landreth* and *Ruefenacht* rejected the sale-of-business doctrine.

The following subsections discuss these points, that *Gustafson* (Section C.i) did not change transactional practice and (Section C.ii) is not responsible for the financial crisis of 2008. Section D shows that the *Gustafson* regime is better than the regime designed by the drafters of the 1933 Act.

i. Transactional Practice Does Not Change

In private transactions, if the issuer does not comply with the disclosure obligations of the 1933 Act, then the issuer may face rescission under Section 12 and misrepresentation liability under the antifraud provisions of the securities laws. The issuer may also lose the shelter of an SEC safe harbor. To comply, the standard practice is to compile a long document providing the information required by the 1933 Act plus cautionary statements about all the possible risks that the investment entails. This is the "private placement memorandum" (PPM).

The elimination of rescission in private sales by *Gustafson* removed the first reason for these memoranda – rescission is no longer a concern.[39] Yet PPMs continue to be used. The cause for the continued use of PPMs is the rest of securities laws, mostly the SEC safe harbor for private sales[40] and avoiding securities fraud liability. Thus the *Gustafson* tempest is restricted to the teapot of Section 12.

ii. Cannot Attribute the Subprime Mortgage Crisis to Gustafson

One is tempted to think of the subprime mortgage crisis as a consequence of *Gustafson*'s libertine expansiveness. The reasoning begins with the realization that selling mortgage-backed securities occurred through private transactions. *Gustafson*'s elimination of the rescission remedy made private sales less risky and thus more appealing. The reasoning closes by connecting *Gustafson* to the reckless issuance of mortgage-backed securities that created the crisis.

Although this reasoning is logical, it does not correspond to reality. After *Gustafson*, issuers continue to produce PPMs for private sales generally and for

39 *Gustafson* applies only to exempt transactions of Section 12(b) because only Section 12(b) refers to "prospectus." A transaction that is not exempt needs to comply with Section 5 and obtains rescission pursuant to Section 12(a) that does not mention prospectus. Thus the delivery of a PPM required by SEC rules (see notes 4–8 and accompanying text) in order for the transaction to be exempt is necessary to trigger *Gustafson* and avoid rescission.

40 Primarily Regulation D, rules 501 et seq., 17 CFR §§ 230.500 et seq.

sales of mortgage-backed securities specifically.[41] The adverse movement of home values was an obvious cautionary disclosure to include in these memoranda. The mere disclosure of the possibility of drops in home prices would prevent buyers from claiming that they bought the mortgage-backed securities through a materially misleading communication. Therefore, even if *Gustafson* had retained the rescission remedy, buyers of mortgage-backed securities would not have received it. *Gustafson* did not contribute to the financial crisis.

D. *GUSTAFSON* CONTAINED?

Gustafson flies in the face of the registration process established in Section 5, ignores the statutory text, and could have undermined the entire regime of the securities laws. Instead, *Gustafson* merely eliminated rescission in private sales. Chapter 7 assesses this effect of *Gustafson* and finds it surprisingly desirable.

[41] See, e.g., *In re Nat'l Century Fin. Enters., Inc.*, 504 F.Supp. 2d 287, 295 (S.D. Ohio 2007); *Vannest v. Sage, Rutty & Co.*, 960 F.Supp. 651, 653–5 (W.D.N.Y. 1997); *Fisk v. Superannuities, Inc.*, 927 F. Supp. 718, 729–31 (S.D.N.Y. 1996).

7

Gustafson Works!

After 12 years, *Gustafson* keeps looking better despite a devastating financial crisis and heaps of unanimous condemnation.[1] To appreciate the resulting regime, consider the four distinct stages that produced it. First, before *Forman*, the sale-of-business doctrine did not exist. Rescission applied to all sales of securities, and sales of control were securities. Second, after *Forman*, many circuits adopted the sale-of-business doctrine. As a result, sales of control were not about securities and did not trigger rescission. Third, then *Landreth* and *Ruefenacht* repealed the sale-of-business doctrine and reproduced the pre-*Forman* regime. Fourth, finally, *Gustafson* repealed rescission as a remedy in private sales of securities. Because rescission in sales of control is unsupportable (the buyer can inspect and will control), the pre-*Forman* period and the period between *Landreth*(/*Ruefenacht*) and *Gustafson* are unstable, and the analysis can ignore them. Two regimes matter – one with the sale-of-business doctrine but without *Gustafson* and one without the sale-of-business doctrine but with *Gustafson*. These are the only two circumstances under which buyers of control in private transactions cannot rescind, which makes them the only workable regimes. Rather than react viscerally to *Gustafson*'s disregard of the text of the 1933 Act, the salient question is, which regime is better?

Revisit the analysis of securities transactions in Chapters 4 and 5 that justified the departure from buyer beware and the transition to seller disclose. The regime's desirability depends on who has information and control. Buyers of noncontrolling stakes cannot inspect the entire enterprise and will not control it, justifying the securities regime of seller disclose. However, private sales of control are different. The buyer has the bargaining power, has the economic incentives to inspect the entire enterprise, and will control the enterprise. Therefore, the remedies and disclosure obligations of securities law are not justified – they would be excessive and inapt because the seller likely does not know the synergies or perks that motivate the buyer. Sales of control should give rise to neither disclosure obligations nor rescission.

[1] See notes 37 and 38 in Chapter 6.

TABLE 7.1 *The Regimes of* Gustafson *and of the Sale-of-Business Doctrine*

<table>
<tr><th>Transaction type:</th><th>Gustafson</th><th>Sale of Business</th></tr>
<tr><td>Control in private sale.</td><td rowspan="2">No section 12 rescission.
Securities fraud applies.
Disclosure applies (PPM).</td><td>No section 12 rescission.
No securities fraud.
No disclosure.</td></tr>
<tr><td>Non-controlling stake in private sale.</td><td></td></tr>
<tr><td>Any public sale.</td><td colspan="2">Section 12 rescission.
Securities fraud applies.
Disclosure applies (prospectus).</td></tr>
</table>

While both the regime of the sale-of-business doctrine and the existing regime of *Gustafson* are alike in not granting rescission for private control transactions, the existing regime is slightly more exacting. It treats private sales of control as securities, thereby (1) obligating the seller to disclose and (2) granting securities fraud protection to the buyer. In contrast, the sale-of-business doctrine does not treat them as securities, thus imposing (1) no obligation on the seller to disclose and (2) leaving such sales to the lesser protection of state law deceit only.[2]

Table 7.1 captures the differences. The table compares the two regimes in three settings: (1) the acquisition of control in a private transaction, (2) the acquisition of a noncontrolling stake in a private transaction, and (3) the acquisition of a noncontrolling stake in a public transaction, an initial public offering (IPO).[3] The cells track three rules: (1) the existence of rescission, (2) the application of securities laws, and (3) the seller's disclosure obligation. An important difference is evident in the middle row, the private sale of noncontrolling stakes.

The following paragraphs explain that the existing *Gustafson* regime is superior to that of the sale-of-business doctrine.

2 Securities antifraud protection arises from multiple sources, including Sections 11 and 12 and more generally Section 17 of the 1933 Act as well as Section 10(b) of the 1934 Act and Rule 10b-5 promulgated thereunder. See Thomas L. Hazen, LAW OF SECURITIES REGULATION §§ 7.01 et seq. and 12.4 et seq. (6th ed. 2009); Kun Young Chang, *Multinational Enforcement of U.S. Securities Laws: The Need for the Clear and Restrained Scope of Extraterritorial Subject-Matter Jurisdiction*, 9 FORDHAM J. CORP. & FIN. L. 89, 93 (2003).

3 Omitted is the possibility of the acquisition of a controlling stake at an IPO, which does not arise. However, as an intellectual exercise, it suggests a potential additional weakness for the sale-of-business doctrine. If the sale-of-business doctrine were to apply to such transactions and exempt them from securities regulation, it could produce an undesirable result. Arguably, the acquirer would not have truly had the negotiating power to inspect the business, making the rescission remedy appropriate.

A. REPEALING RESCISSION BEYOND CONTROL TRANSACTIONS WAS CORRECT

Table 7.1 shows that under the sale-of-business doctrine, although rescission was not available in sales of control, it was available in private sales of noncontrolling stakes. In private sales that do not involve control, buyers may well not have the bargaining power and economic incentives to examine the entire enterprise. Moreover, the buyers will not control the administration of the enterprise. This suggests that buyers in private sales deserve the protection of securities law, but a caveat is necessary.

In 1953, the Supreme Court decided *SEC v. Ralston Purina*, in which it stated that for an offering to be private (and therefore exempt from the registration process of Section 5), the investors receiving it must be "able to fend for themselves."[4] This, along with SEC rules about private offerings (mostly Regulation D[5]), ensures that buyers in private sales have the sophistication and the information to "fend for themselves."[6] According to the corresponding SEC rules, private sale participants must be "accredited investors," defined as sophisticated and wealthy institutions or individuals.[7] Moreover, the substance of the disclosure required in private sales largely matches that of the disclosure in public offerings, giving accredited investors the information they need to fend for themselves.[8]

Thus *Ralston Purina* rendered obsolete the rescission remedy in private offerings, and *Gustafson* eventually eliminated it completely. The rescission remedy of Section 12 was drafted at the initial passage of the 1933 Act, and the drafters could not have anticipated the protection that *Ralston Purina* would provide in private offerings. The text of the 1933 Act did not require that buyers in private offerings be able to fend for themselves. If the private offering exemption turned on the mere privacy of the offer, as it did according to the text of the act before *Ralston Purina*, then buyers may not have been able to protect themselves and would merit the rescission remedy. Then Section 12 appropriately included rescission. However, *Ralston Purina* and Regulation D ensure that the private offering exemption is only available if the offerees "can fend for themselves" through financial

4 *Securities and Exchange Commission v. Ralston Purina Co.*, 346 US 119 (1953).

5 Rules 501 et seq., 17 CFR § 230.501 et seq. (2012).

6 *Ralston*, 346 US at 124 ("An offering to those who are shown to be able to fend for themselves is a transaction 'not involving any public offering.'").

7 See Rule 501, 17 CFR § 230.501 (2012) (defining accredited investors in Section (a) to include under (1) any bank, under (7) "Any trust, with total assets in excess of $5,000,000," under (5) "Any natural person whose individual net worth ... exceeds $1,000,000," and under (6) "Any natural person who had an individual income in excess of $200,000.").

8 See Rule 502, 17 CFR § 203.502 (specifying under [b][2][B] that the issuer must furnish, e.g., in offerings greater than $7,500,000 "[t]he financial statement as would be required in a registration statement filed under the [1933] Act"). Indeed, even the toxic securities that led to the crash had adequate disclosure; see Steven M. Davidoff, *Reading the Fine Print in Abacus and Other Soured Deals*, N.Y. Times DealB%k, November 2, 2012, available at http://dealbook.nytimes.com/2012/11/02/reading-the-fine-print-in-abacus-and-other-soured-deals/ (accessed February 15, 2017).

sophistication and information. The capacity for self-protection makes rescission excessive. Thus *Gustafson* was correct to override the letter of the 1933 Act and abolish rescission in private offerings.

Not only is the protection of *Ralston Purina* and Regulation D superior to what the drafters of the 1933 Act could have expected for private sales, it is more effective protection than that provided by Section 5 itself in public offerings. Section 5 allows sales before even the delivery of the prospectus and the delivery of securities and puffery contemporaneously with the delivery of the prospectus.[9] In contrast, the transaction practice that *Ralston Purina* and Regulation D have produced results in delivery of the PPM (with information equivalent to that of the prospectus) before the sale. Thus buyers in private sales have the fuller protection of actually having the chance to digest the information, whereas Section 5 allows sales without this opportunity.

B. FRAUD PROTECTION IS NOT EXCESSIVE

The second difference of the current regime from that of one with *Gustafson* but without the sale-of-business doctrine is that private sales of control are deemed sales of securities and therefore receive securities fraud protection. Unlike rescission, securities fraud protection for private sales of control is not excessive. Fraud protection merely ensures that the buyer obtains correct information from the seller, unlike rescission, which shifts the entire risk of the transaction to the seller. Consider how a misleading omission gives rise to different results under rescission compared with (only) fraud protection. Rescission turns the obligation to make full disclosure into risk for the seller that the buyer may rescind. The buyer, by pointing to the seller's omission to warn about a risk that materialized, can rescind for surprises that the buyer would not have considered material at the time of the transaction. Under fraud protection, the buyer must show actual reliance on the misrepresentation or omission at the time of the transaction. For the buyer to recover for an omission, therefore, the seller must have knowledge – actual or constructive – of the reasons behind the buyer's desire for the transaction.

To illustrate, consider a variation on the 2009 acquisition of Marvel by Disney.[10] Suppose that Marvel characters had a structural incompatibility with three-dimensional (3D) films. Further, suppose that (1) Disney acquired Marvel in a private sale, (2) Disney intended to produce 3D movies with the characters, (3) Marvel did not know Disney's intent, (4) Marvel knew that its characters were incompatible with 3D filmmaking and (5) omitted to disclose it. Under fraud

[9] See text accompanying notes 26 and 27 in Chapter 6.

[10] Brooks Barnes & Michael Cieply, *Disney Swoops into Action, Buying Marvel for $4 Billion*, N.Y. TIMES, September 1, 2009, at B1; Ethan Smith & Lauren A. E. Schuker, *Disney Nabs Marvel Heroes – Company Bulks Up with $4 Billion Deal but Must Contend with Tangle of Licenses*, WALL ST. J., September 1, 2009, at A1.

protection only, if Marvel did not have knowledge that Disney intended to make 3D movies with the characters, then Disney cannot show reliance on the seller's silence about the characters' incompatibility with 3D and cannot claim fraud.[11] If Disney has the right to rescind the transaction, however, then proof of reliance is unnecessary. Disney would simply exercise its right to rescind. Thus fraud protection lets the transaction stand, as is desirable, because the onus should be on Disney as only Disney can establish how Disney can use Marvel. Rescission places the risk of the transaction on the seller.[12]

11 Thus, under fraud protection, for Disney to ensure that it can recover, it must announce to Marvel during the negotiations that Disney intends to make 3D films.

12 If Marvel were to conduct a public offering, however, buyers could rescind if it did not disclose its characters' incompatibility with 3D. Thus public offerings continue to operate in a legal environment of seller disclose. A caveat regards tracing. See Hillary A. Sale, *Disappearing without A Trace: Sections 11 and 12(2) of the '33 Act*, 75 WASH. L. REV. 429 (2000).

8

Definition Conclusion

The legal definition of a security turns on an imputed motive. Something is a security if, as a matter of law, its buyers invest money in a common enterprise with the expectation of profits mostly from the effort of others. However, the facts that should lead courts to conclude that buyers had these expectations and motivations remain unspecified.

As a consequence of this definition, if something is a security, it will not be subject to the buyer beware regime of contract law but rather the seller disclose regime of securities law. The functional change is appropriate because buyers of ordinary goods can inspect them and will control them, whereas buyers of securities cannot inspect the common enterprise and will not control its management. The law is mostly in harmony with the reality of access to information and future control.

However, private sales of control, although typically taking the form of stock transactions, occur in an environment apt for buyer beware rather than seller disclose. Buyers of control extract nonfinancial value from the target, such as perks and synergies. The seller cannot know what values the particular buyer appreciates and therefore cannot meaningfully bear an obligation to disclose information about them.

The decisions in *Howey* and *Forman* set the interpretation of securities laws on a solid course of substance over form, but substance has since suffered in the subsequent cases regarding sales of control, *Landreth*, *Ruefenacht*, and *Gustafson*. The sale-of-business doctrine placed substance over form, but the Supreme Court struck down this doctrine in *Landreth* and *Ruefenacht* only to reinstate it implicitly and countertextually in *Gustafson*. While *Gustafson* reestablishes the consequences of the sale-of-business doctrine, it does not adhere to the substance-over-form tradition that is the strength of the interpretation of securities laws. Despite this drawback, in combination with *Ralston*, *Gustafson* results in a regulation of private sales of securities that is surprisingly appealing from a normative perspective and superior to what the 1933 Act drafters could have envisioned for private sales.

PART II

Disclosure

Why Subsidize Informed Traders?

9

Introduction

This second part of the book seeks to appraise at a general level the disclosure provisions of securities laws, which require lengthy and audited disclosure on the issuance of a security and annually, supplemented by summary quarterly disclosures.[1] The puzzle that these rules present is that (to a significant extent) they impose disclosure in order to achieve accurate prices for securities. Theory, however, has been ambivalent about this regulatory mission. The chapters in this part explain that disclosure rules are justified in ensuring the accuracy of prices and that firms would not provide this service sufficiently without regulation.

This realization is instrumental in seeing how disclosure rules facilitate the virtuous cycle that securities law promotes, the cycle from lower cost of trading to greater liquidity and more accurate prices, which, in turn, lowers the cost of trading. Disclosure rules do so by ensuring the accuracy of prices.

Chapter 10 offers an overview of the theories that justify disclosure rules. These traditional theories, while they justify some disclosure rules, fail to explain those that promote accurate prices. Despite the theory behind the capital asset pricing model (CAPM)[2] and the evidence of efficiency, more recent theory and evidence suggest that false prices (due to irrational trading) are plausible. Disclosure rules make sense if we reenvision them as subsidies to rational informed traders. This subsidy is initially justified to ensure that the traders and the markets are not overcome by irrationalities. Chapter 11 argues that this subsidy must come from the legal system because corporations and shareholders themselves would underprovide disclosure. The price accuracy that results from disclosure is to the advantage of short-term uninformed shareholders. Corporations would not find it advantageous to disclose for the benefit of short-term shareholders and would rather not bear the cost of

1 In the United States, disclosure regulations for corporations consist primarily of the Securities Act of 1933 and the Securities Exchange Act of 1934, as implemented by the rules that the Securities and Exchange Commission (SEC) has promulgated thereunder. The 1933 Act and the 1934 Act are codified, respectively, in 15 USC § 77a et seq. and § 78a et seq. The regulations of the SEC thereunder are codified in 17 CFR § 230.100-703(T) for the 1933 Act and 17 CFR § 240.0-1-31-1 for the 1934 Act.

2 See Chapter 5.

subsidizing the liquidity (of the market) that their frequent trading creates. In other words, corporations will disclose less than the social benefits of liquidity require.

These chapters justify mandatory disclosure against the Coase-theoretical counterargument that the unregulated marketplace will provide the optimal amount of disclosure. In an unregulated marketplace, corporate decision making would be dominated by long-term shareholders who have less use for the benefits of disclosure – efficiency and liquidity – and who will therefore underprovide it. Instead, a mandatory disclosure regime fosters short-term shareholdings and thus a large trading volume. This, in turn, leads to more liquid markets, a result that is of interest to short-term shareholders but not corporations.[3]

[3] This argument could be considered related to that of Andrei Shleifer & Robert W. Vishny, *Equilibrium Short Horizons of Investors and Firms*, 80 AM. ECON. REV. 148 (1990). Shleifer and Vishny formulate the danger of irrationalities and the ensuing greater inefficiency of long-term assets into a theory that suggests that managers may react too much to estimates of short-term corporate performance, which are more accurately reflected in short-term assets' prices. Short-term securities (e.g., short-term debt), being more efficient than long-term securities (e.g., shares), are also more sensitive to the short-term prospects of the firm. Shleifer and Vishny, however, do not use their argument to justify legal measures, such as disclosure, that increase the efficiency of equity markets. The argument here, which shows that disclosure not only attempts to make equity markets more efficient but also does so by shortening holding periods, is complementary to that of Shleifer and Vishny.

10

An Overview of Disclosure Theories

The question of whether disclosure rules are justified has received significant attention from the legal and economic academy. The attempts to find their theoretical justification span decades and cover a great variety of approaches. A slight generalization allows the justifications of disclosure rules to fall into three categories: disclosure (1) averts fraud, (2) reduces shareholder collective action problems, or (3) assists the market's accurate pricing.

A. FRAUD PREVENTION

The fraud-prevention justification of disclosure rules is the oldest and most conventional[1] but no less problematic than the others. Disclosure makes fraudulent activity by management more likely to be detected, strengthening the deterrent effect of the rules that penalize such activity. Under the deregulatory approach, this reasoning does not justify the mandatory nature of disclosure rules because investors, fearing fraud, would negotiate for protection. Firms that refuse to protect investors, whether by disclosing or otherwise, would face a higher cost of capital. Under this line of reasoning, only if investors and firms are free to contract about fraud-prevention measures will those measures be provided to the extent demanded. Granted, market failures occur, suggesting that fraud-prevention measures are underprovided, but private contracting often shows sufficient ingenuity to overcome market failures.[2] This logic conforms to the "Coase theorem," which argues that

[1] The classic quote, "Sunlight [is] the best of disinfectants," originates in a book of (later Justice) Louis D. Brandeis, OTHER PEOPLE'S MONEY AND HOW BANKERS' USE IT 92 (1914). Notable contemporary support of the fraud-prevention justification comes from Joel Seligman, *The Historical Need for a Mandatory Corporate Disclosure System*, 9 J. CORP. L. 1 (1983), although he uses primarily historical arguments.

[2] Consider, e.g., the market-for-lemons problem. Although it puzzled theory, in practice, it is easily overcome with guarantees. See George A. Akerlof, *The Market for "Lemons": Quality Uncertainty and the Market Mechanism*, 84 Q.J. ECON. 488, 489 (1970) (If buyers cannot distinguish high-quality goods from "lemons" and sellers face high costs in conveying the quality of their products, the result is that all sellers are forced to sell "lemons" because no buyer pays the higher price; guarantees, however,

private contracting will even address externalities given an economy without transaction costs.

Thus the Coase theorem eliminates the need for regulation.[3] Even if the disclosure rules that exist would have been the outcome of free contracting between investors and firms, they should still only serve as a default rule from which firms may opt out.[4] Therefore, a stronger justification of disclosure rules is necessary to defend their mandatory character. One response is to transfer the (weak) argument for mandatory corporate law to disclosure requirements. The reasoning is that market failures would allow too many firms to opt out of disclosure and that disclosure rules should therefore be mandatory. Even if this counterargument is correct, however, the fraud-prevention motive justifies only a fraction of the numerous disclosure provisions.

B. COLLECTIVE ACTION

The argument that disclosure rules resolve a collective action problem focuses on shareholder decision making. When shareholders must make decisions for the corporation, they must expend significant resources to gather and process the information required to reach the best decision for the corporation.[5] Each member of the dispersed group of shareholders would rather see other shareholders carry this burden. The feared result is that no shareholder will undertake the expense of making an informed decision that would benefit the whole. Even if some shareholders did pursue an informed decision, they would not spend as much as the group as a whole in order to ascertain it. According to this argument, disclosure rules resolve this collective action problem by forcing the corporation to spend the

overcome this problem because they allow sellers to effectively promise quality, at 499: "[M]ost consumer durables carry guarantees to ensure the buyer of some normal expected quality.").

3 One of the most readable explanations of the Coase theorem is A. Mitchell Polinsky, An Introduction to Law and Economics (2011). See also Werner Z. Hirsch, Law and Economics: An Introductory Analysis (1988); Richard A. Posner, Economic Analysis of Law § 1.1 (8th ed. 2011).

4 The debate whether corporate and securities law should be mandatory or enabling, and to what extent, has been vigorous. Compare, e.g., Jeffrey N. Gordon, *The Mandatory Structure of Corporate Law*, 89 Colum. L. Rev. 1549 (1989); Roberta Romano, *Answering the Wrong Question: The Tenuous Case for Mandatory Corporate Laws*, 89 Colum. L. Rev. 1599 (1989); John C. Coffee, Jr., *The Mandatory/Enabling Balance in Corporate Law: An Essay on the Judicial Role*, 89 Colum. L. Rev. 1618 (1989); Joel Seligman, *The Case for Federal Minimum Corporate Law Standards*, 49 Md. L. Rev. 947 (1990); Mary E. Kostel, *Note, A Public Choice Perspective on the Debate over Federal versus State Corporate Law*, 79 Va. L. Rev. 2129 (1993).

5 The voluminous literature begins with Adolf Berle & Gardiner Means, The Modern Corporation & Private Property (Harcourt, Brace & World 1932) (Adolf Berle & Gardiner Means. 1932. The Modern Corporation and Private Property. New York: Macmillan). Some of the more recent additions include Bernard S. Black, *Shareholder Passivity Reexamined*, 89 Mich. L. Rev. 520 (1990); Frank H. Easterbrook & Daniel R. Fischel, The Economic Structure of Corporate Law (1991); and Jeffrey N. Gordon, *The Mandatory Structure of Corporate Law*, 89 Colum. L. Rev. 1549 (1989).

resources to collect, process, and disseminate the information that shareholders need to make the corporate decision.[6] While this may be a compelling argument, it only justifies provisions that impose disclosure in anticipation of corporate governance decisions by shareholders. As with fraud prevention, these rules too are but a fraction of the disclosure system.

C. ACCURATE PRICING

Even after the aforementioned two justifications (i.e., preventing fraud and solving shareholders' collective action problems), a significant number of disclosure provisions remain unjustified. Consider, for example, a firm's obligation to describe its business, discuss its operation, and project its future performance (item 100 of Regulation S-K). No evidence of past wrongdoing can come to light by discussing future prospects. Therefore, such provisions cannot be motivated by fraud prevention. Neither can their motivation be the elimination of the shareholders' collective action problem because this disclosure is not related to any shareholder decision. This disclosure requirement is likely motivated by a desire to facilitate accurate pricing. Traditional economic theory, however, does not justify such a motivation. Older economic theory suggests that firms would voluntarily disclose. A newer theory suggests that forcing firms to disclose actually obstructs the firms' ability to send implicit signals to investors as to information about which firms cannot make credible explicit disclosures.

The early financial models tried to determine whether businesses have sufficient incentives to disclose information and found that all firms will disclose. Businesses remaining silent would be penalized because investors would assume the worst and discount the price of their shares. Soon every firm would be led to disclose because its information would not be worse than the market's assumptions.[7]

6 The Coase theorem points to the objection that shareholders would overcome their collective action problem without regulation. Indeed, market remedies to the collective action of gathering information exist in various markets (the most obvious example is CONSUMER REPORTS, which spends resources to test products and then sells its results; no individual consumer would undertake the expense, but the market provides a substitute). In the context of shareholder voting, there are firms that provide the service of determining how shareholders should vote. Professor Bernard Black (note 5, at 573), an active participant in the shareholder-activism discussion of the eighties and nineties, offers a list of services that resolve this collective action problem.

7 Models using the assumption of costless information include Stephen A. Ross, *Disclosure Regulation in Financial Markets: Implications of Modern Finance Theory and Signaling Theory*, in ISSUES IN FINANCIAL REGULATION 177 (Franklin R. Edwards ed., 1979); Sanford J. Grossman, *The Information Roles of Warranties and Private Disclosure about Product Quality*, 24 J.L. & ECON. 461 (1981); Paul R. Milgrom, *Good News and Bad News: Representation Theorems and Applications*, 12 BELL J. ECON. 380 (1981). Models using costly information include Boyan Jovanovic, *Truthful Disclosure of Information*, 13 BELL J. ECON. 36 (1982); Robert E. Verrecchia, *Discretionary Disclosure*, 5 J. ACCT. & ECON. 179 (1983).

This model in which all firms are led to disclose is quite simple. A much more elaborate and recent model is that of Teoh and Hwang.[8] They suggest that forcing firms to disclose actually obstructs the firms' ability to send implicit signals to investors as to information about which firms cannot make credible explicit disclosures. However, a different interpretation of this model is that firms can use the framework of mandated periodic disclosures to convey information they cannot credibly communicate directly.

Teoh and Hwang build their model by dividing information into two types: verifiable information that firms can credibly disclose and unverifiable information, such as managerial quality, that firms cannot credibly disclose. All firms seek superior sales growth, for example, and all believe their management team or their research and development (R&D) to be excellent. However, statements about sales growth are verifiable, whereas those about the quality of management or R&D are not.

Once a piece of information is not subject to credible disclosure, firms and investors face a complex problem. Firms want to communicate their positive information to investors in order to attract capital, and investors want to allocate their capital to the better firms. Lack of credibility, however, means that all firms, regardless of the truth, can boast about excellent but unverifiable information, which does nothing to help investors.

Teoh and Hwang argue that firms *can* communicate unverifiable information to investors and do so credibly. Firms achieve this result indirectly, by implication, through a signaling process. Investors need to have the appropriate expectations: that the firms with poorer unverifiable information will rush to disclose good verifiable information, whereas firms with better unverifiable information will disclose verifiable information in a leisurely, nonboastful way. Thus firms can credibly signal the unverifiable information by timing the disclosure of verifiable information. Firms with good unverifiable information put on a show of "wasting" (verifiable) good news by delaying its release. Firms with bad unverifiable information cannot afford to mimic the good firms. They need to disclose good news without delay.

If the model accurately captures the interaction of firms and investors regarding disclosure, it would imply that regulations should allow firms enough leeway to time their verifiable disclosures and thereby signal their unverifiable information. Whether disclosure rules currently provide this flexibility is debatable. A firm cannot choose to omit some information from a quarterly report in order to signal management's confidence in its prospects, but the firm can postpone such a disclosure until the next – usually quarterly but perhaps annual – report is due.[9]

[8] Siew Hong Teoh & Chuan Yang Hwang, *Nondisclosure and Adverse Disclosure as Signals of Firm Value*, 4 REV. OF FIN. STUDIES 283 (1991).

[9] Postponing disclosure is only possible if the safe harbor of Section 21E for "forward-looking" statements is not available and no previous "forward-looking" statement is rendered misleading by the new

Still, the question remains as to why the disclosure of so much verifiable information is mandated. The following chapters will build up to the argument that firms would not disclose optimally because that would only benefit their shorter-term minority shareholders. The foundation of this argument is that noise trading makes pricing errors occur.

D. EVIDENCE OF EFFICIENCY, INEFFICIENCY, AND IRRATIONALITIES

Mandating disclosure to ensure accurate prices is a paradox in several ways. The theory of pricing capital assets (the capital asset pricing model [CAPM]; Chapter 5) suggests that each security can have only one price, which is dictated by its risk and future returns. The body of empirical evidence that suggests that capital markets are "efficient" implies that prices are accurate. Why then impose disclosure?

To begin with, neither the theory of the CAPM nor the evidence of efficiency ensures that prices would never be wrong. Prices can be wrong due to inaccurate information or frictions.

The CAPM does not really talk about price but about a theoretical value: an asset with given risk (beta) should be valued by discounting its future income stream using a specific rate, determined by the asset's beta. In fact, however, neither the risk nor the future prospects of firms are known with certainty. Uncertainty allows inaccuracies of prices.

Furthermore, the CAPM ignores the frictions of the market, the explicit and the structural transaction costs that are the object of the field of financial market microstructure and that do influence pricing.[10] The presence of frictions reduces the accuracy of the CAPM.

The evidence of efficiency also does not imply accurate prices but rather merely accurate changes of prices in response to new pieces of information.[11] Principled evidence that prices are absolutely accurate is hard to see.

Furthermore, modeling has shown that systematically erring traders (irrational or noise traders) may survive or even dominate the market,[12] that even rational traders

information, per *Backman v. Polaroid, Inc.*, 910 F.2d 10 (1st Cir. en banc 1990) (Liability for nondisclosure does not arise unless the statement that is rendered misleading was "forward looking.").

10 The effect of transaction costs on prices is explored by Yakov Amihud & Haim Mendelson, *Asset Pricing and the Bid-Ask Spread*, 17 J. FIN. ECON. 223 (1986).

11 See James Tobin, *On the Efficiency of the Financial System*, LLOYDS BANK REV. 1 (July 1984); also accepted by the leading proponent of efficiency, Eugene F. Fama, *Efficient Capital Markets: II*, 46 J. FINANCE 1575, 1575–6 (1991).

12 De Long et al. (1991) (If the error of noise traders consists of a systematic underestimation of the risk of their portfolios, then they may survive or dominate in a market that compensates risk; the same result follows the noise traders' underestimation of their risk aversion). The economic literature names irrational traders "noise traders." This term is confusing because both irrational and uninformed liquidity traders cause the random fluctuations called "noise" in prices.

may intentionally trigger euphorias or panics among irrational traders,[13] that risk aversion may drive investors to take smaller positions that may not be enough to correct irrationalities,[14] that structural agency costs may drive rational investment managers to do the same,[15] and that errors in prices may exist without giving rise to an opportunity for arbitraging them away.[16] Empirical work supports the contention that the markets have displayed inefficiencies or irrationalities.[17] Experimental evidence agrees.[18]

13 J. Bradford DeLong, Andrei Shleifer, Lawrence Summers, & Robert Waldman, *Positive Feedback Investment Strategies and Destabilizing Rational Speculation*, 45 J. FINANCE 379 (1990) (The existence of noise traders that "follow the crowd," as, for example, does portfolio insurance, may induce rational traders to anticipate such trends, enter in their beginning, and initiate them.). See also David M. Cutler, James M. Poterba, & Lawrence H. Summers, *Speculative Dynamics and the Role of Feedback Traders*, 80 AM. ECON. REV. 63 (1990).

14 J. Bradford De Long, Andrei Shleifer, Lawrence H. Summers, & Robert J. Waldmann, *Noise Trader Risk in Financial Markets*, 98 J. POL. ECON. 703 (1990) (The existence of noise traders increases risk; rational traders take that risk into account and, therefore, take smaller positions, which may be insufficient to correct the effect on prices of noise traders.).

15 Andrei Shleifer & Robert W. Vishny, *The Limits of Arbitrage*, 52 J. FINANCE 35 (1997) (Building a model where the concern for a period of poor performance – in which case the under their management may be withdrawn – may lead investment managers to refrain from large positions.).

16 *Kenneth A. Froot & Maurice Obstfeld, Intrinsic Bubbles: The Case of Stock Prices*, 81 AM. ECON. REV. 1189 (1991) (Building a model of bubbles based on the rate of increase of dividends, which resembles the historical path of stock prices better than a model without bubbles.).

17 J. Bradford De Long & Andrei Shleifer, THE BUBBLE OF 1929: EVIDENCE FROM CLOSED-END FUNDS (National Bureau of Economic Research Working Paper No. 3523, 1990) (Evidence that compares the ratio of the closed-end fund premium before the two crashes, 1929 and 1987, to its historical level supports the existence of bubbles. In 1929, the fund premiums averaged 60%; from this the authors suggest that a bubble larger than 30% existed before the crash. The authors' data do not reach 1987, but in 1985, as well as in 1969–70, closed-end funds were selling at premiums.); Gordon Gemmill & Dylan C. Thomas, *Noise Trading, Costly Arbitrage, and Asset Prices: Evidence from Closed End Funds*, 57 J. FINANCE 2571–94 (2002) (The difficulty of arbitrage allows the price of closed-end funds to deviate from asset values.).

Even attempts to rationalize market breaks do not contradict but support the existence of irrationalities. Thus the explanation of the October 1987 market crash as a readjustment of stock prices to an increase in perceived risk, as in Fischer Black, *An Equilibrium Model of the Crash*, in NBER MACROECONOMICS ANNUAL 1988, at 269 (Stanley Fischer ed., 1988), is consistent with the irrationalities theory that the market underestimated risk before the crash. According to Black's explanation, investors underestimated either volatility or risk aversion in the months preceding the crash and woke up, to wit, with a crash.

Evidence of efficiency, moreover, does not preclude irrationalities in parts or sectors of the market that cancel out when averaged over the entire market. That conclusive evidence of irrationalities accompanies rare market breaks does not preclude much more frequent partial irrationalities.

18 Vernon Smith's 2002 Nobel Prize celebrated his accumulation of voluminous experimental evidence on persistent bubble creation. For a discussion of its support of financial regulation, see, e.g., Erik F. Gerding, *Laws against Bubbles: An Experimental-Asset-Market Approach to Analyzing Financial Regulation*, 2007 WIS. L. REV. 977; and Erik F. Gerding, LAW, BUBBLES, AND FINANCIAL REGULATION (Routledge, 2011); see also Amitai Aviram, *Bail-Ins: Cyclical Effects of a Common Response to Financial Crises*, 2011 U. ILL. L. REV. 1633 (the errors that the experimental evidence leads us to expect aggravate the consequences of legal reactions to crises). For the argument that this evidence (but more generally, behavioral evidence) does not justify regulation, see Fred

Nevertheless, pointing at the theory and evidence of irrationalities does not suffice to justify mandatory disclosure. The counterargument is that businesses would take into account the undesirability of irrationalities and would disclose to reduce them. The optimal amount of disclosure is a determination that listed corporations would make, and mandatory disclosure precludes them from making that determination. Rather, the argument that irrationalities justify mandatory disclosure requires a showing that the decision-making dynamics in the corporation leads to less disclosure than is socially optimal. Chapter 11 demonstrates this.

First, however, it is necessary inquire into merely alleviating the problems created by irrationalities. The solution is to provide information to the market: information of great precision, in great quantities, and with little cost to traders. This will strengthen rational, informed traders, whose trading drives the market toward efficiency.[19]

E. DISCLOSURE SUBSIDIZES INFORMED TRADING

Unfortunately, irrational traders and false prices (irrationalities) occasionally appear. They are obviously undesirable because they at least interfere with the optimality of the market's allocation of capital among competing firms.[20] As vividly felt in 2008, they also expose the economy to the risk of depressions.[21] Regulation that would directly hinder irrational trades is, however, impracticable. Ex ante, they are indistinguishable from rational, informed trades.

Disclosure rules solve this problem by performing two functions beneficial to rational trading. First, they ensure the uniform appearance of the information about corporations – compliance with generally accepted accounting principles, for example – which renders the information easier to understand.[22] More important,

S. McChesney, *Behavioral Economics: Old Wine in Irrelevant New Bottles?*, 21 SUP. CT. ECON. REV. 43 (2013).

[19] Informed traders do not correct exclusively irrationalities, nor do they only trade to correct prices on releases of new information (notice how exchange structure favors the release of information during off-trading hours, favors suspension of trading in information events, and provides information directly to the floor to reduce such trading). The principal role of informed traders is to counter the random effects on prices that the trading of uninformed liquidity traders has (see note 1). Thus, effectively, the informed traders provide an "outside spread," a high and a low price beyond which they buy or sell so that they resist price fluctuations outside it. See also notes 1 and 2.

[20] For an extensive discussion of the social benefits of efficiency, see Marcel Kahan, *Securities Laws and the Social Costs of "Inaccurate" Stock Prices*, 41 DUKE L.J. 977 (1992).

[21] The 1929 stock market crash is the typical example of a financial crisis that spread into the nonfinancial economy with devastating effects. The sudden drop of securities' prices that were used as collateral for heavy borrowing led to many banks' failure as well as to the ruin of many nonbanking productive entities. The failure or the perceived weakness of the banks led to a "run" on the banks by depositors, leading to a general dissolution of the economy into the Great Depression; see, generally, John Kenneth Galbraith, *THE GREAT CRASH OF 1929* (1997).

[22] Michael J. Fishman & Kathleen M. Hagerty, *Disclosure Decisions by Firms and the Competition for Price Efficiency*, 44 J. FINANCE 633 (1989).

however, disclosure eliminates any cost or effort on the part of the shareholders to search for and find information about corporations. Rather, anybody can obtain very detailed information at no cost.

Thus disclosure rules function as a subsidy to informed traders because they lower the costs informed traders would otherwise bear.[23] Instead, this cost is borne by the corporations and thus effectively by all shareholders. The informed traders are only a fraction of active traders, which are, in turn, only a fraction of all shareholders.

When the cost of an activity drops, more of it will occur. We should expect disclosure rules to intensify informed trading. This has a positive-feedback effect. The intensification of informed trading attracts entry of competing informed traders.[24] Informed trading intensifies, and the likelihood of irrationalities drops because the augmented ranks of informed traders trade against – and thus resist – false prices. The reduced likelihood of irrationalities, in turn, is a further attractor of informed trading because as risk-averse informed traders fear irrationalities less, their trading becomes more intense and is more likely to correct pricing errors. Effectively, the fear of false prices operates as a structural transaction cost. Disclosure reduces it and attracts informed trading. Cheaper trading, however, also attracts uninformed trading, further increasing market liquidity.

Finally, besides assisting rational, informed traders, disclosure rules are also likely to cause some irrational traders to revise their actions in view of the information. By almost force-feeding irrational traders with information, disclosure rules school some irrational traders. Thus disclosure promotes the domination of rational, informed traders not only by reducing their costs but also by reducing the ranks of irrational traders.

Even if informed trading is desirable because it increases efficiency directly as well as indirectly by mitigating irrationalities, the puzzle of the mandatory nature of disclosure provisions remains. Firms could choose the optimal degree of efficiency for their shares.[25] By contrast, Chapter 11 argues that the structure of corporate decision making indicates that without a legal mandate, corporations would provide a suboptimal amount of disclosure.

[23] Disclosure rules also ensure that the information provided to the traders is accurate. This accuracy, however, is not a result of disclosure rules themselves but of the rules that prohibit fraud, the mainstay of which is Rule 10b-5. To the extent that even without disclosure rules, rational, informed traders would be able to "buy" statements from the corporations (which would have the same high accuracy that mandated disclosures have due to antifraud rules), disclosure rules only reduce the cost of these accurate statements.

Most probably, this "buying" of information would not be direct and explicit but indirect and implicit. For example, corporations that would provide adequate indications that they would disclose relevant information would attract the demand of informed traders and would command higher share prices. The disclosing corporation is compensated for disclosure by having a lower cost of capital.

[24] See Anat R. Admati & Paul Pfleiderer, *A Theory of Intraday Patterns: Volume and Price Variability*, 1 REV. FIN. STUD. 3 (1988) (theorizing that the more informed traders will be attracted). See Chapter 11, notes 2 and 3.

[25] Indeed, Lynn A. Stout, *The Unimportance of Being Efficient: An Economic Analysis of Stock Market Pricing and Securities Regulation*, 87 MICH. L. REV. 613, 617–18 (1988), has argued that securities regulation provides excessive efficiency.

11

Failure of the Corporate Disclosure Decision

The beneficial nature of imposing disclosure on corporations appears to follow from the conclusions of Chapter 10: given the danger of irrationalities, which rational, informed trading averts, and given that disclosure rules are a subsidy to rational, informed traders, the reduction of irrationalities appears to justify rules imposing disclosure. Before concluding, however, that disclosure rules are necessary, we must apply the Coase theorem and ask whether private initiative would reach the same outcome. If so, the legal mandate is superfluous. It is only necessary if private initiative would fail.

A. DISCLOSURE POLICY AND HOLDING PERIODS

Chapter 10 categorized shareholders into rational, informed traders, and irrational traders. This bifurcation, which served the purpose of explaining the dynamics behind the subsidy function of disclosure rules, also explains the necessity for disclosure rules. Now, a third but fundamental category, the uninformed traders who trade for liquidity or lifecycle reasons regardless of price appeal, must enter the scene.[1] In addition, we must take into consideration that holding periods may differ. Thus shareholders will hold for the long or short term and either trade rationally

[1] The existence of uninformed/liquidity trading is obvious. Not only do people trade for lifecycle needs (e.g., automatic investment of paycheck fraction in pension plans and liquidation for retirement), but also the legal system itself provides for forced liquidations. Trading without any attempt to exploit information, however, is much more frequent than retirements, bankruptcy liquidations, or margin calls. A portion of daily trading volume is "index arbitrage," both "legs" of the trade of which are uninformed because the arbitrageur does not bet on a price movement. Other uninformed trades are those of "portfolio insurance" or other "dynamic hedging" or "synthetic" instrument strategies, where trading is automatically triggered by market moves. For example, an option to buy stock at a certain price can be recreated, "synthesized," by automatically buying that amount of stock as price rises and passes that price. See, generally, John Hull, Options, Futures, and Other Derivative Securities (7th ed. 2009). Similarly uninformed, but less prevalent, are the trades of index funds, which simply purchase stocks that are part of an index, as well as the trades of ordinary mutual funds, which are made when redemptions and new subscriptions by clients do not cancel out.

with information, without information for liquidity and lifecycle reasons, or finally, irrationally.

To begin, assume a simplified world where all shareholders expect to be uninformed traders.[2] When these shareholders liquidate their holdings, they depend on accurate market pricing (efficiency) and liquidity to provide a liquidation price that reflects their shares' value. An illiquid market would react to their selling by lowering the price. An inefficient market would allow them to trade at a price that might differ from their stock's value.[3] Disclosure, as Chapter 10 showed, reduces irrationalities. Also, as we will see, disclosure causes a shorter holding period (more frequent trading) and thus greater market liquidity. Therefore, disclosure helps uninformed sellers sell at a price closer to value. Shareholders would then estimate the likelihood that they would have to liquidate along with the cost of providing the disclosure that would ensure adequate informed trading and choose their optimal disclosure policy

[2] One can argue that shareholders, even the founding entrepreneurs, may expect to also be informed traders with some probability. However, it is not clear whether informed traders prefer more or less disclosure. Although it turns out that more disclosure would lead to shorter holding periods for the uninformed and, hence, more uninformed trading and noisier prices and one could imply that the increased opportunities for informed trading this would give rise to informed traders to favor disclosure, the reasoning of Admati & Pfleiderer, *A Theory of Intraday Patterns*, 24 (empirically supported by Michael J. Barclay, Robert Litzenberger, & Jerold B. Warner, *Private Information, Trading Volume, and Stock-Return Variances*, 3 REV. FIN. STUD. 233, 1990), suggests the opposite. More uninformed trading would increase aggregate informed trading profits, but this would attract entry into informed trading and competition. This competition would reduce their per-trader profits, so the informed may be indifferent to the uninformed traders' holding period. This runs counter to the application of the argument that interest groups drive disclosure regulation, an argument that has been made extensively in other fields of securities and corporate law (see, e.g., Jonathan R. Macey, *The Myth of "Reregulation": The Interest Group Dynamics of Regulatory Change in the Financial Services Industry*, 45 WASH. & LEE L. REV. 1275 (1988); Jonathan R. Macey & David D. Haddock, *Shirking at the SEC: The Failure of the National Market System*, 1985 U. ILL. L. REV. 315; Jonathan R. Macey & Geoffrey Miller, *Toward an Interest-Group Theory of Delaware Corporate Law*, 65 TEX. L. REV. 469, 1987; Nicholas Wolfson, A *Critique of Corporate Law*, 34 U. MIAMI L. REV. 959, 1980). Indeed, I have found no reference to disclosure rules as being the result of lobbying by the professional investment community, as opposed to other parts of securities and corporate law (Schedule 13D disclosure, however, is distinguishable as motivated by change-of-control concerns).

[3] Although direct empirical evidence for the proposition that trading volume leads to liquidity is sparse (but see Venkat R. Eleswarapu & Chandrasekar Krishnamurti, *Liquidity, Stock Returns and Ownership Structure: An Empirical Study of the BSE*, Federal Reserve Bank of St. Louis, IDEAS database, 1995, available at http://ideas.repec.org/p/wpa/wuwpfi/9507005.html, who associate a liquidity premium with trading volume), this relation is intuitive and generally accepted. The paucity of evidence must be attributed to the difficulty of quantifying the effects of liquidity due to the complementary nature of trading delays and price concessions (dividing a trade and spreading it in time may reduce its price impact). Indirect evidence of the connection between trading volume and liquidity exists in Barclay, Litzenberger & Warner, note 2 (1990), who support empirically the theoretical model of Admati & Pfleiderer, A *Theory of Intraday Patterns*. Admati and Pfleiderer show that the liquidity caused by increases in trading volume leads to increased profits for the informed and stronger competition among them, leading to greater efficiency. See also discussion on insider trading below.

accordingly. Provided that all shareholders expect to hold their shares for periods of equal length, the result of this process would be optimal. An example illustrates.

Example 11.1 Shareholders' Choice of a Disclosure Policy

Consider that two possible disclosure strategies are available to the corporation: "cryptic" and "detailed." If the corporation chose cryptic disclosure, its disclosure expenses would be 1% of its capitalization annually, whereas detailed disclosure would cost the corporation 2%. Shareholders' motivation for providing more disclosure is that by preventing irrationalities it ensures less of a deviation of price from the true value of the stock. Consider that cryptic disclosure allows price to fluctuate up to 20% from value, whereas detailed disclosure reduces the possible inaccuracy to 10%. Suppose that shareholders' risk aversion is such that they equate (uninformed) trading at prices subject to 20% error to a 4% reduction in wealth and trading at prices subject to 10% error to a 1.5% reduction in wealth. The expected holding period[4] at which these shareholders will be indifferent between the two disclosure regimes is 2.5 years. If they expect to hold their shares for only 2 years, detailed disclosure would cost them 5.5% (2 years at 2% plus 1.5% due to error aversion), whereas cryptic disclosure would cost 6% (2 years at 1% plus 4% error aversion). If, by contrast, they expect to hold for 3 years, cryptic disclosure is preferable because it costs 7% (3 years at 1% plus 4% error aversion) versus the 7.5% cost of detailed disclosure (3 years at 2% plus 1.5% error aversion).

The optimality of the shareholders' disclosure decision erodes with different holding periods. Shorter holding periods lead to more frequent trading. Since the benefits of liquidity and efficiency are enjoyed at each trade, shareholders who trade more frequently derive more value from disclosure. Thus short-term shareholders are likely to favor more disclosure than their long-term counterparts, as the following example illustrates.

Example 11.2 Why Short-Term Shareholders Prefer More Disclosure than Their Long-Term Counterparts

Given the same choice as in Example 11.1 between cryptic disclosure, which costs 1% annually and allows a 20% price error, and detailed disclosure, which costs 2% but reduces price error to 10%, compare the reaction of a long- and a short-term shareholder to the disclosure choice of a firm that is expected to have a 10% annual return before disclosure expenses (i.e., a 9% return after expenses if it chooses cryptic disclosure or an 8% return if it chooses detailed disclosure).

The short-term shareholder will hold for 1 year. If the firm chooses cryptic disclosure, this shareholder expects a return between 31% and a loss of 13%.[5] If the firm chooses detailed

[4] "Expected holding period" is defined as the average holding period given an uninformed sale, considering only the possibility of selling without information. Thus, even if a shareholder is very unlikely to ever sell without information, the possibility of bankruptcy implies an expected holding period given an uninformed sale. Of course, the example's analysis is greatly simplified because the possibility of using the disclosed information to become an informed trader would also be considered. But the analysis holds under the assumption that informed trading earns zero profits because of perfect competition.

[5] The value of the firm will increase 9%, but price may fluctuate ±20% from this 109%, which gives a range of prices from 130.8% to 87.2%.

disclosure, the return will lie between 19% and a loss of 3%.[6] Neither choice is dominant, but even a mildly risk-averse shareholder would prefer to see the firm choose detailed disclosure, in which it gives up 1% of expected return to halve the range of price error.

The long-term holder's horizon is 10 years. Were the firm to choose detailed disclosure, the expected 8% annual return with annual compounding would translate into a total return of 116%.[7] The ±10% fluctuation would give a range of total return from 73% to 159%.[8] If the firm were to choose cryptic disclosure, the firm would offer an expected return of 9%, for a total return of 137%. With the ±20% fluctuation of price from value, cryptic disclosure offers a range of total return from 90% to 184%, which is preferable to the result of detailed disclosure unless the long-term shareholder has exorbitant risk aversion.[9]

Since disclosure is costly, corporations will tend to provide as little as necessary. This tendency, which works to the benefit of long-term shareholders, gives shareholders with the median holding period the ability to dominate the disclosure determination. Corporate policy is set by directors who are subject to elections by shareholder majority. If a short-term minority proposes more disclosure than the median shareholder desires, the longer-term shareholders (who prefer less disclosure) will propose a disclosure policy that matches the median shareholder's preference, and this proposal will receive the majority vote.

B. HOLDING PERIOD DRIFT

The corporation's disclosure decision is not a one-time event. The dynamics of the preceding interaction provide a disincentive for short-term investment in the stock and an incentive for all holders to lengthen their holding periods. This leads to longer holding periods and a longer median holding period. The result is a spiral toward less disclosure.

In sum, the dynamics of shareholders with different holding periods have several consequences. First, they lead to a corporate policy of the least disclosure that will sustain the group of long-term holders. Second, they lead to neglect of the disclosure needs of short-term shareholders. This allows greater deviation of prices from true value. Third, they lead to the impracticability of uninformed trading because shareholders need to evaluate each security they trade. Since transaction costs include the cost of acquiring information, the need to become informed functions

6 The value of the firm will increase 8%, but price may deviate ±10% from this 108%, which gives a range from a high of 118.8% to 97.2%.

7 The investment would increase by 1.0810 = 2.159. A $100 investment would turn into $216.

8 The value of the firm, which has increased to 216% of the original investment, will fluctuate between 0.8 × 216% = 172.7% and 1.2 × 216% = 259.2%.

9 Assuming that a uniform distribution of the price deviations and a utility-of-wealth function with constant relative risk aversion leads to the conclusion that a short-term shareholder would be indifferent between the two disclosure regimes if he or she had a risk-aversion coefficient of 1.8 (a coefficient of 0 means risk neutrality), while a long-term holder would need a risk-aversion coefficient of 33.5. (For realistic estimates of risk-aversion coefficients range from 1 to 2, see Mehra and Prescott, 1985, p. 154.)

as an increase in transaction costs. Finally, the dynamics of shareholders with different holding periods results in a disincentive to invest in shares for all but the longest-term investors. If all short-term investors exit the securities market, the disclosure policy will readjust to that of a longer-term majority. This process would repeat itself, in theory, until the only shareholder constituency was perpetual holders, institutions such as university endowments and pension funds. All four results of the dynamics of unregulated disclosure reduce trading in the stock market. The market even closes at the theoretical limit of perpetual shareholders.

In sum, by forcing corporations to disclose more than without regulation, mandatory disclosure indirectly helps short-term uninformed shareholders. Their frequent trading drives market liquidity.

C. CONCLUSION: DISCLOSURE REVEALS SECURITIES REGULATION AS THE CONGRUENT LAW OF LIQUIDITY

It should be no surprise that disclosure rules, by increasing the accuracy of prices, promote liquidity. The connection of accurate prices to liquidity is a key part of the virtuous cycle that securities regulation furthers. As we will see in Parts III and IV (Chapters 12 to 15 and 16 to 19), the intensity of deterrence and the prohibition of insider trading come to the same result – they serve the virtuous cycle by promoting liquidity, which begets more accurate prices, which foster trading by making it safer, which leads to greater liquidity. A closer look shows liquidity to be the inverse of a transaction cost. An increase in liquidity means easier trading; larger trades produce less of a price concession and take less time in more liquid markets.

Reductions in transaction costs are desirable not only from the corporations' perspective but also from a social one. Lower transaction costs lead to higher security prices and a lower cost of capital.[10] More important, however, liquid markets lead to more accurate pricing and allow easier, cheaper, and faster movements of assets among uses. Thus effective securities regulation not only lowers the cost of capital but also increases its mobility.

Accurate prices, in turn, encourage trading because accurate prices make trading less risky and, hence, more appealing. Thus disclosure rules serve the virtuous cycle at the point of greater price accuracy, leading to lower costs of trading and from there to greater liquidity. We will see when analyzing insider trading that greater liquidity itself fosters accurate prices, closing the virtuous cycle.

10 See Amihud & Mendelson (1986) (A theoretical explanation of the effect of transaction costs on holding periods and pricing, validated by empirical data. Smaller transaction costs result is shorter holding periods and lesser rates of return. Short-term investors cannot enjoy the higher returns of the hightransaction-cost assets because they are eroded by their transaction costs. A clientele effect arises, where funds get the highest return in assets with transaction costs that dictate a holding period that corresponds to the investment horizon of the funds.).

PART III

Deterrence of Securities Fraud

12

Introduction to Deterrence Intensity

In 1976, the New York Nets had a very gifted basketball player, Julius "Dr. J" Erving. After including Dr. J in their season ticket advertising, the Nets traded their star. Several season ticket buyers, who alleged that they bought the tickets to see Dr. J, attempted to bring a class-action lawsuit for deceit on behalf of all who bought tickets before the trade. The court refused to certify the class because questions of individual reliance on the ads predominated over questions common to the class.[1] Had the tickets been securities, the "fraud-on-the-market theory" of securities law would have presumed the ticket-buyers' reliance, and the class action would have been certified. Why should reliance differ so radically between deceit and securities fraud?

This part (Chapters 12 to 15) shows how deterrence of securities fraud fits in the virtuous cycle of securities law. Preventing fraud furthers accurate pricing. Accurate pricing makes trading appealing, which is akin to reducing a cost of trading. More trading increases liquidity. The more liquid market attracts trading that makes prices more accurate, completing the virtuous cycle.

This part compares the two torts that may arise from a misrepresentation. A lie about a security may give rise to securities fraud liability,[2] whereas a lie in a nonfinancial setting may give rise to liability under the common-law tort of deceit.[3] The tort of deceit and securities fraud are very similar, as is apparent from

1 *Strauss v. Long Island Sports, Inc.*, 401 NYS.2d 233, 235–6 (N.Y. App. Div. 1978).

2 Throughout this part of the book, "securities fraud" will refer to fraud in a nameless transaction on an organized exchange. Face-to-face transactions are analytically equivalent to the type of transactions that common-law deceit addresses, and securities fraud jurisprudence applies deceit-like rules to them. Therefore, they will not be distinguished from common-law deceit. These chapters justify the strictness of securities fraud via the desirability of liquidity and efficiency in securities markets. The absence of these features from face-to-face transactions obviates a departure from common law. The paradigmatic securities fraud rule is Rule 10b-5, 17 CFR 240.10b-5, issued by the Securities and Exchange Commission (SEC) under the authority of Section 10(b) of the Securities and Exchange Act of 1934. Other frequently arising securities fraud rules include 14e-3 and 12b-20, 17 CFR 240.14e-3 and 12b-20.

3 Some jurisdictions have codified the tort of deceit. See, e.g., Ala. Code § 6-5-104 (Westlaw current through the end of the 2013 Regular Session); Cal. Civ. Code § 1710 (West, Westlaw current with all 2013 Regular Session laws, all 2013–14 1st Extraordinary Session laws, and Res. c. 123 [S.C.A.3]);

their shared elements. Both require (1) a misrepresentation, (2) the appropriate state of mind (scienter, i.e., knowledge of falsity and intent to deceive), (3) reliance on the misrepresentation, and (4) injury (5) caused by actions taken in reliance on the misrepresentation.[4]

The two torts, however, have different standards for reliance that are quite significant. For liability in common-law deceit, reliance on a misrepresentation must be actual and justifiable. By contrast, for liability in securities fraud, reliance may be presumed according to the fraud-on-the-market theory, provided that the misrepresentation is material.

Chapter 13 constitutes the heart of the analysis of the two torts. This analysis concludes that despite assertions that securities fraud is overprotective of investors,[5] misrepresentations about financial goods must be more rigorously deterred than misrepresentations about real goods. The fraud-on-the-market presumption increases deterrence in two ways. First, securities fraud class actions become easier to certify, increasing their probability. Second, the presumption increases the size of the class, increasing the size of damage awards.[6] The argument for more deterrence

Ga. Code Ann. § 51-6-2 (West, Westlaw current through the end of the 2013 Regular Session); Okla. Stat. Ann. Tit. 76, § 2 (West, Westlaw current First Extraordinary Session of the 54th Legislature [2013]); S.D. Codified Laws § 20-10-1 (Westlaw current through the 2013 Regular Session and Supreme Court Rule 13-17).

4 See, e.g., Louis Loss, Fundamentals of Securities Regulation 712 (2d ed. 1988) (enumerating knowledge of falsity and justifiability separately). The environment of securities markets causes different weight to be given to each of these elements as they are transferred into the world of securities fraud. Materiality substitutes for justifiability. See, e.g., *Huddleston v. Herman & MacLean*, 640 F.2d 534, 543 (5th Cir. 1981) (listing elements of private action in direct and personal transactions as "(1) misstatement or an omission (2) of material fact (3) made with scienter (4) on which the plaintiff relied (5) that proximately caused his injury"); 3 Alan R. Bromberg & Lewis D. Lowenfels, Bromberg & Lowenfels on Securities Fraud and Commodities Fraud 195 (categorizing private-action elements in open-market impersonal transactions into misrepresentation and nondisclosure, materiality, scienter, privity, reliance, causation, and closed transaction). Not listed is the closed-transaction element that Bromberg and Lowenfels admit has many exceptions and "is being whittled away." *Id.* at 222.1. The fate of privity is similar. *Id.* at 206.

5 The lead article favoring relaxation of securities fraud rules while also focusing on fraud-on-the-market reliance is Paul G. Mahoney, *Precaution Costs and the Law of Fraud in Impersonal Markets*, 78 Va. L. Rev. 623 (1992). In a similar spirit are Daniel R. Fischel & David J. Ross, *Should the Law Prohibit "Manipulation" in Financial Markets?*, 105 Harv. L. Rev. 503 (1991); Daniel R. Fischel, *Efficient Capital Markets, the Crash, and the Fraud on the Market Theory*, 74 Cornell L. Rev. 907 (1989); Jonathan R. Macey et al., *Lessons from Economics: Materiality, Reliance, and Extending the Reach of Basic v. Levinson*, 77 Va. L. Rev. 1017 (1991); Jonathan R. Macey & Geoffrey P. Miller, *The Fraud-on-the-Market Theory Revisited*, 77 Va. L. Rev. 1001 (1991); Jonathan R. Macey & Geoffrey P. Miller, *Good Finance, Bad Economics: An Analysis of the Fraud-on-the-Market Theory*, 42 Stan. L. Rev. 1059 (1990); Richard A. Posner, *Law and the Theory of Finance: Some Intersections*, 54 Geo. Wash. L. Rev. 159 (1986).

6 Securities fraud is easier for the plaintiff to prove for other reasons as well. An example is the evidentiary standard. Securities fraud must be proved only by a preponderance of the evidence, while deceit must be shown with clear and convincing evidence. See *Herman & MacLean v. Huddleston*, 459 US 375, 387–8 (1983).

of misrepresentations about financial goods than about real goods rests on the differences between the price-formation mechanisms of the two goods.

Chapter 14 applies the preceding analysis to the rules of securities fraud. Section A reminds us that reliance in a deceit action is a test of causation: whether the deceived party's actions were caused by the misrepresentation. Section B contends that the fraud-on-the-market reliance presumption is just an adaptation of conventional legal causation testing to a new environment. In modern securities markets, injury can occur without actual reliance. Section B also argues that securities fraud jurisprudence has neglected to fully adapt the presumption of reliance to its new surroundings. While uninformed investors are adequately protected against fraud, informed speculators are inexplicably exposed to it with no recourse. If informed traders invoke the presumption of reliance, it may be rebutted due to their failure to trust the integrity of the market, but this rebuttal is undesirable.[7] This analysis concludes that fraud-on-the-market is an appropriate but incomplete development that could be improved by a rapprochement to the traditional defense of avoidable consequences in order to protect informed traders.

[7] *Zlotnick v. TIE Communications*, 836 F.2d 818, 823 (3d Cir. 1988) (holding an informed trader, short-seller, could not use the presumption of reliance because, while the presumption's premise is market efficiency, the short-seller believed that the market price overestimated the stock's true value; therefore, he did not trust in the integrity of the market).

13

Comparing the Economic Function of Deceit to That of Securities Fraud

This chapter compares the economic rationale for the torts of deceit and securities fraud. The justification for each tort rests on how prices form in the corresponding market, which Chapter 5 discusses. Section A introduces the argument by describing these pricing mechanisms. In the market for real goods, price equals the valuation of only the last buyer and seller regardless of other market participants' subjective valuations. By contrast, all buyers and sellers value financial goods equally, but this valuation is uncertain because it rests on expected future performance.

Section B builds the foundation of the argument, arguing that the danger of false prices due to misrepresentations is greater in financial markets than in markets for real goods. Misrepresentations about financial goods tend to influence price more, last longer, attract wider (potentially global) attention, be more frequent, and be more costly to uncover than misrepresentations about real goods.

A. PRICE FORMATION

As we saw in Chapter 5, financial goods differ from real goods in that they do not provide a direct benefit to their owner. Stocks, bonds, and bank deposits are merely vessels for value, held until liquidation. Real goods are ends in themselves, owned for direct use. Buyers of real goods decide whether to buy them based on how much utility they will derive from the goods. Buyers of financial goods decide to invest based on the expected proceeds from their eventual sale.

To prepare for the analysis of a misrepresentation, consider the formation of a real good's price in a simple supply-and-demand example.

Example 13.1 Example of a Real Good's Pricing

Let's say a real good has nine potential buyers and nine sellers. Buyer 1 would receive \$1 of use from a unit of the good, buyer 2 would receive \$2, and so on. A second unit is of negligible use to any of the buyers (which is a manifestation of diminishing returns). Seller 1 produces a single unit of the good for a cost of \$1, seller 2 for \$2, and so on.

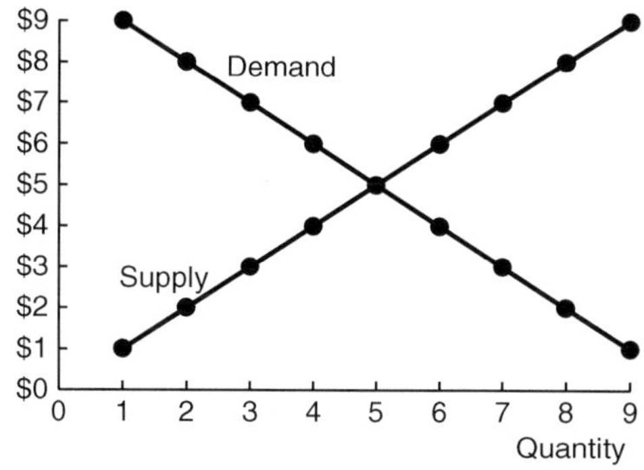

FIGURE 13.1 The supply/demand pricing mechanism for real goods.

The cost of producing a second unit is extraordinary for all sellers (again, diminishing returns). In this market, the price for the good will be $5, and five units of the good will be produced. Because they receive utility of $5 or more from the good, the high-valuing buyers (buyers 9, 8, 7, 6, and 5) will buy the units that would be sold by the low-cost sellers (sellers 1, 2, 3, 4, and 5). Figure 13.1 depicts the supply and the demand curves to show how many goods will be bought or sold at each price. The market "clears" at the price for which the number bought equals the number sold.

The point of the example is that each market participant has a subjective valuation of the good that is different from its price, while price coincides with the valuations of the "marginal" buyer and seller.[1] Some buyers value the good more than its market price. Yet they cannot profit from this disparity. Their diminishing returns ensure that additional units would produce less value for them than the market price. Sellers face the same predicament. They cannot profitably sell additional units.

The supply-and-demand pricing mechanism does not disappear in financial goods. The assumption of costless arbitrage and the disappearance of diminishing returns, however, change the picture dramatically. Supply and demand curves are horizontal. Any decrease in price results in unlimited buying; any increase results in unlimited selling. Figure 13.2 depicts the supply-demand interpretation of the capital asset pricing model (CAPM). According to the CAPM, everyone values the securities equally, here as having the value p_o. Any price above p_o leads to infinite selling, as depicted by the horizontal supply curve going to infinity at prices above p_o. Any price below p_o leads to infinite demand. According to the CAPM, no trading takes place if price is at p_o. Thus the graphical representation of the CAPM also hints at the paradox that in a market that the CAPM describes, trading ceases when price becomes perfectly accurate, the "efficiency paradox."[2]

1 The *marginal* buyer and seller are the very last buyer and seller, the ones who are indifferent about whether they enter into the transaction. In other words, the marginal buyer would not buy if the price were any higher, and the marginal seller would not sell if the price were any lower.

2 See Grossman & Stiglitz, *On the Impossibility of Informationally Efficient Markets*, 70 AM. ECON. REV. 393 (1980); see also Chapter 14, note 27.

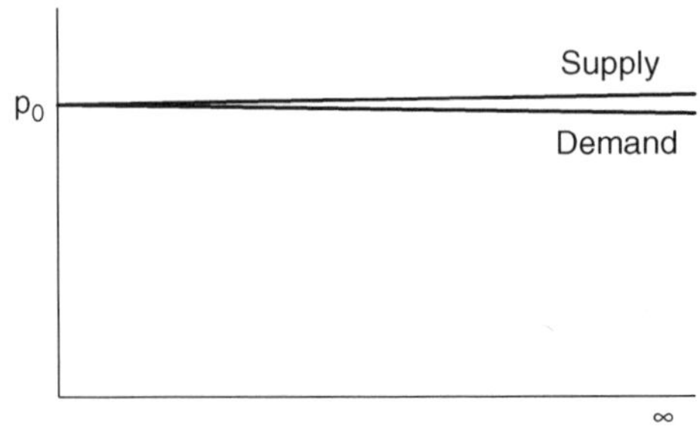

FIGURE 13.2 The horizontal supply and demand of the CAPM.

To evaluate the effects of misrepresentations, we need to understand the economic explanation for the undesirability of fraud. Although this undesirability seems obvious, its economic basis is not intuitive. Looking at social welfare in the aggregate, when fraud moves value from the defrauded party to the maker of the misrepresentation, no social wealth is lost. Waste arises because the fear of fraud induces investors to protect against it – fraud creates an incentive to verify. Precautions against fraud typically involve expending resources to verify information when those resources could be spent on other goods. The waste is easier to see in theft, which has an analogous economic harm. The theft itself merely moves resources among members of the society – from the owner to the thief – without destroying the resources themselves. The reaction, however, is to install locks and alarm systems, which do not produce welfare for their owner – they merely protect against theft. If the legal system can eliminate the fear of theft, then society can expend the resources that it once devoted to the production of locks and alarm systems to produce what is actually desired, for example, food, clothing, shelter, art, or luxuries. Similarly, if fraud were perfectly deterred, society would redirect resources from verification to the production of truly desired goods.

Recognizing that the purpose of the two torts, deceit and securities fraud, is to eliminate wasteful verification, let us examine how verification incentives are different in the two underlying markets. Section B shows how this incentive is stronger in financial markets. Subsection B.i then goes on to argue that the heightened concern about verification waste in financial markets is appropriate. Securities fraud rules, therefore, are properly more severe than those of deceit.

B. DIFFERENCES IN THE INCENTIVE TO VERIFY

It is intuitive that misrepresentations have an adverse impact on participants in both real and financial markets. Consider those misrepresentations in the context of the preceding example (see Example 13.2).

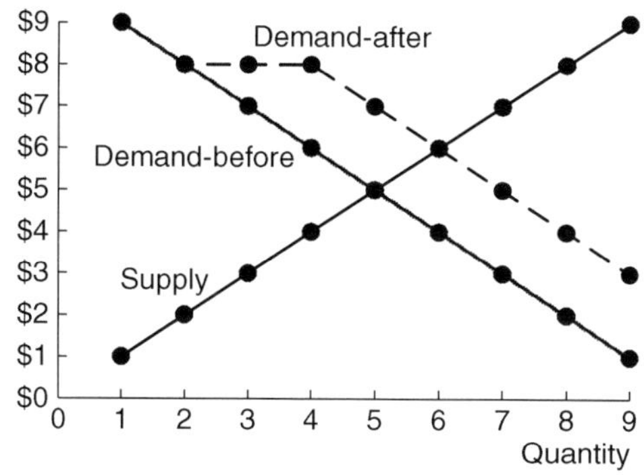

FIGURE 13.3 A misrepresentation's interference with supply and demand.

Example 13.2 A Misrepresentation about a Real Good

In the nine-buyer/seller example used to illustrate the pricing mechanism of real goods (Example 13.1), assume that a lie reaches two potential buyers and changes their beliefs about the good's usefulness. Suppose that these buyers valued the good at \$1 and \$2, respectively. This misrepresentation persuades them to value the good at \$8.[3] At a price of \$8, demand exists for four units, two by the victims of the misrepresentation and two by the buyers who originally valued the good at \$8 and \$9. At a price of \$7, demand for a fifth unit arises, at \$6 for a sixth, and so on. Effectively, the misrepresentation shifts the infected segment of the demand curve to the right by two units, as Figure 13.3 illustrates. Without the misrepresentation, this market produces a price of \$5. With the misrepresentation, the price shifts to \$6.

This example reveals two of the striking features of misrepresentations in real goods. First, if the misrepresentation had reached the buyers who value the good at \$5 or more, it would have had no impact on conduct or price. The misrepresentation influences buyers' conduct and thus price because its recipients would not have bought the good *but for* the misrepresentation. This illustrates that misrepresentations about real goods may well have no effect depending on who receives

[3] This example is distinguishable from *Strauss v. Long Island Sports, Inc.*, 401 NYS.2d 233 (N.Y. App. Div. 1978), where the Nets advertised Erving as a member of the team and then traded him. The misrepresentation there, "Come see Erving play for the Nets," may imply higher utility for some basketball fans and lower utility for others, such as the fans of the Nets' opponents. Thus the misrepresentation may not influence prices, even though it may result in the tickets' highest-valuing users not buying them.

The Nets example is more complex than the one in the text, but it underlines one more difference between real and financial goods. The complexity is that the single statement of the Nets has two different results, one on Nets' fans and one on their opponents' fans. Once the two effects are separated, the analysis is analogous to the one in the text.

The different ways that the same piece of information subjectively influences the goods' desirability is a characteristic of real goods that *Strauss* brings to focus. The only relevant statements about financial goods concern their risk and future returns. Two investors who agree on the meaning of a statement cannot then value the asset differently. If the statement implies higher returns or lower risk, it makes the asset more desirable for every investor.

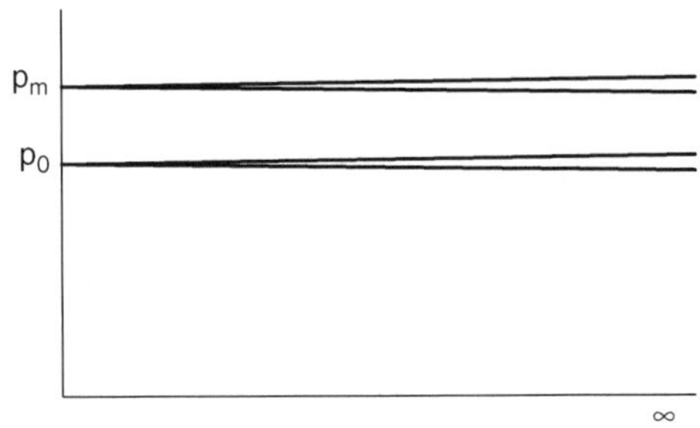

FIGURE 13.4 Effect of misrepresentation on supply and demand per the CAPM.

them. Second, the size of the misrepresentation is much larger than its effect on price. It changed the buyers' valuation from $2 or $1 to $8, a $6 or $7 change. The price, however, changed by only $1. This illustrates that misrepresentations about real goods may well have a much smaller impact on price than their content implies. Further investigation reveals more striking differences between the effects of a misrepresentation on real and financial markets.

Predicting the effect of a misrepresentation about a financial good is difficult. The framework of the analysis is the CAPM, but its horizontal supply and demand curves confound the analysis. The trading of those who believe the misrepresentation will form horizontal supply and demand curves at the price indicated by the misrepresentation (p_m in Figure 13.4). Those who do not believe it will form horizontal supply and demand curves at the original price (p_o). At any price between the two, the group that believes the misrepresentation would engage in unlimited buying, and the group that does not believe in it would engage in unlimited selling. Neither the CAPM nor supply and demand curves offer any insight as to what the price would be in such a market. Figure 13.4 illustrates this lack of an equilibrium.

The inability of the CAPM to deal with heterogeneously informed traders in financial markets is answered by a method of finance that focuses on the interaction between market participants in even more detail than microeconomics. It is known as "market microstructure," and its disciples use game-theoretic methods. The quest is not for the equilibrium price but rather for the equilibrium strategy. Once such a strategy is devised, every participant must react to the others' strategies without giving other investors grounds to improve their strategies. Every strategy is the best response to every other strategy.

Decades of microstructure work reduce the shortcomings of the CAPM by drawing some important conclusions. The risk aversion of informed traders reduces their impact on price. At the same time, the market's liquidity increases the number of informed traders and intensifies their competition, thereby increasing their impact on price. Finally, time pressure (e.g., an impending public announcement of information) increases the impact of informed traders because they need to reap the benefits of their information before it becomes public.

Market microstructure suggests that the market will react to misrepresentations. Only a fraction of informed traders needs to believe the misrepresentation for them to face significant competition and trade aggressively. Only some risk aversion by nonbelieving informed traders is enough to keep them from completely resisting the new price movement. Only some time pressure is enough for the informed traders who believe the misrepresentation to rush to take advantage of it. Moreover, the liquidity of each security determines the likely number of informed traders. The greater the liquidity, the larger is their number, and the more likely it is that just persuading a fraction of them will create competitive pressure.

Notice that the courts applying the fraud-on-the-market presumption of reliance have been sensitive to similar concerns. If the market is not liquid (and hence not efficient), courts have refused to apply the presumption.[4] Furthermore, if informed traders are persuaded that the misrepresentation is not true, the presumption of reliance may be rebutted.[5]

The analysis of the effects of a misrepresentation in the markets for real and financial goods lays the foundation for their comparison. Stricter securities fraud rules would be justified if the securities markets created stronger incentives to verify information.[6] The following subsections argue that misrepresentations in financial markets tend to create stronger verification incentives than misrepresentations in real markets.

False statements in markets for real goods are less detrimental than in markets for financial goods for the following reasons. First, false statements influence the price of real goods for a shorter time and only when their recipients participate in the market. The prices of financial goods are influenced continuously until the false statements are corrected. Second, the influence of false statements on the price of real goods is smaller than the change in value implied by the misrepresentation. Few safeguards prevent the price of financial goods from

4 See, e.g., *Freeman v. Laventhol & Horwath*, 915 F.2d 193, 199 (6th Cir. 1990) (holding that the market for municipal bonds is not efficient enough for statements to be reflected in price, so the fraud-on-the-market presumption of reliance is rebutted).

5 See, e.g., *In re Donald J. Trump Casino Sec. Litig.*, 7 F.3d 357, 371–3 (3d Cir. 1993), cert. denied sub nom. *Gollomp v. Trump*, 114 S.Ct. 1219 (1994) (concluding other cautionary statements in offering sufficiently warned investors of risk so that no liability arose for some omissions); *Roots Partnership v. Lands' End, Inc.*, 965 F.2d 1411, 1420 (7th Cir. 1992) (finding inaccurate statements by Land's End of its performance did not create liability when the market knew the actual results); *In re Apple Computer Sec. Litig.*, 886 F.2d 1109, 1115 (9th Cir. 1989), cert. denied sub nom. *Schneider v. Apple Computer, Inc.*, 496 US 943 (1990) (Despite Apple's misrepresentations, the press had credibly informed investors about the failure of new products.).

6 The economic undesirability of fraud lies in the wasteful incentive it creates to verify statements. See above.

reflecting the entire change in value suggested by the misrepresentation. Third, the misrepresentation about a real good is often local and tends to only draw local attention and verification efforts, while financial misrepresentations receive global attention and verification attempts. Fourth, misrepresentations about financial goods should be expected to be more frequent than misrepresentations about real goods. Finally, verification costs are smaller in the case of real goods.

i. Duration

The false prices that misrepresentations create in real goods are corrected as soon as the deceived participants leave the market. Deceived parties influence price through their contribution to demand or supply. As soon as the deceived parties leave, the price should return to its predeceit level. By contrast, when prices of financial goods change due to a misrepresentation, more than the simple absence of the deceived parties is necessary for price correction. Corrective information must reach a critical mass of market participants.

According to economic theory, the price of real goods is associated with the concept of "market clearing." Prices will be set so that everyone who would buy or sell at that price has done so.[7] Clearing, however, is not well defined in practical terms. For instance, does the market for groceries clear every evening or when the season's produce sells out? To the extent that this question about market clearing can be answered, the answers will have caveats about continued sales. Grocers need not sell out at the end of the day; they can sell the next day. Even at the end of the season, produce can be frozen or canned for further sales.

To see how the influence of deceit depends on the presence of the deceived party in the market, imagine a good that is too costly to carry across time the way a grocer can. Markets for this good must clear independently at the end of each period. Imagine, also, that the good is useful for three periods, while three periods are also necessary for its production. A buyer of this good is likely not to return to the market for two periods after a purchase. Deceiving one buyer may influence price in the current period, but it will not influence prices in the following two periods. Consider the earlier example of nine buyers and sellers (Example 13.1). The shift in the demand curve only occurs in the period when the deceived buyers participate in the market (see Example 13.3).

[7] Those who have not bought or sold have not done so because the price is too high to buy or too low to produce and sell. This supply/demand analysis is frequently used in economics textbooks to show that price regulation causes the market not to clear, in which case excess supply or demand exists. See, e.g., William J. Baumol & Alan S. Blinder, ECONOMICS: PRINCIPLES AND POLICY 70–6 (12th ed. 2012); Paul A. Samuelson &William D. Nordhaus, ECONOMICS 54 (19th ed. 2010).

Example 13.3 Failure to Equalize Prices Due to Costly Carrying

Consider a good that lasts for three periods, and assume that the supply and demand of the good in each period are identical to Example 13.1. If two buyers have been deceived in period 1, we now assume that they will return in periods 4, 7, and so on. The result is a price of $6 in period 1 with the misrepresentation, while the price was $5 before.

Assume that carrying the good from one period to the next costs $2 per unit (for storage, maintenance, or refrigeration). Since the price in the periods affected by deceit will be $6 and will be $5 at other times, carrying is not profitable and will not occur. Therefore, the price differential across periods will persist. The price in periods 2 and 3 will be $5, while during period 4 and every third period thereafter, as long as the deceived buyers remain misinformed, the price returns to $6.

This example illustrates the temporary influence of deceit on prices. Its temporary nature, however, is limited by the degree of separation between periods, that is, the cost of carrying goods to subsequent periods. The speed with which the deceived party discovers the truth may also reduce the duration of deceit's influence on prices. If I were told that an elixir would increase my strength within a month, the falsity of this statement would be obvious one month later. My disillusionment would eliminate my contribution to the shift in the demand curve. Thus the effect of deceit on prices tends not to be permanent for two reasons: deceived parties tend not to buy continuously, and deceived parties tend to recognize the truth sooner or later.

Neither of these two effects is present in the securities markets. Not only does carrying securities across trading periods have negligible cost (because securities need no costly storage), but also the recipient of the misrepresentation is rarely able to recognize a statement's falsity.[8] It is impossible to distinguish an accurately priced security from one that is erroneously priced. The accuracy of the price depends on

8 The problem is most acute for "forward-looking" information about a firm's future prospects, the most important type of information for determining the price of its securities. Investments are made for future returns. Information about future performance determines the price at which investments are desirable. The uncertainty associated with estimating future performance effectively prohibits management from predicting the firm's performance. Any such prediction runs the risk of securities fraud liability. Given this problem, and acknowledging that forward-looking information is most important for accurate pricing, Congress has created a safe harbor for forward-looking statements identified as such in Section 21E of the 1934 Act and Section 27A of the 1933 Act. The Securities and Exchange Commission (SEC) has tried to encourage predictions by shielding them from liability in several ways. For example, SEC Rule 175, 17 CFR 230.175 (1994) provides a safe harbor for forward-looking statements by immunizing their makers from liability if they are in good faith. See SEC, Safe Harbor Rule for Projections, Securities Act, Release No. 6084 [1979 Transfer Binder] Fed. Sec. L. Rep. CCCH) 82,117 (June 25, 1979). The treatment of appraisals is analogous. Appraisals are uncertain because they concern assets that have not yet been liquidated. As with predictions, professionals are afraid to make appraisals for fear of incurring liability. The SEC has reduced the likelihood that appraisals made in good faith will give rise to liability by removing them from the note to SEC Rule 14a-9, which listed them as examples of misleading statements. See also Adoption of Amendments to Proxy Rules, Exchange Act, Release No. 5276 [1956 Transfer Binder] *Fed. Sec. L. Rep.* (CCH) 76,380 (January 17, 1956). The SEC's efforts, however, do not solve the problem of investors trying to verify the valuation of securities.

the accurate calculation of the probability with which each different future price will materialize. Even after the fact, however, one cannot know whether the probabilities were correct. The outcome that materialized is irrelevant information with regard to the probability that this outcome would materialize, which is the information that matters for accurate pricing.

In sum, misrepresentations about real goods should influence prices for a shorter time than misrepresentations about financial goods for two reasons: (1) the influence on prices lasts only as long as the deceived parties' presence in the market, and (2) the statement's falsity is usually ascertainable relatively quickly.

ii. Price Impact

We saw in Example 13.2, illustrating the movement of the demand curve caused by a lie, that the price of a real good tends not to change as much as the deceptive statement implies. The small effect of misrepresentations on the prices of real goods has two causes. First, a misrepresentation tends not to influence all potential buyers, especially when made face-to-face. Second, unless supply is perfectly inelastic, the rise in prices will induce an increase in supply that mitigates the effect of the misrepresentation.[9]

Securities markets provide a very different environment, one in which local and national borders are crossed at little, if any, cost. The additional fact that a central clearing corporation holds all securities in most exchanges eliminates any storage cost.[10] Therefore, securities can be held for the long term at no cost. The lack of diminishing returns in securities markets – another fundamental distinction from real goods markets – dramatically increases the capacity of small, misinformed groups of buyers or sellers to influence prices. Because buying more units of the financial good, that is, more shares, does not make additional shares any less desirable, even small groups who think a security is undervalued have an incentive to buy as much of it as they can and exert great buying pressure on prices. This stands in stark contrast to the situation of real goods, where each buyer can use only a limited amount of the good due to diminishing returns and thus exerts limited pressure on prices. Even if many potential buyers were convinced that a real good was worth more than its price, each would buy only a few units.

Even when all buyers of a real good believe the misrepresentation and the demand curve shifts by the entire amount of the misrepresentation, prices will rarely change as much as the misrepresentation implies. The reason lies in the production

[9] This mitigation is embedded in the slope of the supply curve. It does not involve a shift of the supply curve because the costs of production do not change.

[10] See, e.g., Egon Guttman, *Federal Regulation of Transfer Agents*, 34 Am. U. L. Rev. 281 (1985). The regulation of clearing houses and transfer agents is controlled by the 1934 Act, Section 17A, 15 USC 78q-1 (1994), and the SEC rules promulgated thereunder.

increase that usually follows a price increase. Increased production counters the inflationary effect of the misrepresentation.

In economic theory, this point is illustrated by the upward (positive) slope of the supply curve, showing that an increase in prices leads to an increase in the quantity supplied. The downward (negative) slope of the demand curve shows that prices fall in response to more supply. Therefore, the mitigation of increases in supply depends on the slopes of the supply and demand curves.[11]

A special case occurs when a horizontal supply curve interacts with a horizontal demand curve, a phenomenon that is practically unique to the securities markets of the CAPM. A misrepresentation may affect price fully if its believers are willing to take enough risk.[12]

iii. Area of Impact

Markets for real and financial goods also differ in size and scale. Financial markets are international, whereas markets for real goods are often local. A financial misrepresentation by a Connecticut snowblower manufacturer with stock traded on the New York Stock Exchange is as relevant in California or Germany as it is in Connecticut. German and American investors are equally interested in the firm's valuation because they can all trade shares in the corporation at equal cost. By contrast, a misrepresentation about an impending snowstorm will only influence the demand, and thus price, of snow-removal equipment in the affected area. Misrepresentations have different impacts because of the difference in the size of the markets.

The source of the difference, again, is carrying costs. Real goods must be moved to the place where they are needed, and this carrying cost is significant. A misrepresentation about a snowstorm may increase demand for snowblowers in Hartford, Connecticut, allowing dealers to increase profits, but snowblower dealers in Boston, Massachusetts, and Albany, New York, cannot satisfy the unexpected demand without cost. They must absorb the cost of moving their inventory to Hartford before selling it. They will not move their snowblowers unless the Hartford price is higher than their local price plus carrying costs. Furthermore, if additional snowblowers arrive in Hartford, these will alleviate the effect of the misrepresentation by increasing supply and decreasing prices. The carrying cost sets how close prices in Hartford can be to prices in Boston and Albany.

11 A more horizontal supply curve would lead to a smaller price change in response to the movement of the demand curve (provided that it slopes down). A horizontal supply curve means that sellers have unlimited production ability at the current price. At the opposite extreme, a more vertical supply curve would fully translate any movement of the demand curve to a change in prices. A vertical supply curve means that producers are unable to increase production in the face of higher prices.

12 See Figure 13.4.

The difference in snowblower prices between Hartford and the other markets cannot profitably be reduced below the carrying cost.

Financial goods, by contrast, are traded in organized transfer and clearing systems that eliminate the need to physically deliver the certificates underlying the securities. When investors buy a security, regardless of their location, a simple entry in the books of the clearing corporation will transfer ownership of the security. With this lack of physicality, the reach of financial misrepresentations – and the incentive to avoid them – is global. All investors want to know the truth about the security they buy. In contrast, a snowblower buyer in Colorado is virtually indifferent to misrepresentations that influence snowblower prices in the northeastern United States and has no incentive to verify such statements.

The lesson for the law of deceit is that fear of misrepresentations in financial markets tends to induce more verification than in markets for real goods. Distrust in statements about a security will induce verification around the world. Distrust in statements about a real good may only lead to verification by local buyers. Since verification is waste, the misrepresentation that produces less of it is comparatively benign, and the law should treat it more leniently.

iv. Frequency

Financial misrepresentations can produce greater gains for their makers than misrepresentations about real goods. Therefore, we should expect financial misrepresentations to have greater frequency, under the extraordinary assumption of all else being equal.[13] The wasteful incentive to verify is directly influenced by the expected frequency of misrepresentations. Moreover, because fraud would in any case be relatively rare, the natural aversion to risk that individuals have aggravates its fear, and individuals prefer that fraud is rarer.[14]

[13] We must imagine identical rules in both financial and real misrepresentations. It is not possible to go back in time and compare real and financial markets before securities laws were developed. Furthermore, such a comparison would be inconclusive because the securities markets have evolved dramatically in the meanwhile. Attempts to empirically judge the reaction to the passage of federal securities laws favor the notion that investors raised their value of securities in reaction to the additional disclosure requirements. See, e.g., Michael Greenstone, Paul Oyer, & Annette Vissing-Jorgensen, *Mandated Disclosure, Stock Returns, and the 1964 Securities Acts Amendments*, Q. J. ECON. 399, 446–7 (2006); Gregg A. Jarrell, *The Economic Effects of Federal Regulation of the Market for New Security Issues*, 24 J.L. & ECON. 613, 624–50 (1981); Rafael La Porta, Florencio Lopez-de-Silanes, & Andrei Shleifer, *What Works in Securities Laws?*, 61 J. FINANCE 1, 27–8 (2006) (Mandatory disclosure rules improve stock market performance.); Carol J. Simon, *The Effect of the 1933 Securities Act on Investor Information and the Performance of New Issues*, 79 AM. ECON. REV. 295, 313 (1989) (Mandatory disclosure benefited unseasoned, non-NYSE-traded firms but not seasoned NYSE-traded firms.).

[14] Compare two uncertainties, one leaving the individual with \$1,001 with a 99% probability or \$901 with a 1% probability to one leaving the individual with \$1,050 or \$950 with a 50% probability each. While a risk-neutral person would consider the two equivalent, a risk-averse one would prefer the former. In technical terms, assume that individuals' risk aversion takes the form of a utility of wealth function

Misrepresentations about real goods offer small gains to their maker. The price changes caused by the misrepresentations, and hence the profits they generate for their makers, tend to be small, temporary, and local, as we saw in the preceding subsections. Financial misrepresentations tend to have a larger impact. Although the benefits of financial misrepresentations are less direct, the sizes of the gains are staggering compared with those that misrepresentations about real goods produce.

Since financial misrepresentations are undesirable, the legal system must increase penalties, increase the probability that financial misrepresentations will be penalized, or both. Class actions provide recourse to those with small claims that would not be cost-justified to litigate individually. Their participation in the class increases the potential damage award. Moreover, the greater damage award makes the litigation more appealing for attorneys compensated by contingency fees. This increases the probability that a claim will be pursued. The fraud-on-the-market presumption of reliance, which allows securities fraud class actions to go forward more easily than deceit class actions, increases both the size of the damage award and the probability that financial misrepresentations will be penalized. This increased probability and magnitude of liability leads to greater deterrence.

v. Verification Cost

How costly is it to verify information about real goods? Consumers can verify information about many real goods, even if they do not have the expertise to do so, at relatively little cost. For example, used-car buyers can verify the condition of the vehicle's mechanical operation at a garage.[15] Home buyers can check the house's mechanical and structural soundness by hiring an inspector.[16] The cost of inspections as a percentage of price is very small.

Verifying information about securities, however, is prohibitively expensive and practically impossible. Numerous examples of financial fraud litigation show that the false information could not have been verified without the cooperation of its maker. Consider the example of Equity Funding, an insurance company that

U(w) that has constant relative risk aversion by having a slope that changes at the same rate relative to wealth at every level of wealth. In mathematical terms, this family of functions derives from their slopes by the method of differential equations. See, generally, Kenneth J. Arrow, *The Theory of Risk Aversion*, reprinted in 3 COLLECTED PAPERS OF KENNETH ARROW 147 (1984); John W. Pratt, *Risk Aversion in the Small and in the Large*, 32 ECONOMETRICA 122, 134 (1964). Thus, depending on whether the coefficient of risk aversion a is smaller than one, one, or larger than one, the form of the utility of wealth function is w^{1-a}, $\log w$, or $-w^{-(a-1)}$. Compare expected utilities as in the preceding example. The more rare fraud incidence will correspond to greater expected utility.

15 For example, eBay has arranged for $99 inspections of cars to be sold on eBay Motors; see *Inspect that Car before Buying!* (2009), available at www.edmunds.com/car-buying/inspect-that-used-car-before-buying.html (accessed February 15, 2017).

16 Internet searches indicate that home inspections in 2013 cost from $300 to $500 depending on house size.

overstated its assets. The fraud of several years was finally exposed by disgruntled ex-employees.[17]

Consistent with what the preceding subsections argued, the effect of the misrepresentation on the price of Equity Funding's stock was full, persistent, and global. The stock traded at a price that fully reflected the misrepresentation. The misrepresentation influenced price for at least three years.[18] Equity Funding was based in California, but the fraud influenced investors around the world.

Although huge profits were in store for whomever uncovered the misrepresentation, the fraud persisted until insiders revealed it to Raymond Dirks, a securities analyst. The costs that Dirks undertook to uncover the misrepresentation were significant. After he received the tip, he left his New York office and went to California to interview several employees of Equity Funding. Despite the fact that senior management denied wrongdoing, he pursued his efforts for weeks until he could corroborate the allegations of fraud.[19] Even government auditors had missed the fraud.[20] Certainly no investor could have uncovered it without the help of an insider.

This example shows that financial frauds can be prohibitively expensive and nearly impossible to uncover. Equity Funding is not unique. Examples of financial misrepresentations that stay hidden for years abound, including more recently Enron, WorldCom, and Bernie Madoff's Ponzi scheme.[21]

To summarize, financial misrepresentations have a larger and longer impact on prices, have a more global audience, are presumably more frequent, and are costlier to verify than misrepresentations about real goods. Clearly, financial fraud poses a greater threat than real fraud, and its rules should increase the likelihood that a securities fraud plaintiff succeeds.[22] Fear of fraud will also tend to reduce the

17 The ex-employees disclosed the fraud to Raymond Dirks, a securities analyst. When Dirks tried to bring the information to light, respected newspapers and the SEC ignored him. When he had his clients trade on it, the SEC prosecuted him for insider trading. *Dirks v. Securities and Exch. Comm'n*, 463 US 646 (1983). For the place of the case in insider trading law, see Chapter 17 note 9.

18 The SEC first received information about fraud at Equity Funding in 1971. The discovery led the New York Stock Exchange to suspend trading in Equity Funding on March 27, 1973. *Id.* at 650 & n. 3.

19 *Id.* at 649–50.

20 *Id.* at 652 ("Largely thanks to Dirks one of the most infamous frauds in recent memory was uncovered and exposed, while the record shows that the SEC repeatedly missed opportunities.").

21 See *United States v. Ebbers*, 458 F.3d 110 (2d Cir. 2006) (WorldCom falsified financial reports.); *SEC v. Madoff*, 2008 WL 5197070 (SDNY) (Madoff embezzled more than $50 billion.); *United States v. Skilling*, 638 F.3d 480 (5th Cir. 2011) cert. denied, 132 S.Ct. 1905 (2012) (Skilling transferred losses of the retail division to the wholesale division of Enron to make its financial reports appear appealing.).

22 One cannot argue that fraud in secondary securities markets does not decrease social welfare and therefore efforts to curb it are unnecessary. Such a contention would be false because uninformed and informed investors are hurt by misrepresentations and can only compensate for the fear of trading at false prices by not trading or trading more rarely. Thus the fear of fraud functions as a transaction cost, and the strong deterrence of securities fraud reduces a transaction cost, similarly to disclosure rules.

amount of capital available to firms because of the lengthening of holding periods it will force on investors, further increasing the cost of capital for businesses and reducing productivity.

The confidence generated by a strict securities fraud regime, however, does not also imply that the current securities fraud rules are perfect. While Chapter 14 shows how the interpretation of securities fraud increases deterrence, it also argues that the current fraud-on-the-market presumption of reliance, the source of securities fraud deterrence, can be improved.

14

Reliance in Deceit and Securities Fraud

Chapter 13 showed that from a policy perspective, the securities markets need stricter, more austere measures against misrepresentations than real goods markets. This chapter applies these conclusions to the law, specifically the fraud-on-the-market presumption of reliance of securities fraud. In order to understand this doctrine, we must start with its common-law ancestor, the reliance required for liability in deceit.

A. JUSTIFIABLE RELIANCE IN COMMON-LAW DECEIT

Deceit is one of the more logically intricate torts. The plaintiff's own actions cause the plaintiff's injury. Nevertheless, recovery for self-inflicted injury is possible because the plaintiff alleges that his actions came in response to the defendant's false statement.[1] Thus deceit involves two causal chains: one from the false statement to the plaintiff's act and another from the plaintiff's act to his own injury. Justifiable reliance is only relevant to the first link.

i. Reliance as a Test of Causation

Reliance is an essential element in the chain of causation connecting the misrepresentation to the plaintiff's injury. The misrepresentation influences the plaintiff only if the plaintiff relies on the misrepresentation in acting or refraining from action. Without the requirement of reliance, any misstatement by a defendant might give

[1] The defendant must also have made this statement with scienter – he must know that it is false or disregard its accuracy – and with the intent to influence the plaintiff's actions. Although scienter and intent are controversial topics that deserve analysis, they are secondary to the virtuous cycle and this book. Therefore, the necessary intent for culpability is assumed in this chapter. For more on intent, see, generally, William Landes & Richard Posner, The Economic Structure of Tort Law (1987); Steven Shavell, Economic Analysis of Accident Law (2007); David W. Robertson, *Negligence Liability for Crimes and Intentional Torts Committed by Others*, 67 Tul. L. Rev. 135 (1992); Steven Shavell, *An Analysis of Causation and the Scope of Liability in the Law of Torts*, 9 J. Legal Stud. 463 (1980) (hereinafter Shavell, *Analysis of Causation*).

rise to crushing liability.[2] All possible plaintiffs whose actions by chance coincided with the action suggested by the misrepresentation would benefit. Hence the element of reliance is a test of causation.[3]

ii. *Justifiability as a Test of Avoidable Consequences*

Reliance, however, is not the only element of causation. Even if the plaintiff undertook the injurious actions because she believed in the defendant's statements, this response may be defective. The plaintiff may not be justified in believing the statement. A reasonable plaintiff would know it was false, irrelevant, or insignificant. Either the error of believing the misrepresentation or the error of responding to it interrupt the chain of causation. In these cases, the plaintiff's actions and the resulting damage are the plaintiff's error. They cannot be attributed to the misrepresentation. The defendant is not held liable for those damages for the same reason that defendants are not liable for avoidable-consequence injuries.[4]

An example illustrates this point. Imagine that the misrepresentation suggests to the plaintiff that to reach the top of a rocky ledge, he should confidently climb the rocks because they are stable. If the plaintiff overlooked the existence of an obviously superior alternative to climbing, such as a nearby ladder, and was injured by unstable rocks, his deceit action will fail because the reliance is unjustified. The plaintiff made an independent error by adjusting his actions to information that, however deceptive, was immaterial. His reliance exists but is not justified. The injury cannot be traced to the deceptive statement because the plaintiff's own error interrupts the chain of causation. Therefore, the climber cannot recover for his injuries.

In sum, the justifiable reliance element of the common-law tort of deceit is not different from causation. The plaintiff must plead that his actions were, in effect, caused by the defendant because he relied on the misrepresentation. The defendant can rebut this allegation by claiming that the plaintiff's actions were due to his own error. The defendant will claim that the injury was an avoidable consequence by pleading that the plaintiff's reliance was not justifiable. Thus reliance is identical to causation, and justifiability is identical to avoidable consequences.

The incorporation of justifiable reliance as an element of the securities fraud offense may not have given rise to any problems if modern stock exchanges had not developed. However, the efficiency of securities markets changes the way in which

[2] The term "crushing liability" is used by Steven Shavell in his pioneering article on economic analysis of causation to mean that if legal causation concepts are relaxed excessively, then the tortfeasor will be liable for an extraordinary number of remote consequences of the tort. This liability would crush any tortfeasor. See Shavell, *An Analysis of Causation*, in note 1.

[3] One of the most respected corporate law commentators, calls reliance "a part of the causal chain from violation to injury." Robert C. Clark, CORPORATE LAW 329 (1986).

[4] See W. Page Keeton et al., PROSSER AND KEETON ON THE LAW OF TORTS § 65, at 458 (5th ed. 1984).

a statement can cause injury. In an efficient market, a misstatement can change prices and thus cause injury without reliance. The courts respond to this problem not by abolishing the reliance requirement in securities fraud actions, which would be the straightforward solution, but by presuming the securities fraud plaintiffs' reliance.

B. SECURITIES FRAUD RELIANCE: FRAUD-ON-THE-MARKET PRESUMPTION

In the transition from common law to modern securities law, reliance loses much of its importance. Though causation retains its central role, the process by which modern markets set securities' prices results in a more objective causation test than reliance, which seeks to subjectively establish the cause of plaintiffs' decisions. The following discussion shows that according to securities fraud jurisprudence, an individual's actions in the modern securities markets may be influenced by a misrepresentation even if the individual has not heard the misrepresentation.

In an efficient securities market, available information is assimilated into securities prices.[5] Each piece of information adds to or subtracts from the price of the security. This does not mean that there is, by definition, one "true" price for a security. The price tends to be the market's best, yet imprecise estimate of the present value of the future income stream that the security will produce.[6] Furthermore, statistical methods can only point to the accuracy of price changes in response to information; true price cannot be derived.

Public misrepresentations are assimilated into price as one more piece of information. By influencing prices, such misrepresentations influence all investors who trade at those prices. Without the misstatement, all investors would have transacted at different prices, regardless of reliance on the misrepresentation or even awareness of it, because in an efficient securities market the effect of an erroneous statement influences prices. Traders act on the statement (and may be injured by it) without having heard it because they transact at a price that is influenced by the statement.

[5] See, generally, Ronald J. Gilson & Reinier Kraakman, *The Mechanisms of Market Efficiency*, 70 VA. L. REV. 549, at 568 (1984); Eugene F. Fama, *Efficient Capital Markets: A Review of Theory and Empirical Work*, 25 J. FINANCE 383 (1970). But see Eugene F. Fama, *Efficient Markets: II*, 61 J. FINANCE 1575 (1991) (finding exceptions to market efficiency). See, generally, James H. Lorie et al., THE STOCK MARKET: THEORIES AND EVIDENCE (2d ed. 1985); Benoit Mandelbrot, *Forecasts of Future Prices, Unbiased Markets, and "Martingale" Models*, 39 J. BUS. 242 (1966); Paul A. Samuelson, *Proof That Properly Anticipated Prices Fluctuate Randomly*, 6 INDUS. MGMT. REV. 41 (1965). The Nobel Prize in Economics for 2013 included as a laureate Eugene Fama for his work on market efficiency (as well as Robert Shiller for his work against efficiency; see, e.g., note 28).

[6] That the price will tend to equal the discounted future income stream of the security is a generally accepted principle of financial economics. See, e.g., Robert A. Schwartz, EQUITY MARKETS IN ACTION: THE FUNDAMENTALS OF LIQUIDITY, MARKET STRUCTURE, AND TRADING 33–58 (2004).

In contrast, misstatements in the common-law environment injure only those whose actions are actually influenced by the misinformation.

The fraud-on-the-market presumption of reliance evolved in response to this reasoning. The presumption was developed loosely and concurrently in several federal circuits with little homogeneity or consistency, starting with dicta in the early 1970s.[7] The theory was established in the early 1980s.[8] The US Supreme Court offers a single coherent source for the theory in *Basic, Inc. v. Levinson*.[9] In *Basic*, the Court started from the premise that investors have confidence in the integrity of the market price and went on to construct a presumption of reliance on all public misrepresentations:

> An investor who buys or sells at the price set by the market does so in reliance on the integrity of that price. Because most publicly available information is reflected in market price, an investor's reliance on any public material misrepresentations, therefore, may be presumed for the purposes of a Rule 10b-5 action.[10]

Reliance on the misrepresentation is presumed because of investors' "reliance on the integrity of [the market] price."[11] The dissenters in *Basic*, in an opinion by Justice White, objected to what they saw as a claim that the market price becomes equal to "true value" through some "metaphysical process," the existence of which courts cannot ascertain: "While the scholastics of the medieval times professed a means to make such a valuation of a commodity's 'worth', I doubt that the federal courts of our time are similarly equipped."[12]

Justice White's objection was probably founded on a view that fraud-on-the-market meant that traders would be allowed to rely on the market for accurate pricing of their securities and therefore indirectly rely on the statements that may influence these valuations. Fraud-on-the-market, however, is distinguishable from indirect reliance.[13]

7 See, e.g., *Reeder v. Mastercraft Elec. Corp.*, 363 F.Supp. 574, 581 (S.D.N.Y. 1973).

8 See *Finkel v. Docutel/Olivetti Corp.*, 817 F.2d 356, 361 n. 11 (5th Cir. 1987); *Peil v. Speiser*, 806 F.2d 1154, 1161 n. 11 (3d Cir. 1986). A lone forerunner appeared in 1975, *Blackie v. Barrack*, 524 F.2d 891 (9th Cir. 1975), cert. denied, 429 US 816 (1976).

9 485 US 224 (1987). This was a class action of sellers who allegedly sold at prices depressed because of Basic's fraudulent denials of rumors about merger negotiations. The Supreme Court reversed the circuit court's finding that statements denying rumors were per se material, as well as the district court's bright-line test that statements about corporate combinations are not material before a preliminary agreement. The Court also set case-by-case standards of materiality, defined a rebuttable fraud-on-the-market presumption of reliance, and remanded.

10 *Basic*, 485 US at 247.

11 *Id.* Some circuit courts have considered this phrase not to define reliance but to be a license to develop their own fraud-on-the-market theories. See, e.g., *Abel v. Potomac Ins. Co.*, 858 F.2d 1104, 1120 (5th Cir. 1988) (stating that "*Basic* essentially allows each of the circuits room to develop its own fraud-on-the-market rules . . . a new, largely undefined, version of this presumption of reliance").

12 *Basic*, 485 US at 255 (footnote omitted) (White, J., dissenting).

13 Common-law deceit, which does not accept the presumption of reliance, accepts indirect reliance. Restatement (Second) of Torts 2d 533:

i. Distinguishing Fraud-on-the-Market from Indirect Reliance

Justice White's objection sounds reasonable: courts should not determine the accuracy of market prices. However, the fraud-on-the-market presumption of reliance does not require that the courts establish a security's worth. The investors' reliance on the integrity of market price is different from relying on the accuracy of that price. The presumption is merely a claim that investors assume that formation of the price accounts for all information, an assumption that *Basic* acknowledges to be legitimate and protected by Rule 10b-5.[14] The courts only need to determine that a fraudulent statement has influenced price to the plaintiff's disadvantage.[15] Courts do not appraise the security's "true" value.[16] Justice White's concern that the fraud-on-the-market presumption of reliance operates as a guarantee of accurate prices is wrong because the presumption operates only as a guarantee that prices are not manipulated. Prices may be incorrect for other reasons.

Confusion of fraud-on-the-market with indirect reliance also seems to be at the center of the disagreement between the majority and the dissent in *Mirkin v. Wasserman*.[17] The dissent appears to disagree with the majority's refusal to adopt the fraud-on-the-market presumption of reliance in deceit, arguing that indirect reliance has already been adopted and proclaiming the two principles "fully consistent."[18]

> The maker of a fraudulent misrepresentation is subject to liability for pecuniary loss to another who acts in justifiable reliance upon it if the misrepresentation, although not made directly to the other, is made to a third person and the maker intends or has reason to expect that its terms will be repeated or its substance communicated to the other, and that it will influence his conduct in the transaction or type of transaction involved.

14 See *Basic*, 485 US at 245 (stating that "the presumption of reliance employed in this case is consistent with, and, by facilitating Rule 10b-5 litigation, supports, the congressional policy embodied in the 1934 Act; in drafting that Act, Congress expressly relied on the premise that securities markets are influenced by information, and enacted legislation to facilitate an investor's reliance on the integrity of those markets").

15 *Id.* Both the existence of an influence and its size can easily be measured by statistical methods of finance. See, e.g., Stephen J. Brown & Jerold B. Warner, *Using Daily Stock Returns: The Case of Event Studies*, 14 *J. Fin. Econ.* 3 (1986).

16 Notice that "true" value is distinguished from the price that the shares would command absent the misrepresentation. The courts must find the price that would prevail absent the misrepresentation, a much easier feat than ascertaining "true" value.

17 *Mirkin v. Wasserman*, 858 P.2d 568 (Cal. 1993).

18 *Id.* After discussing the case law on indirect reliance, the dissent concludes:

> As this review of the relevant authorities demonstrates, the fraud-on-the-market principle that the federal courts developed in rule 10b-5 cases is fully consistent with the Restatement (Second) of Torts [533] and with California law. In actions for intentional misrepresentation, our law has never required direct or "eyeball" reliance to sustain a claim, but has recognized the principle of indirect reliance, under which a fraudulent statement is no less actionable because it has passed through an intermediary and in the process has undergone a change in form before inducing reliance by a party who thereby suffers injury. The price of a security traded in an open and developed market may express the effect of a fraudulent statement just as surely as a credit rating (Rest.2d Torts, 533, com. f), governmental certification (*Learjet Corp. v. Spenlinhauer*, 901 F.2d 198), doctor's prescription (*Allen v. G.D. Searle & Co.*, 708 F.Supp. 1142), or even a child's importuning of a parent to purchase a particular breakfast

Indirect reliance as an element of deceit, however, is distinguishable because the causal chain and the injury are different from those in fraud-on-the-market. Plaintiffs in deceit actions seek to undo the consequences of their reliance, usually by rescinding the transaction into which the misrepresentation led them. By contrast, securities fraud plaintiffs do not seek to undo their trades but seek to recover the portion of the price that they paid or did not receive due to the inflation or depression of price that the misrepresentation caused. Instead of reliance causing the transaction (transaction causation), reliance in securities fraud litigation causes a trading loss (loss causation).[19] Whether the price would have been perfectly accurate without the misrepresentation is irrelevant. At issue is the influence that the misrepresentation had on price. Under common-law indirect reliance, parties whom the misrepresentation did not reach, directly or indirectly, cannot recover any overpayments they made due to the misrepresentation. By contrast, under the fraud-on-the-market presumption of reliance, parties who ignore the misrepresentation can still recover resulting overpayments.

To illustrate, envision a hypothetical investor who purchases a security. Unknown to our investor, a false statement has elevated the price of this security. The investor has only two choices: to buy or not to buy. Price cannot be negotiated. If the investor buys, the misstatement will affect her personal finances because it inflated the price at which she bought the securities. In the buyer beware environment of the common law, the investor would have no recourse because the misstatement did not cause the investor to purchase the security. Under securities law, it is understood that the investor paid more based on the misstatement, thereby acting on it. It does not matter that the investor did not hear the statement. The market "heard" it and priced the security accordingly, while the investor perforce "relied" on the market's information and paid the inflated market price.

The "loss causation" function of fraud-on-the-market must be distinguished from indirect reliance leading to "transaction causation." It is easy to think that the role of the fraud-on-the-market presumption is to allow reliance on the market valuation. If that were the only result of the fraud-on-the-market presumption, its novelty would be marginal. An example shows that acceptance of reliance on the market's valuation is not a significant change from the common-law concept of reliance. Consider that a pedestrian had recommended tires to drivers, allowing a local shop to sell tires at an inflated price of $10, while they would otherwise have sold for $5. Under deceit rules, the tire purchasers who do not rely directly or indirectly on the pedestrian's statement

cereal (*Committee on Children's Television, Inc. v. General Foods Corp.*, 35 Cal.3d 197). In all such cases, the chain of causation is unbroken, and the element of reliance is established.

Id. at 590.

19 Because the fraud-on-the-market presumption attributes the loss due to the inflated or depressed portion of the price to the misrepresentation, courts and commentators use the term "loss causation" in referring to this reliance. This term contrasts with "transaction causation," which refers to the function of reliance in deceit (and securities fraud in face-to-face transactions).

have no recourse against him for the $5 loss they suffer when buying the tires.[20] The fraud-on-the-market theory, however, would allow recovery on the premise that the extra $5 was paid because the market was influenced by the misstatement. The difference is that common-law reliance operates under the assumption that the drivers who do not like the price of tires will try to find a different shop or negotiate the price and that each individual's reasons for participating in a transaction in real goods are purely subjective and may be unrelated to price. However, investors who must trade securities face essentially a single integrated market, and price is not negotiable. In the example of Dr. J's trade by the NY Nets, the Court noted that season ticket buyers may have wanted to see the opposing teams or to provide business entertainment rather than to see Dr. J play.[21]

In economic terms, as Chapters 5 and 13 explained, buyers are expected to buy if the utility they derive from the good exceeds its price. Sellers sell if prices cover their costs or their lost utility. If all buyers and sellers behave this way, goods are allocated optimally. Artificial prices, as in the tire example, are unsustainable in the long term.[22] The Dr. J. example is distinguishable because it is not certain that the Nets would have charged less for tickets without Dr. J. The tickets' value would be lower for buyers who wanted to see Dr. J, but the demand of buyers with other motives may have sustained the same price. Indeed, it is not hard to imagine nonnative New Yorkers who may be fans of other teams and therefore prefer the Nets without Dr. J. The Nets advertisement may have resulted in tickets being bought by the wrong buyers – those who wanted to see the Nets with Dr. J instead of those wanting to see them without him – but not necessarily at a wrong price.[23]

20 See, e.g., *Strauss v. Long Island Sports, Inc.*, 401 NY S.2d 233 (NY App. Div. 1978) (holding that buyers of New York Nets' season tickets had insufficiently homogeneous motives for buying tickets for certification of class action alleging Nets' deceit in advertising Julius Erving as a member of the team and trading him before the season started). See also, e.g., *Varwig v. Anderson-Behel Porsche/Audi, Inc.*, 141 Cal. Rptr. 539 (Cal. Ct. App. 1977) (holding that final buyer of an automobile had cause of action for deceit against initial seller who misrepresented car's title because of indirect reliance on the initial seller's statement to the intermediate buyer); *Committee on Children's Television, Inc. v. General Foods Corp.*, 673 P.2d 660 (Cal. 1983) (finding that children watched misleading advertisements and requested they buy cereal, sufficiently pleaded reliance in their cause of action for deceit because of indirect reliance on the statement that was made to the children, even if the children were not alleged to have repeated the statement to their parents). In *Children's Television*, the court noted that "repetition . . . should not be a prerequisite to liability; it should be sufficient that defendant makes a misrepresentation to one group intending to influence the behavior of the ultimate purchaser, and that he succeeds in this plan." Id. at 674; see also *Restatement (Second) of Torts* 533 (1977): The maker of a fraudulent misrepresentation is subject to liability . . . to another who acts in justifiable reliance upon it if the misrepresentation, although not made directly to the other, is made to a third person and the maker intends or has reason to expect that its terms will be repeated or its substance communicated to the other, and that it will influence his conduct.

21 See note 1; *Strauss* at 236.

22 See above, on the duration of the influence of misrepresentations.

23 Notice that the contract-law remedy of rescission addresses the misallocation of real goods – they return to their seller and reenter the market.

Common law appears not to allow buyers to draw the inference that since the tires' or the tickets' price is high, their utility to the buyers is also high. The refusal of common law to allow inferences about the goods' usefulness (the quality, value, or utility they offer) from their price is in perfect agreement with the economic theory of pricing nonfinancial goods. Under that theory, as the Dr. J case illustrates, the utility each buyer derives from the good is unique and different from its price. The case with financial goods is exactly the opposite, as Chapter 13 explained.

ii. The Problematic Requirement of Blind Trust in the Market's Integrity: The Zlotnick *Paradox*

Justice White's objection to the fraud-on-the-market presumption of reliance raises a different issue, perhaps unwittingly: why the fraud-on-the-market presumption of reliance requires a blind trust in the integrity of the market. The *Basic* opinion made the presumption of reliance rebuttable rather than absolute. In the rebuttable presumption, defendants can interrupt the chain of reasoning that yields reliance. There are two points in this chain where the presumed reliance can be rebutted. The first is "market efficiency." Efficiency means that prices react to information. Absent market efficiency, a misstatement would not distort prices, and the fraud-on-the-market presumption would not operate. Since efficiency is far from ubiquitous, this rebuttal is appropriate.[24] More interesting, however, is whether the presumption

[24] The issue of whether price was influenced by the false statement is central to this step in the fraud-on-the-market presumption and to its rebuttal, and the misrepresentation's materiality plays an important role in determining whether the price was influenced. Materiality is tested by whether the information in the misrepresentation would significantly alter the total mix of available information about the firm. See *TSC Indus. v. Northway, Inc.*, 426 US 438, 449 (1976); see also *Basic*, 485 US at 232 ("We now expressly adopt the *TSC Industries* standard of materiality for the 10(b) and Rule 10b-5 context."). Presumably, significant altering of information results in price changes. Hence, it is connected to the issue of whether prices were, in fact, influenced under the fraud-on-the-market reliance presumption. The purpose of the element of materiality appears to be different from that of reliance. Instead of testing causation, materiality has the dual purpose of shielding trivial misrepresentations from liability and testing whether the misrepresentation is likely to influence price. By showing materiality, the plaintiff implicitly shows that the defendant's statements are likely to have influenced price. This rebuttal of the presumption of reliance allows the defendant to answer that, while his statements were likely to influence prices, they did not actually affect prices; therefore, the plaintiff was not injured by the statement. Maybe the market was inefficient and did not take the misrepresentation into account, or maybe the market was perfectly efficient and saw through the statement's falsity. If the misstatement did not influence market price, the plaintiff cannot have been injured by simply transacting at the market price.

In practice, this rebuttal is intertwined with the "alteration of the total mix of information" test of materiality. Thus, if prices were not influenced, plaintiffs whose actions fail for lack of presumed reliance fail for immateriality of the false statements, even if the statements were important but the market determined that they were false. See, e.g., *In re Apple Computer Sec. Litig.*, 886 F.2d 1109, 1115 (9th Cir. 1989), cert. denied sub nom. *Schneider v. Apple Computer, Inc.*, 496 US 943 (1990):

> We conclude that in a fraud on the market case, the defendant's failure to disclose material information may be excused where that information has been made credibly available to the

of reliance should be rebuttable even if the market price was influenced by the misrepresentation. *Basic* allowed rebuttal under those circumstances by hinging the presumption of reliance on the investor's trust in the integrity of market price.[25] Therefore, if the plaintiff does not trust that the market price was a fair appraisal of the security's worth, the defendant may rebut the presumption of reliance and force the plaintiff to plead and prove actual reliance, even if the market price was influenced by the misstatement.

The following paragraphs will use an actual rebuttal scenario to argue that rebuttal should not be allowed on the grounds that the plaintiff did not trust the integrity of the market price. I will explain that this rebuttal exposes informed traders to fraud,[26] which is undesirable because informed traders are the source of market efficiency.[27] This rebuttal is not only undesirable from a policy perspective, as

> market by other sources. The issue with regard to the bulk of Apple's misstatements is whether, in light of the press' documentation of [the project's] risks, a rational jury could nonetheless find a "substantial likelihood" that full disclosures by Apple would have "significantly altered the 'total mix' of information made available."

Id.; see also *In re Convergent Technologies Sec. Litig.*, 948 F.2d 507, 513 (9th Cir. 1991) (following the *Apple* reasoning); *Hanon v. Dataproducts Corp.*, 976 F.2d 497, 503 (9th Cir. 1992) (applying the *Apple* reasoning but rejecting defendants' contention that the market had been otherwise informed). Notice, by contrast, that an appropriate solution is to reject the presumption itself due to prices not being influenced. See, e.g., *Freeman v. Laventhol & Horwath*, 915 F.2d 193, 198 (6th Cir. 1990) (stating that nonexistence of an efficient market makes the presumption of reliance unavailable); *Reingold v. Deloitte Haskins & Sells*, 599 F.Supp. 1241 (S.D.N.Y. 1984). An important development here is that the market for initial public offerings is considered not to be efficient; see *In re Initial Public Offerings Securities Litigation*, 471 F.3rd 24, 42 (2nd Cir. 2006) ("[T]he market for IPO shares is not efficient.").

25 The language of *Basic* is clear. Rebuttal is possible if there was either no influence on price or if the plaintiff did not trust the fairness of the market price: "Any showing that severs the link between the alleged misrepresentation and either the price received . . . or [the plaintiff's] decision to trade at a fair market price, will be sufficient to rebut the presumption of reliance." *Basic*, 485 US at 248. The Court then gives examples of possible rebuttals very similar to those about to be analyzed:

> For example, a plaintiff who believed that [the defendant's] statements were false . . . and who consequently believed that [the defendant's] stock was artificially underpriced, but sold his shares nevertheless because of other unrelated reasons, e.g., potential antitrust problems, or political pressures to divest from shares of certain businesses, could not be said to have relied on the integrity of a price he knew had been manipulated.

Id. at 249.

26 These informed traders are not "insiders" under either Section 16 of the Securities Exchange Act of 1934, 15 USC 78j-78p (1994) or SEC Rule 10b-5.

27 The activity of informed traders is desirable and beneficial in most securities markets. However, there can be too much informed trading. If all market participants are informed, then prices will be accurate but trading volume will be negligible. As mentioned earlier, Chapter 13, text accompanying note 2, this leads to a state known as the "efficiency paradox," where trading ceases. In markets that approach this theoretical state, nearly all participants should be presumed to have information. At that point, large trades will move prices excessively to the trader's disadvantage. Because of this feature, uninformed traders would find participation to have high cost and small rewards. By contrast, some researchers, primarily Professor Robert Shiller, see the US stock market as excessively volatile. See Robert J. Shiller, Irrational Exuberance (2000); Robert J. Shiller, Market Volatility (1989)

Chapter 13 showed, but it is also logically inconsistent because market efficiency is the premise of the fraud-on-the-market presumption. Despite the time that courts have had to recognize this paradox, few decisions support the sensible position that trading to make a profit does not produce a rebuttal of the presumption of reliance.[28]

This rebuttal is also unnecessary from a doctrinal perspective. In common law, reliance corresponded to causation. The presumption of reliance is justified because the causal link practically always exists in securities fraud. In extraordinary circumstances where causation may be absent, the defendant must rebut the presumption to show its absence. The common-law equivalent of this rebuttal is the avoidable consequences defense: that the plaintiff could have avoided the misrepresentation's injury.

When examining the rebuttal to the presumption of reliance, we must keep the presumption's function as a causal link in mind. The rebuttal's role is to replicate the common-law avoidable-consequences defense in the securities fraud setting, recreating the same logical relationship seen in tort between causation and avoidable consequences. Table 14.1 illustrates these equivalences. The function that proximate cause plays in a negligence suit in common-law deceit is played by reliance; in securities fraud, the corresponding test of causation is performed by the presumption of reliance. The function that avoidable consequences plays in negligence is played by justifiability in common-law deceit; in securities fraud, the rebuttal of the presumption of reliance tests for the corresponding interruption of the causal chain.

The following paragraphs show that returning to common-law causation concepts and pleading a traditional avoidable-consequences defense to reliance captures the rebuttal's only useful function.

(collecting his earlier work); Robert J. Shiller, *Market Volatility and Investor Behavior*, 80 Am. Econ. Rev. 58 (1990); Robert J. Shiller, *Speculative Prices and Popular Models*, 4 J. Econ. Persp. 55 (1990). I see volatility as a healthy sign of uninformed trading that prevents the efficiency paradox. In essence, it is the mix of informed and uninformed traders that ensures proper operation of the markets. Informed traders bring efficiency; uninformed traders save the market from the efficiency paradox. See also Chapter 13, note 2 and accompanying text.

28 The clearest attempt to put the jurisprudence in this area back on the correct course is an opinion authored by Judge Easterbrook, *Schleicher v. Wendt*, 618 F.3d at 684 (7th Cir. 2010) ("That the class includes short sellers ... also is irrelevant. A person buys stock (goes long) because he thinks the current price too low ... a person sells short ... because he thinks the price too high ... These positions are mirror images. If a long can participate in a class, so can a short."). See also *Argent Classic Convertible Arbitrage Fund L.P. v. Rite Aid Corp.*, 315 F.Supp.2d 666 n. 13 (E.D. Pa. 2004) ("For example, *Zlotnick*' s reasoning would lead to the conclusion that a plaintiff who bought stock believing that it was undervalued – like Zlotnick, who sold short because he believed that stock was overvalued – would not be entitled to the fraud on the market presumption of reliance."); *In re CMS Energy Sec. Litig.*, 236 FRD 338, 344 (E.D. Mich. 2006)("[I]t seems possible ... that a covering purchase by a short seller could be made in reliance on the integrity of the market price."); *Gordon v. Sonar Capital Management LLC*, 962 F.Supp.2d 525 (S.D.N.Y., 2013).

TABLE 14.1 *Equivalence between Avoidable Consequences and Justifiability of Reliance*

	Normal tort (e.g., negligent accident)	Common-law deceit	Securities fraud
Defendant's act	Negligent action	Misrepresentation	Misrepresentation
Causal link	Causation of harm	Believing and acting on the misrepresentation	Trading at influenced price
Legal test	Proximate cause	Reliance	Presumed reliance
Victim's precaution	Avoidance precaution	Independent determination of falsity	Interruption of causal link between misrepresentation and trade at false price
Legal test	Avoidable consequences, last clear chance	Justifiability of reliance	Rebuttal of presumption of reliance

Zlotnick v. TIE Communications[29] illustrates that requiring the plaintiff to show blind trust in the integrity of the market before presuming reliance is wrong because it denies protection to the very class of traders that ensures this integrity: informed traders. Zlotnick sold short[30] and then repurchased at a loss the fraudulently inflated stock of a majority-owned subsidiary of TIE Communications. By the time Zlotnick repurchased the stock, TIE had manipulated the price of its subsidiary, causing Zlotnick's loss. The court held that by selling short, Zlotnick had manifested his disbelief in the accuracy of the market price not only at the time of the sale but also at the time of his later repurchase. Since he did not trust the integrity of the market price, he could not use the fraud-on-the-market presumption.

This reasoning produces an awkward result. According to the *Zlotnick* court, if investors trade because they think a price is attractive, they deny faith in accurate

[29] *Zlotnick v. TIE Communications*, 836 F.2d 818 (3d Cir. 1988). Subsequent cases have narrowed the *Zlotnick* holding and have not followed it. See, e.g., *Schleicher v. Wendt*, 618 F.3d 679, 684 (7th Cir. 2010) ("A person buys stock (goes long) because he thinks the current price too low and expects it to rise; a person sells short . . . because he thinks the price too high and expects it to fall. These positions are mirror images. If a long can participate in a class, so can a short."); *Argent Classic Convertible Arbitrage Fund L.P. v. Rite Aid Corp.*, 315 F.Supp.2d 666 n. 13 (E.D. Pa. 2004) ("For example, *Zlotnick*' s reasoning would lead to the conclusion that a plaintiff who bought stock believing that it was undervalued – like Zlotnick, who sold short because he believed that stock was overvalued – would not be entitled to the fraud on the market presumption of reliance."); *In re CMS Energy Sec. Litig.*, 236 FRD 338, 344 (E.D. Mich. 2006) ("[I]t seems possible . . . that a covering purchase by a short seller could be made in reliance on the integrity of the market price.").

[30] Short sellers sell shares they do not yet own. First they borrow the shares, betting that the price of the shares will decline, which will allow the short seller to repurchase the shares they owe at a lower price and thus profit from the price drop.

pricing and waive the use of the presumption of reliance. The very market participants who correct market inefficiency are thereby deprived of the benefit of a legal rule based on market efficiency. In essence, *Zlotnick* allows manipulators such as TIE Communications to outwit those who are in the best position to uncover the manipulation.

The reasoning behind *Zlotnick* and *Basic* is consistent but wrong.[31] If the plaintiff does not believe that the market is efficient, he cannot use the fraud-on-the-market presumption of reliance. Under this theory, the presumption exists, in essence, only for the benefit of uninformed investors, typically long-term diversified investors. Short-term informed traders who bet on fast price fluctuations presumably believe that prices are wrong and lose the benefit of the fraud-on-the-market presumption. Yet the efficiency of financial markets depends on the existence of these traders. They do not trust the integrity of market prices; they create it. As a policy matter, informed traders must be protected against manipulators because their participation guarantees the efficiency that allows uninformed investors to participate.

That said, it is not only on policy grounds that we must allow informed traders to use the fraud-on-the-market presumption of reliance. The causal chain that fraud-on-the-market represents exists in the case of informed traders; therefore, it is logically consistent that their reliance be presumed as well.

iii. The Causal Chain behind Informed Trading: Reliance Exists, but an Avoidable-Consequences Rebuttal May Still Be Desirable

As explained earlier, the causal chain connecting the defendant's misrepresentation to the plaintiff's damage is simpler in a developed securities market than in transactions in real goods. In a securities market, the plaintiff trades at a price influenced by the defendant's statement. The injury caused by trading at the disadvantageous price is attributable to the defendant's statement regardless of the plaintiff's trust in the market's integrity or efficiency.

Instead of an elaborate theory of rebutting the presumption of reliance, we have a simpler substitute theory: the common-law defense of avoidable consequences.[32] If the defendant shows that the trader had the information that the trade would be

[31] *Basic* upholds *Zlotnick* by allowing the presumption of reliance to be rebutted in instances where the plaintiff has not relied on the integrity of the market. See *Basic Inc. v. Levinson*, 485 US 224, 249 (1988) (finding "petitioners also could rebut the presumption of reliance as to plaintiffs who would have divested themselves of their Basic shares without relying on the integrity of the market"). Another case that refuses to protect informed traders in an even more perverse way is *Gianukos v. Loeb Rhoades & Co.*, 822 F.2d 648 (7th Cir. 1987), where, after Loeb Rhoades succeeded in persuading Gianukos to trade on information it had fabricated, Loeb Rhoades was able to rebut Gianukos' presumption that he relied on the information.

[32] For an explanation of the defense, see, generally, PROSSER AND KEETON, note 4: the theory of avoidable consequences "denies recovery for any damages which could have been avoided by reasonable conduct on the part of the plaintiff … It is suggested, therefore, that the theories of contributory negligence and avoidable consequences are in reality the same." *Id.* at 458–9.

disadvantageous, then the trader must show overriding reasons for the disadvantageous trade.

In other words, the complication in using the avoidable-consequences defense is the argument that some informed traders should be allowed to recover even if they knew the misrepresentation was false because they could not avoid trading. At issue is how to determine which traders may recover and which may not.

Consider, for example, a setting inverse to that of *Zlotnick*. A corporation makes a misrepresentation that depresses the price of its stock. A trader identifies the stock as undervalued and buys it on margin (i.e., credit). Then the corporation aggravates the misrepresentation, depressing prices further, with the result that the trader's position is liquidated automatically.[33] The liquidation happens via a forced sale, making the trader sell at the depressed price. Thus the trader becomes a plaintiff claiming securities fraud and using the fraud-on-the-market presumption of reliance. The defendant counters that the trader knew the price was artificially depressed. The trader should be allowed to recover because there was no voluntary action that interrupted the chain of causation.

Other examples abound: (1) an index arbitrageur knows that a certain stock price in the index she is trading is inflated because of a misrepresentation but buys it because her investment strategy requires it; (2) a corporation about to launch a takeover must divest shares for antitrust reasons and sells the stock knowing that its price is depressed by a misrepresentation; (3) a university fund manager knows that some stock prices are artificially depressed but must sell due to political pressures to divest. *Basic* offers the last two examples as clear rebuttals of the fraud-on-the-market theory showing a lack of trust in the market's integrity.[34] The argument here suggests that these rebuttals are not necessarily desirable.

From a policy perspective, having uninformed trading in the market is beneficial in a different way from having informed traders. The uninformed provide liquidity. The index arbitrageur is a prime example of such a trader. His automatic trading of all the stocks in the index ensures a large trading volume that facilitates other trading.[35] The benefits of liquidity argue against rebutting his presumption of reliance.[36]

33 Traders must maintain a specific balance when they borrow on margin or their broker liquidates their holdings. See 12 CFR § 220.4(a)(4)(d) (2017) ("If any margin call is not met in full within the required time, the creditor shall liquidate securities sufficient to meet the margin call.").

34 *Basic*, 485 US at 248–9.

35 The increased liquidity associated with a stock being part of a popular market index is a likely source of the price rise and drop associated with inclusion or exclusion from the Standard & Poor's 500 Index. A 3% price increase is associated with inclusion in the index. See, e.g., Lawrence Harris & Eitan Gurel, *Price and Volume Effects Associated with Changes in the S&P 500 List: New Evidence for the Existence of Price Pressures*, 41 J. FINANCE 815 (1986); Prem C. Jain, *The Effect on Stock Price of Inclusion in or Exclusion from the S&P 500*, FIN. ANALYSTS J., January–February 1987, at 58.

36 Uninformed trading saves the capital markets from falling into the efficiency paradox trap, see also note 27.

To assess causation, then, we must examine what caused the trades in the examples. In each one, the defendant's misrepresentation created a price that injured the traders. They saw the danger and did not avoid it. The defendant argues that the cause of the traders' injury is not the defendant's statement but the traders' own decisions to trade at the disadvantageous price. These are decisions subsequent to the misrepresentation and appear to interrupt the chain of causation.[37] Although the avoidable-consequences defense would bar recovery, if these traders could not avoid trading, then the causal chain is not broken, the misrepresentation is the proximate cause of the injury, and the traders should recover. Their presumption of reliance should not be rebutted. Section B.ii presented an intuitive theory of reliance based on absolute loss causation that is only one small step ahead of the fraud-on-the-market theory but much closer to common-law concepts of causation.[38] If a misrepresentation causes price movement, there is an injury to each plaintiff. The plaintiff's knowledge that the statement was false is a defense that functions like avoidable consequences. The plaintiff's voluntary trade is an intervening cause interrupting the chain of causation connecting the misrepresentation to the plaintiff's injury. Plaintiffs can overcome this defense by showing that they were forced to trade. Eventually, the degree of force necessary to overcome the avoidable-consequences defense should be set by accounting for the benefit that trading has for liquidity.

[37] See Prosser and Keeton, note 4: "The greater number of courts have explained [contributory negligence] in terms of 'proximate cause,' saying that the plaintiff's negligence is an intervening, or insulating, cause between the defendant's negligence and the result," at 452.

[38] Analogous arguments in favor of pure loss causation have previously been made. See, e.g., Daniel R. Fischel, *Efficient Capital Markets, the Crash, and the Fraud on the Market Theory*, 74 CORNELL L. REV. 907 (1989); Daniel R. Fischel, *Use of Modern Finance Theory in Securities Fraud Cases Involving Actively Traded Securities*, 38 BUS. LAW. 1 (1982). In contrast to previous arguments, this argument connects reliance in securities fraud to its common-law counterpart and shows that loss causation is not a radical step but one that follows by necessity if common-law causation principles are applied to securities markets.

15

Conclusion of Deterrence Intensity

The chapters in this part argued that the fraud-on-the-market reliance presumption conforms to the causal chains observed in markets for financial goods. The benefits that result from the fraud-on-the-market presumption address social concerns over false statements about financial goods by reducing the danger of transacting at manipulated prices. This is analogous to the structure that actual reliance imposes on the tort of deceit. Actual reliance conforms to the causal chains observed in markets for nonfinancial goods and addresses social concerns about false statements in those markets: false statements result in the allocation of goods to users other than those who value them most.

Consider the remedies available to deceit plaintiffs: rescission or out-of-pocket damages.[1] Rescission directly remedies the misallocation caused by the deceit. Out-of-pocket damages compensate the victim of the misallocation and substitute for rescission when it is unavailable or impractical. For example, the buyer of a good who would derive $1 of use from it but buys it for $3 due to a misrepresentation would receive, if rescission were unavailable, out-of-pocket damages of $2. This compensates the $1 user buying a $3 good but does not remedy the misallocation as rescission would.

Neither remedy is appropriate in securities fraud. The social concern in securities fraud is not misallocation of capital but traders' fear of manipulated prices. Allowing only those who traded in actual reliance on the misrepresentation to recover does not encourage others to overcome their fear. It has no effect on the fear of erroneous prices felt by uninformed traders. Only if everyone who traded at the influenced price can recover will all traders' fear of incorrect prices be subdued. This is what fraud-on-the-market achieves. Notice that this remedy does not correspond to any of the conventional measures of damages. It is not rescission, because rescission would

[1] See W. Page Keeton et al., PROSSER AND KEETON ON THE LAW OF TORTS at 765 (5th ed. 1984). Benefit-of-the-bargain damages are also awarded in deceit actions. But their use has to be attributed to those circumstances where deceit is not easy to distinguish from a breach-of-contract claim. In that case, their economic justification would take us into the economics and law of contracts.

prevent the defrauded buyers from retaining any profits from the trade earned after the misrepresentation is uncovered. Nor is it out-of-pocket damages, which would mitigate the amount that the misrepresenter owes by any gains his victims may have derived. Nor is it benefit-of-the-bargain, which should give the stock's implied value according to the misrepresentation to those who were aware of the misrepresentation and thus weaken their incentive to trade to correct prices.

Analogously, neither should a fraud-on-the-market presumption apply in common-law deceit. If fraud-on-the-market rules were to apply in deceit, a misrepresenter about real goods would have to pay all buyers the difference in price they paid due to the misrepresentation. But since the misrepresentation could have marginal or could have had no effect on price, damages could be little or none, producing trivial or no incentives not to misrepresent. Conversely, if actual reliance was required in securities fraud, an issuer misrepresenting the value of its stock would expect to pay minimal damages because the issuer would be liable only to those who traded in reliance on the false statement. Carrying this logic to the extreme, the issuer could ask for a trading halt, make the false announcement, and expect the new opening price to reflect the misrepresentation. This would be a price at which no speculator who believed the misrepresentation would trade. Thus this issuer would avoid all liability.

The understanding suggested here is not only desirable from a policy perspective and consistent with the causation function of reliance, but it is also simple for courts to apply. Consider the alternative. First, determining the price that a nonfinancial good would have had *but for* a misrepresentation is extremely difficult. By contrast, it is easy in the case of financial goods, where standard statistical methods can answer the question.[2] Second, rescinding a real goods transaction is simple, while a financial goods rescission may involve a series of subsequent transactions. Third, admittedly, it may be difficult to determine out-of-pocket damages in real goods because it is hard to quantify the owner's actual benefits and costs. But it is nearly impossible to quantify damages in financial goods because it is anyone's guess how the injured investors would have traded without the misrepresentation. The gain that would have resulted from these other transactions would be their damages in an actual reliance, out-of-pocket damage calculation. Conversely, were the courts to consider benefit-of-the-bargain damages in a securities fraud case, the courts would again have absolutely no guidance in determining the price that the stock should have attained had the misrepresentation been true. The proposed analysis of the current regime raises none of these complexities.

[2] See, e.g., Stephen J. Brown & Jerold B. Warner, *Using Daily Stock Returns: The Case of Event Studies*, 14 J. FIN. ECON. 3 (1986).

PART IV

Insider Trading

16

Introduction to Insider Trading

After deterrence intensity (which came after the definition of a security and the analysis of disclosure), securities law turns to the contentious prohibition of "insider trading." The chapters in this part offer a law and economics analysis that builds on the theoretical discussion of insider trading.[1]

Understanding the economic function of prohibiting insider trading is key to understanding the virtuous cycle of securities regulation. Prohibiting insider trading reduces a cost of trading, which increases liquidity. Rather than making prices less accurate, the prohibition against insider trading promotes liquidity, which makes the markets appealing to competing informed traders, who, in turn, make prices more accurate. This closes the virtuous cycle. More accurate prices make the market more attractive by eliminating a risk of trading at wrong prices. Thus they reduce transaction costs, increasing liquidity.

After a literature review in the following paragraphs, Chapter 17 provides a summary of the law on insider trading, emphasizing that insider trading is not synonymous with "informed trading": the prohibition of insider trading prohibits the trading of only some informed traders, allowing market participation by informed noninsiders. Chapter 18 examines the interaction of informed and uninformed traders generally. In this context, it first explains how the profits of informed traders are a cost to the uninformed, asks whether this cost may be reduced by regulatory measures, and examines insider trading regulation as a means to reduce the disadvantage (i.e., the cost) of uninformed trading. Chapter 19 concludes by pointing out that insider trading rules are complemented by the regulations forcing corporations to disclose information.

The law and economics discussion about "insider trading" began in 1961, soon after the Securities and Exchange Commission (SEC) decided *Cady, Roberts & Co.*,[2]

1 A much earlier version of the analysis in these chapters appears in Nicholas L. Georgakopoulos, *Insider Trading as a Transaction Cost: A Market Microstructure Justification and Optimization of Insider Trading Regulation*, 26 CONN. L. REV. 1–51 (1993).

2 *Cady, Roberts & Co.*, 40 SEC 907 (1961).

which introduced the possibility that securities fraud provisions may be violated by trading with "material nonpublic" information. From the law and economics perspective, the initial reaction to *Cady Roberts* was negative.[3] Trading with superior information is desirable because it pushes prices toward their true value and thus promotes the optimal allocation of capital. This straightforward argument against the prohibition of insider trading ran counter to legal intuition. This tension spurred researchers to a series of more complex theories about the effect that insider trading may have on corporate operations and governance.

One line of analysis explores the managers' service to the corporation and how insider trading may interfere. A license to trade on inside information as part of the management contract is argued to have the beneficial effect of causing only the best managers to accept such a contract and signal their skill.[4] The counter to this signaling argument is obvious: acceptance of contingent pay does not necessarily denote a skilled manager but rather an optimistic or overconfident one. Furthermore, managers, due to their risk aversion, may not value contingent pay as much as it costs to risk-neutral shareholders and would prefer certainty of compensation. In such a case, the signaling argument is reversed

[3] See, generally, Henry B. Manne, INSIDER TRADING AND THE STOCK MARKET (1966) (Insider trading increases market efficiency because it produces desirable incentives on corporate managers.).

[4] See Michael J. Carney, *Signalling and Causation in Insider Trading*, 36 CATH. U. L. REV. 863, 886–93 (1987) (Insider trading signals competent managers.). For a discussion of insider trading and its effect on management, see, generally, Frank H. Easterbrook, *Insider Trading as an Agency Problem*, in PRINCIPALS AND AGENTS: THE STRUCTURE OF BUSINESS 81 (John W. Pratt & Richard J. Zeckhauser eds., 1985) (describing the effects of insider trading on the agency relationship); Manne, INSIDER TRADING AND THE STOCK MARKET (1966) (Insider trading profits are a better management incentive than options or bonuses.); Dennis W. Carlton & Daniel R. Fischel, *The Regulation of Insider Trading*, 35 STAN. L. REV. 857 (1983); Frank H. Easterbrook, *Insider Trading, Secret Agents, Evidentiary Privileges, and the Production of Information*, 1981 S. CT. REV. 309 (hereinafter Easterbrook, *Insider Trading, Secret Agents*) (insider trading and the incentives to disclose and produce information); David D. Haddock & Jonathan R. Macey, *A Coasian Model of Insider Trading*, 80 NW. U. L. REV. 1449 (1986); Kenneth E. Scott, *Insider Trading: Rule 10b-5, Disclosure and Corporate Privacy*, 9 J. LEGAL STUD. 801 (1980); Lucian A. Bebchuk & Chaim Fershtman, *Insider Trading and the Managerial Choice Among Risky Projects*, 29 J. FIN. & QUANTITATIVE ANALYSIS 1 (1994) (Unfettered insider trading leads managers to riskier projects.); Guochang Zhang, *Regulated Managerial Insider Trading as a Mechanism to Facilitate Shareholder Control*, 28 J. Bus. Fin. & Acct. 35, 36 (2001) (inducing managers to provide shareholders with accurate information); Henry G. Manne, *Insider Trading: Hayek, Virtual Markets, and the Dog that Did Not Bark*, 31 IOWA J. CORP. L. 167, 174 (2005) (arguing that insider trader would inform corporate decision makers); Thomas A. Lambert, *Overvalued Equity and the Case for an Asymmetric Insider Trading Regime*, 41 WAKE FOREST L. REV. 1045 (2006) (arguing that insider trading that decreases prices should be treated differently than price-increasing insider trading); Jonathan Macey, *Getting the Word Out about Fraud: A Theoretical Analysis of Whistleblowing and Insider Trading*, 105 MICH. L. REV. 1899, 1921–40 (2007) (Insider trading is a better signal of corporate wrongdoing than whistleblowing.); Robert A. Prentice & Dain C. Donelson, *Insider Trading as a Signaling Device*, 47 AM. BUS. L.J. 1 (2010) (investigating Manne's arguments along with Macey's proposal that insider trading would be more effective than whistleblowing at signaling corporate wrongdoing).

into the "lottery-ticket argument": insider trading as compensation is equivalent to paying with lottery tickets. Since risk is undesirable to managers, the best managers will prefer compensation packages with greater portions of less risky pay.[5] Furthermore, trading by managers based on information that they acquire or generate about the securities of other corporations (a form of insider trading across corporate boundaries that I have called "cross-trading"[6]) will tend to cause management disloyalty.[7]

Another strain of argumentation is more remote and relates insider trading to firms' decision to issue shares.[8] This analysis shows that it is not necessary to consider investment decisions by firms in the debate on insider trading, the causal relation of which is probably too remote anyway. Thinking that insider trading rules induce conduct that significantly reduces business risk is implausible and unlikely to have

[5] See Easterbrook, *Insider Trading, Secret Agents*, at 332; Scott, *Insider Trading: Rule 10b-5, Disclosure and Corporate Privacy*, at 808. The signaling and the lottery ticket arguments do not necessarily lie on opposite assumptions about managers' risk preferences. Given different risks of individual firms, the signaling argument may be valid if the share price of the firm is relatively stable and not subject to random shocks outside the control or knowledge of management. In high-risk industries, by contrast, the lottery ticket paradigm seems much more forceful. What changes is the risk of the compensation, not the risk preferences of managers.

[6] See Nicholas L. Georgakopoulos, *Classical and Cross Insider Trading: Variations on the Theme of Rule 10b-5*, 28 AM. BUS. L.J. 109 (1990).

[7] Notice, however, that this argument fails to justify regulation opposite the Coase theorem. Firms should have sufficient incentives to prohibit and, in fact, do prohibit cross-trading on their own initiative.

[8] This argument has been approached by a number of commentators. Lawrence Ausubel points out that the expectation of losses to insider trading leads to underinvestment by outsider investors. The elimination of insider trading restores investment incentives, increasing the welfare of both. See Lawrence M. Ausubel, *Insider Trading in a Rational Expectations Economy*, 80 AM. ECON. REV. 1022 (1990). The intuition is that outsiders experience lower gains from their investments, so they invest less, which leads to insiders having less capital for business and less earnings. Both the insiders and the outsiders gain by eliminating insider trading. Therefore, Ausubel's argument would lead one to expect voluntary elimination of insider trading and does not justify regulation.

Hayne Leland builds a model with two classes of informed traders, insiders and outsiders, as well as liquidity traders, and includes the firm's decision to raise capital. Insider trading may be either desirable or undesirable depending on several factors. See Hayne E. Leland, *Insider Trading: Should It Be Prohibited?*, 100 J. POL. ECON. 859 (1992). Some of the conclusions of Leland come relatively close to those of the present analysis. Leland's model, however, is extremely stylized and, being a microeconomic model, is insufficiently close to the trading action. By contrast, the analysis offered here rests on the trade-by-trade examination of the interaction of traders that market microstructure makes possible.

In his work along similar lines, Michael Manove points out that discounting by outsiders for the danger of insider trading affects the internal investment decisions of firms, leading to overinvestment in order to lower the risk of the outcome of the investment and, therefore, lessen the danger of insider trading and the discount by outsiders. This argument is reversed and leads to underinvestment if the risk of the outcome of the corporate investment is so high that it cannot be lessened through additional investment. See Michael Manove, *The Harm from Insider Trading and Informed Speculation*, 104 Q. J. ECON. 823 (1989). The intuition is akin to one where the firm buys insurance to protect outsiders, which is wasteful and produces overinvestment; vice versa, if the project is not insurable, then the outsiders underinvest because they will lose part of the returns to insiders.

any effect on stock prices.[9] Moreover, the scholarship that explores the relation of insider trading to risk-taking assumes an a priori definition of insiders, whereas the analysis here contributes to the optimal definition of an insider.[10]

Commentators have also suggested that insider trading restrictions promote the interests of the professional investment community.[11] When corporate insiders are prohibited from trading, the first traders who will benefit from new information are the professional traders. The same profits that the insiders would reap without the prohibition accrue in favor of the professional investment community. This seems to make the prohibition merely pointless because it does not change the position of the uninformed. However, the prohibition does harm shareholders because corporations must replace executives' foregone trading profits with costly compensation.[12]

The analysis here, in justifying the prohibition of insider trading, rebuts the notion that insider trading rules simply shift the profits of informed trading without reducing them. The prohibition of trading against a narrow group of informed

9 The reason for the remote relevance of arguments premised on the effect insider trading has on prices is associated with the puzzle of the "risk premium," i.e., the excess return of equity over debt after adjusting for risk. Rajnish Mehra and Edward Prescott justify a minuscule portion of the superior returns of equity by risk. Arguments premised on the influence of insider trading on prices are therefore unlikely, particularly since insider trading will not nearly eliminate the 20% volatility that justifies that small portion of the equity premium. See Rajnish Mehra & Edward C. Prescott, *The Equity Premium: A Puzzle*, 15 J. MONETARY ECON. 145 (1985); Rajnish Mehra & Edward C. Prescott, *The Equity Premium in Retrospect*, in 1 HANDBOOK OF THE ECONOMICS OF FINANCE 889 (George M. Constantinides et al. eds., 2003).

10 A seemingly related analysis of insider trading using microstructure tools was also attempted by Albert Kyle. See Albert S. Kyle, *Continuous Auctions and Insider Trading*, 53 ECONOMETRICA 1315 (1985). Kyle's work, however, analyzes the strategy of insiders who are faced with an end to trading and does not consider the possibility of changes in their numbers and their competition. While Kyle finds that insiders, still exogenously defined, correct prices at the end of trading, this finding has little impact on the regulation of insider trading. Properly understood, the end of trading for Kyle's insiders happens only if trading in the corporation ceases permanently, e.g., if the corporation is delisted from the exchange or if it is liquidated in a Chapter 7 proceeding (as opposed to a Chapter 11 reorganization, where the insider's knowledge retains its importance in the surviving reorganized entity). The date of public disclosure is not equivalent to the end of trading in Kyle's model because the insiders can still trade after the disclosure of their information, since they will still have greater familiarity with it. Both empirical evidence and theoretical work support this analysis and refute Kyle's conclusions. See note 15 at page 176 and note 17 at page 177.

The competition among informed traders is also considered by the seminal article written by Admati and Pfleiderer, *A Theory of Intraday Patterns*. Their model, however, does not examine legal constraints on informed trading and, therefore, although very closely related, does not address the issue of the desirability of an insider trading prohibition.

11 See Haddock & Macey, *A Coasian Model of Insider Trading*, at 1458–9.

12 In contrast to the inconclusive theoretical debate, legal practice has almost unanimously favored the prohibition of insider trading, considering it an "unfair" practice. See, e.g., Victor Brudney, *Insiders, Outsiders, and Informational Advantages Under the Federal Securities Laws*, 93 HARV. L. REV. 322 (1979); Roy A. Schotland, *Unsafe at Any Price: A Reply to Manne, Insider Trading and the Stock Market*, 53 VA. L. REV. 1425, 1441–2 (1967) (providing various statements relating investor confidence to the proscription of insider trading). Schotland's article can also be read as giving a concrete law and economics explanation – or translation – of the intuition of "unfairness" invoked by practitioners.

traders ("insiders") leaves a broader group as the first informed traders (say, investment analysts). This causes more competition among informed traders, which, in turn, reduces their aggregate profits. A reduction in the profits of informed traders reduces the invisible transaction cost that burdens uninformed trading.[13] Reduction of this trading cost is where the insider trading prohibition facilitates the virtuous cycle.

13 A closely related point has been made by William Wang. See William K. S. Wang, *Trading on Material Nonpublic Information on Impersonal Stock Markets: Who Is Harmed and Who Can Sue Whom under SEC Rule 10b-5?*, 54 S. CAL. L. REV. 1217, 1234–5, 1247–8 (1981). This, however, was done before the financial tools for further analysis of these transaction costs were developed.

17

Insider Trading Law

Insider trading liability has several sources. Liability first arises directly from the prohibitions under Section 16 of the Securities Exchange Act of 1934 (1934 Act)[1] and Rule 14e-3.[2] In addition, three other theories support the imposition of liability for insider trading under antifraud rules: the classical approach that treats insiders as fiduciaries of their shareholders, the interpretation that insider trading represents a type of misappropriation akin to stealing, and the interpretation that insider trading is a violation of the mail and wire fraud statutes.

A. DIRECT PROHIBITIONS

Although the analysis of insider trading tends to focus on interpretation of the antifraud rules, securities law also contains two direct prohibitions. Rule 14e-3

[1] The relevant text of Section 16(b) of the 1934 Act reads

> (B) For the purpose of preventing the unfair use of information . . . any profit realized by [any insider] from any purchase and sale, or any sale and purchase, of any equity security of such issuer . . . within any period of less than six months . . . shall inure to and be recoverable by the issuer . . . Suit to recover such profit may be instituted at law or in equity in any court of competent jurisdiction by the issuer, or by the owner of any security of the issuer in the name and in behalf of the issuer.

15 USC § 78p(b) (2017).

[2] The text of Rule 14e-3 limits its application to tender offers:

> (a) If any person has taken a substantial step or steps to commence, or has commenced, a tender offer (the "offering person"), it shall constitute a fraudulent, deceptive or manipulative act or practice within the meaning of section 14(e) of the Act for any other person who is in possession of material information relating to such tender offer which information he knows or has reason to know is nonpublic and which he knows or has reason to know has been acquired directly or indirectly from:
>
> (1) The offering person,
> (2) The issuer of the securities sought or to be sought by such tender offer, or
> (3) Any officer, director, partner or employee or any other person acting on behalf of the offering person or such issuer, to purchase or sell or cause to be purchased or sold any of such securities.

17 CFR § 240.14e-3 (2017).

prohibits trading with takeover information. The Securities and Exchange Commission (SEC) adopted it under the antifraud authorization of Section 14(e) of the 1934 Act, which was added in 1968 by the Williams Act.[3] The Supreme Court affirmed its validity in *O'Hagan*.[4] While the analysis of insider trading generally requires an elaborate argument, insider trading on the basis of takeover information has a much simpler analysis. Trading with information about takeovers, even if it were to influence prices, does not further optimal resource allocation in saving, spending, or investment decisions. The brief time between the creation of the takeover information and its revelation does not allow for any such reallocations. Because the most egregious insider trading surrounds takeover news, Rule 14e-3 is the most effective prohibition against insider trading.

Section 16 of the 1934 Act prohibits two narrow types of insider trading.[5] Subsection (a) establishes a reporting requirement for large shareholders, directors, and officers, on whom the remaining subsections apply; subsection (b) has the corporation recover any profits such insiders make due to short-swing trading, that is, any sequence of two trades that occur within six months; finally, subsection (c) prohibits short selling by the same insiders in the stock of their own corporations. Section 16 and the SEC rules under it have changed repeatedly, illustrating the fact that even the "statutory insiders" of Section 16 are subject to a flexible definition.

B. ANTIFRAUD FOUNDATIONS

The limitations of Section 16 and Rule 14e-3 are important to recognize. Under only Section 16 and Rule 14e-3, statutory insiders would be able to buy the stock of their own corporations before positive news (but not takeovers) and reap the corresponding gains, as long as they waited more than six months before selling. Statutory insiders who would have held their shares more than six months would also be able to sell them (but not take a short position) before negative news (but, again, not takeovers). Moreover, insiders who would not meet the statutory definition would face no limitations. This leaves a considerable gap that is filled by the interpretation of antifraud rules, mostly Rule 10b-5 but also mail and wire fraud. The first relevant interpretation, based on fiduciary breach, is known as the "classical interpretation" and only applies to the securities law antifraud provisions. The second, based on the stealing of information, is the "misappropriation theory" and applies to both the securities law antifraud provisions and the mail and wire fraud statutes.

[3] Section 14(e), Purchase of Securities by Issuer:

> (1) It shall be unlawful for an issuer ... to purchase any equity security issued by it if such purchase is in contravention of such rules and regulations as the Commission ... may adopt.

15 USC 78m.

[4] *United States v. O'Hagan*, 521 US 642 (1997).

[5] 15 USC § 78p. The rules under Section 16 are in 17 CFR § 240.16a-1 et seq.

i. The Classical Fiduciary Breach Theory

The original theory used against insider trading was based on the concept that insiders and the persons on the other side of their trades have a fiduciary relationship. Being fiduciaries, the insiders must protect rather than exploit shareholders, and they must disclose their information or their silence is deceptive.

In *Chiarella v. United States*,[6] the seminal case on insider trading law, the Supreme Court stated clearly that the source of a duty to disclose must be a relationship of trust between the trader and her counterpart. *Chiarella* involved a suit against the printer for several acquiring corporations. The printer decoded information concerning the acquisitions and traded in the stock of the target companies. In exonerating the printer, the Court stated

> No duty [to disclose] could arise from petitioner's relationship with the sellers of the target company's securities, for petitioner had no prior dealings with them. He was not their agent, he was not a fiduciary, he was not a person in whom the sellers had placed their trust and confidence. He was, in fact, a complete stranger.[7]

Unlike Chiarella, who worked for one corporation and traded in the stock of others, management and other employees of a corporation have fiduciary duties to its shareholders. For them, trading based on knowledge that is unavailable to shareholders involves a conflict of interests. Because of the bond of trust, employees have a duty to disclose their information.[8] Their silence constitutes fraudulent concealment and violates Rule 10b-5.

The problem with *Chiarella* was that it made the prohibition of insider trading narrower than the SEC's desire. Insider trading could only take place between shareholders and employees of the same corporation and persons receiving tips from employees.[9] Prior cases had established that all holders of material nonpublic

6 445 US 222 (1980). 7 *Id.* at 232–3.

8 Compare the analogous provision of the Restatement (Second) of Torts. Section 551(2)(e) reads

> (2) One party to a business transaction is under a duty to exercise reasonable care to disclose to the other before the transaction is consummated . . .
>
> (e) facts basic to the transaction, if he knows that the other is about to enter into it under a mistake as to them, and that the other, because of the relationship between them, the customs of the trade or other objective circumstances, would reasonably expect disclosure of those facts.

Restatement (Second) of Torts § 551(2)(e) (1977). The third restatement of torts, still in draft form, restates this provision in Section 13, Liability for Economic Harm (tentative draft, 2014).

9 The liability of persons receiving tips was established and circumscribed by *Dirks v. Securities and Exch. Comm'n*, 463 US 646 (1983) and reaffirmed in *Salman v. United States*, 580 U.S. _ (December 6, 2016). The fraud in *Dirks* was discussed in Chapter 13, text accompanying notes 17–20. Recently, the Second Circuit increased slightly the hurdle for state of mind, effectively relieving from liability some remote tippees; *United States v. Newman*, 773 F.3rd 438 (2d Cir. 2014), cert. denied 136, US 242 (2015).

information were bound by a fiduciary relationship to all investors, an interpretation known as the "equal access theory."[10]

ii. Insider Trading as the Stealing of Information: The Misappropriation Theory

The "misappropriation theory" considers insider trading that is profitable to be stealing. In affirming the misappropriation theory, the Supreme Court in *O'Hagan* accepted the proposition that "misappropriators ... deal in deception. A fiduciary who '[pretends] loyalty to the principal while secretly converting the principal's information for personal gain' ... 'dupes' or defrauds the principal."[11] The facts of *O'Hagan* leave little doubt that the agent was prohibited from trading on the information. O'Hagan was a lawyer working on an acquisition for the acquirer and, as did Chiarella, traded in shares of the target. The rules of professional responsibility clearly placed on O'Hagan a duty not to profit from the client's information.[12]

A 2013 transaction offers an interesting example that, by falling outside the misappropriation theory, demarcates its border. A corporation decided to make an issuance of common stock that would dilute the interest of current shareholders. Its chief executive contacted a large shareholder to inform him and ask him to participate. The shareholder disagreed with the desirability of the offering, refused to participate in it, and promptly sold his holdings, avoiding about $750,000 of losses. The SEC pursued him for civil insider trading liability but lost.[13] While this was a jury decision, it serves as a good example of a situation where the information is not public and is valuable but where the recipient neither has a fiduciary relation to the corporation (directly or due to a tip) nor has a confidentiality arrangement.

[10] See *SEC v. Texas Gulf Sulfur Co.*, 401 F.2d 833, 848 (2d Cir. 1968) (en banc) (Rule 10b-5 "is based in policy on the justifiable expectation of the securities marketplace that all investors trading on impersonal exchanges have relatively equal access to material information."), cert. denied, 394 US 976 (1969). *Chiarella v. United States*, 445 US 222 (1980), marked the end of that period. Justice Blackmun's dissent in *Chiarella* supported the dying theory of equal access to information. See *id.* at 249–50 (Blackmun, J., dissenting) (citing *Texas Gulf Sulfur*, 401 F.2d at 848; *Lewelling v. First California Co.*, 564 F.2d 1277, 1280 (9th Cir. 1977); *Speed v. Transamerica Corp.*, 99 F.Supp. 808, 829 (D. Del. 1951)). See also *United States v. Chiarella*, 588 F.2d 1358, 1365 (2d Cir. 1978), rev'd, 445 US 222 (1980); *United States v. Charnay*, 537 F.2d 341, 349–50 (9th Cir. 1976) ("[T]he duty to disclose material information is based on a potential manipulator's duty to the investing public as a whole as well as to particular shareholders."), cert. denied, 429 US 1000 (1976).

[11] 521 US 653–4 (citations omitted). [12] Unless the client had allowed it, and the client had not.

[13] See Ben Protess and Lauren D'Avolio, *Jury Rules for Mark Cuban in Setback for SEC*, N.Y. Times, October 16, 2013, available at http://dealbook.nytimes.com/2013/10/16/mark-cuban-cleared-of-insider-trading/ (accessed February 15, 2017). The dispute produced one appellate opinion, *SEC. v. Cuban*, 620 F.3d 551 (5th Cir. 2010), and nine opinions in total.

iii. Insider Trading as the Stealing of Information: The Mail and Wire Fraud Theory

Courts, when applying mail and wire fraud statutes to insider trading cases, usually base their decisions on the theory that "confidential business information" is property. The profiting on the information becomes a deceptive scheme violating the mail and wire fraud statutes.[14]

In 1987, the Supreme Court decided *McNally v. United States*,[15] which narrowed the applicability of the mail and wire fraud statutes to the taking of "property" rather than the taking of any entitlement. The Court soon clarified *McNally* with its decision in *Carpenter v. United States*.[16] *Carpenter* removed any doubt that mail and wire fraud statutes might be inapplicable to insider trading by including "intangible property" in the *McNally* definition of property. *Carpenter* involved the trading by a WALL STREET JOURNAL columnist on the future content of his column. The WALL STREET JOURNAL's confidential business information was a property right, and the mail and wire fraud convictions of the defendants were upheld unanimously.[17]

The misappropriation theory involves a determination of what types of relationships demand confidentiality of information. Once such a relationship is established, any trading on confidential information is a "misappropriation." In contrast, the "mail and wire fraud theory" involves a determination of whether the source of the confidential information protected it adequately to elevate it to a "property right." The facts of *O'Hagan* and of *Carpenter* fall almost squarely within the limits of each theory, respectively.[18] Thornier settings may involve the doctor-patient

[14] The mail and wire fraud statutes are designed to reach all "fraudulent" activity that may use the mail, the wires, or radiowaves. They are drafted with the same extremely expansive "catchall" notion of the securities fraud provisions. In one long-winded sentence, the *United States Code* makes it a criminal offense to use the mails (1) to further a scheme to defraud, (2) to obtain money or property using false pretenses, or (3) to distribute counterfeit currency, 18 USC § 1341 (2017). See *United States v. Carpenter*, 791 F.2d 1024, 1034–5 (2d Cir. 1986) ("It is clear that 'confidential and nonpublic commercial information' may constitute fraudulently misappropriated 'property' under the mail fraud statute."), aff'd., 484 US 19 (1987); *United States v. Newman*, 664 F.2d 12, 19–20 (2d Cir. 2000) ("[The indictment] clearly charges appellee with fraudulent misappropriation of property that did not belong to him. Intangibles such as 'confidential and nonpublic commercial information' fall within the definition of 'property' under the mail fraud statute"; citing prior cases). The *Newman* court supported its definition of property by noting that confidential business secrets are specifically protected in a number of criminal statutes. 664 F.2d at 19 n. 4; see also *United States v. Victor Teicher & Co.*, 726 F.Supp. 1424, 1433–4 (S.D.N.Y. 1989); *United States v. Reed*, 601 F.Supp. 685 (S.D.N.Y. 1985), rev'd, 773 F.2d 477 (2d Cir. 1985).

[15] 483 US 350 (1987). The Court exonerated a public official who was prosecuted under the mail and wire fraud statutes with the theory that he "stole" the right to "good government" from his constituents. *Id.* at 360. The Court held that the mail and wire fraud statutes apply to "property rights" only, not to entitlements, such as the entitlement to good government. *Id.*

[16] 484 US 19 (1987). [17] *Id.* at 28.

[18] In *Carpenter*, for example, the Court emphasized that the *Wall Street Journal* had prohibited its employees from trading on its information: "The official policy and practice at the Journal was that

relationship[19] or relationships among family members.[20] Once more, the flexibility of the definition of "insider trading" is apparent.

In sum, insider trading – besides its direct prohibitions – is prohibited under three primary legal theories. The first, under which insider trading is a breach of employees' fiduciary duties to shareholders, defines insider trading quite narrowly as the trading of corporate agents in the stock of their employer corporation. The misappropriation theory and the mail and wire fraud theory are founded on the notion that employees' unauthorized trading using their employer's confidential information constitutes theft, whatever stock they trade. Thus these latter two theories have a wider reach.

The definitions of insider trading under the three primary theories, as well as under the statutory prohibition of Section 16 of the 1934 Act, have variable width. Wider definitions would reach more informed traders, and narrower definitions would reach fewer. That some informed trading does not fall under the current definitions shows that insider trading rules currently disallow only part of informed trading. The issue is to determine what subset of informed traders should be prohibited from trading and why.

prior to publication, the contents of the column were the Journal's confidential information ... [The defendant] was familiar [with the rule]." 484 US at 23.

19 *United States v. Willis*, 737 F.Supp. 269 (S.D.N.Y. 1990).

20 *United States v. Reed*, 601 F.Supp. 685 (S.D.N.Y. 1985) (son found guilty of insider trading under mail and wire fraud theory of liability for information he received from his father, a corporate director, based on finding that the father-son relationship was sufficiently confidential to support the proposition that the son "defrauded" his father by trading on the information). The Second Circuit touched on the circumstances where a familial relationship would support a finding of a fiduciary relationship in *United States v. Chestman*, 947 F.2d 551 (2d Cir. 1991) (en banc), cert. denied, 112 S.Ct. 1759 (1992). The court distinguished *Reed* on the grounds that *Reed* involved repeated confidences, which may be sufficient to create the "functional equivalent" of a fiduciary duty: "[W]e limit *Reed* to its essential holding: the repeated disclosure of business secrets between family members may substitute for a factual finding of dependence and influence and thereby sustain a finding of the functional equivalent of a fiduciary relationship." *Id.* at 569. The court ruled that there must be a pattern of sharing business secrets before a fiduciary relationship can be found. More important, frequent sharing of secrets is only a substitute for dependence and influence, which, in the court's opinion, are the essential elements of a fiduciary relationship. *Id.*

18

Defining Insiders

Chapter 17 described insider trading law and pointed out that the law does not forbid all informed trading. The regulation of insider trading consists of a partial prohibition against informed trading – a prohibition against trading by only those informed traders whom the law labels "insiders," and one can easily imagine wider as well as narrower definitions. This chapter uses this understanding and analyzes the prohibition of insider trading as a type of regulation of informed trading.

Informed trading is beneficial because it promotes accurate securities prices. Nevertheless, maybe some informed trading should be prohibited. Section A explains that informed trading, despite its beneficial nature, generates a cost. Informed traders "take" part of the stock market returns from the uninformed traders. Uninformed traders can avoid this by not trading. This "taking" resembles a transaction cost because not trading avoids it. Section B argues in favor of the prohibition against insider trading. Different classes of informed traders "take" different amounts in transforming their information into trading profits and contribute unequally to the accuracy of prices. The amount of profits that a class of informed traders reaps depends on how competitively the class trades. Informed traders with little competition extract large profits with little improvement in price accuracy. Therefore, the prohibition of their trading by calling them "insiders" is desirable. Furthermore, regulation is necessary because neither the firms nor shareholders face sufficient incentives to prohibit this trading themselves.

A. THE TRANSACTION COST GENERATED BY INFORMED TRADING

i. Insiders' Profits as Outsiders' Costs of Trading

Insiders burden the trading of outsiders with a cost. The cost to outsiders as a group is equal to the total profits of insiders. If, in a given time period, insiders outperform the market by $100, then outsiders as a group trail the market by $100. Probabilistically, the expected cost of each transaction by an outsider is equal to the group's loss divided by the number of outsider transactions. Thus, if insiders beat the market by $100 in a period during which outsiders made 100 trades, the outsiders bear a cost of trailing the market by $1 for each trade.[1] The result is that insiders' profits take the form of a transaction cost burdening outsiders. Financial economics uses the term "adverse selection" for this phenomenon: outsiders are *adversely selected* to experience disproportionately more drops of prices and fewer rises.

Trades by outsiders against outsiders, despite the fact that one side may profit at the other's expense, do not influence the calculation. As far as outsiders as a group are concerned, the profits of some cancel out the losses of others. Since the transactions are not motivated by information but are random, the expected profit or loss from them is zero.

Example 18.1 Informed Profits as a Transaction Cost

This example illustrates in greater detail how the losses of the outsider group become a transaction cost. The outsiders' losses are caused by the fact that insiders take advantage of price movements. Insiders, however, cause outsiders as a group to hold less stock before price rises and more before price drops. Assume a firm with a total capitalization of $100, $90 of which is held by outsiders and $10 by insiders. Insiders, predicting a price drop, sell $5 of their holdings, resulting in their holding $5 for the outsiders' $95. Insiders' expectations materialize, and the price falls 20%, leaving outsiders with 95% of $80, or $76, and insiders with $4. Insiders readjust their holdings to 10% ($8) and participate with the initial ratio in dividends until they predict a price rise, whereupon they increase their holdings to 15% ($12). The market rises, returning to its original $100 level. Insiders now hold $15 and outsiders $85. In the course of the two price moves, insiders first avoided losing $1 and, subsequently, gained $1 extra by

[1] The same effect will exist in a market with market makers, but it will be less pronounced. In a market where the participants transact among themselves, the "losses" of the uninformed are by necessity equal to the profits of the informed. The interjection of a market maker (who stands ready to trade with anyone at the bid and ask prices that the market maker sets) complicates the picture because the market maker acts as a "buffer" between the informed and uninformed. Whenever the market maker is forced to trade with an informed trader, the market maker is likely to be entering into a disadvantageous transaction.

The market maker reacts to such losses by widening the difference between the bid and ask prices, i.e., the bid-ask spread. Uninformed traders trading with the market maker "reimburse" his or her losses to informed traders and bear the costs of informed trading in a more tangible way – as a wider bid-ask spread – but are further removed from the informed traders. The correlation between the bid-ask spread and the profits of informed traders indicates that market makers provide traders with a way to extrapolate or approximate their transaction costs that are attributable to their trading without information.

The financial literature on market makers is expansive. See, generally, Lawrence R. Glosten & Paul R. Milgrom, *Bid, Ask and Transaction Prices in a Specialist Market with Heterogeneously Informed Traders*, 14 J. FIN. ECON. 71 (1985) (Bid-ask spread widens to reflect information imbalances.); John P. Gould & Robert E. Verrecchia, *The Information Content of Specialist Pricing*, 93 J. POL. ECON. 66 (1985); Robert A. Schwartz, EQUITY MARKETS: STRUCTURE, TRADING, AND PERFORMANCE 92–5, 387 (1988).

trading on their information. Thus outsiders trail the market by $2, and insiders lead it by $2.[2] Inserting more trading instances and dividing the groups into their individual members do not change this conclusion. If the outsiders traded only among themselves, their group would have followed the market's performance regardless of the fact that some of the members would exceed and some would trail the market. If, in the example time, outsiders entered into two trades, then each trade caused them to trail the market by $1. If outsiders made more trades, then they treat the loss as being spread evenly among their trades because they cannot parse which trades cause loss to insiders from which cause loss to other outsiders. Thus, if outsiders entered into 200 trades, from their perspective, each trade corresponds to an expected loss of 1 cent.

Outsiders who trade do not know whether they have traded opposite an insider, but they do know that they are likely to underperform the market more for every trade they make, specifically by the amount of insiders' profits divided by the total number of outsider trades. This expected loss per outsider trade is the transaction cost of trading without information.[3]

ii. *Informed versus Uninformed Trading*

Example 18.1 pitted insiders against outsiders. However, some outsiders, for example market professionals, are informed, and insiders sometimes trade uninformed for lifecycle reasons. To see the effects of different definitions of "insiders," place informed trading against uninformed trading. The transaction cost is identical. The uninformed trades bear the profits of the informed as a transaction cost. Section B uses this division of trades into informed and uninformed to show how different definitions of "insider trading" will influence the transaction costs of uninformed trading. Given this transaction cost, the ultimate issue is whether regulation – call it "insider trading rules" – can decrease this cost and whether, therefore, this regulation is justified.

[2] The performance of outsiders can be tracked more closely. They started with $90. They had to "borrow" $5 to buy the insiders' sales. Their wealth stays at $90, while their holdings increase to $95. After the 20% drop, their $95 is reduced to $76, and their wealth is $76 minus the $5 debt, i.e., $71. After the sales to insiders, their holdings are reduced to $68 with $8 of proceeds and $5 of debt, resulting in a wealth of $71. After the market returns to $100, outsiders' holdings increase to $85 plus $3 in cash after the $5 debt repayment, for a total of $88. Outsiders are worse off by $2 than if they had not traded.

[3] The transaction cost of trading opposite insiders who report their trades under Section 16 of the 1934 Act has been calculated. See H. Nejat Seyhun, *Insiders' Profits, Costs of Trading, and Market Efficiency*, 16 *J. Fin. Econ.* 189, 200 (1986). Seyhun divided firms into five groups based on size of equity. Despite the higher profitability of insider trades in the smallest group, that group is not the one presenting outsiders with the highest likelihood of trading opposite an insider. Seyhun determined that the likelihood of trading opposite a reporting insider starts at 3.6% for the issuers under $25 million, peaks at 4.5%, and as shareholder equity passes the $50 million mark, abruptly drops to 1.9%, 1.1%, and 0.8% for corporations with over $50 million, $250 million, or $1 billion of equity. *Id.* at 20001. The finding that the insiders of the smallest firms make more profits with fewer trades than those of the next size is in harmony with the explanation here if the smallest firms' illiquidity does not sustain profitable informed trading to compete with the insiders.

B. MONOPOLISTIC AND COMPETITIVE INFORMED TRADING: THE PROHIBITION OF INSIDER TRADING AS A REDUCTION OF INFORMED PROFITS

Although it may seem intuitive that banning the trading of a certain subgroup of informed traders (by defining them as "insiders" and disallowing "insider trading") may reduce the profits of informed traders, this conclusion is simplistic. The prohibition against certain members of the class of informed traders may simply increase profits for the rest of the class, leaving the transaction costs borne by uninformed traders unaffected or even enlarged.[4] The following subsections show how the prohibition against insider trading is desirable because it would reduce the adverse selection transaction cost of uninformed traders.

i. *An Example of Regulating Informed Trading with Uninformed Trading Kept Constant*

Assume different classes of informed traders who participate with numerous uninformed traders in a market for a single security of constant liquidity. The volume of uninformed trading is constant and is not expected to move prices. The different classes of informed traders differ in the speed with which they acquire information and in the competition they face. Thus the first class of informed traders faces no competition.[5] Subsequent classes of informed traders are successively larger. As a result, each class faces not only competition by the members of the previous classes but also more internal competition.

Competition influences the trading decision of informed traders. A trader who knows that no other informed traders exist to correct price can trade repeatedly on the same piece of information. By contrast, traders who face competition know that others' trading will correct prices, thus limiting each trader's opportunities for repeated profitable trades. Therefore, a lone informed trader will have a different trading strategy than competitive ones. Each trader's strategy depends on the number of competitors.

To observe traders' optimization, start with a simplified example of only three trades. The sequence of events is (1) information reaches the insider, (2) the first trade occurs, (3) the market maker selects the counterparty for the next trade, (4) the information reaches the public, (5) the second trade occurs, and so on. While in

[4] Along these lines, commentators have argued that the insider trading rules favor market professionals, who reap the profits that the law prohibits insiders from taking. See Carney, *Signalling and Causation in Insider Trading*, at 897; Haddock & Macey, *A Coasian Model of Insider Trading*, at 1458–9; Jonathan R. Macey & Geoffrey P. Miller, *Toward an Interest-Group Theory of Delaware Corporate Law*, 65 TEX. L. REV. 469 (1987).

[5] This group can be understood as a single CEO who creates information with her actions. No one else has the information or competes for any profits that can be made on it. A cohesive group of corporate directors could have similar dynamics.

actual exchanges trades move prices indirectly by exhausting existing limit orders (known as "walking the book of limit orders").[6] The analysis, however, with barely any loss of realism, follows the convention that trades move price directly.[7]

Imagine that the liquidity of the market makes prices move by $1 for every 100 shares traded. The shares are presently priced at $120, but the new information indicates that their value is $100. Profits consist of gain per share multiplied by the number of shares traded. Start with the strategy of a perfectly competitive trader, that is, one who does not expect to trade again on this information because competitors also seek to trade and because prices will quickly correct. The trader may decide to sell a few shares and push price down a little or sell many shares and push price down a lot. In the first case, the profits will be the result of a large gain per share multiplied by a small number of shares. In the second, profits will be a smaller gain multiplied by a larger number of shares. It turns out that the trade that maximizes profits is to sell 1,000 shares and push price down $10 to $110, halfway to value.[8]

6 For example, the current bid-ask spread is $19.95 by $20, and the following limit orders to sell exist: (a) an order for 200 shares at $20, (b) an order for 300 shares at $20.10, and (c) an order for 200 shares at $20.20. Someone who wants to buy 700 shares immediately will move the price to $20.20 by first filling the order at $20 and moving up the sequence of limit orders.

7 A trade of size s will be executed at a price p_1, which is a function of size s and the previous price p_0 according to the impact λ that trades have on price (called the "liquidity parameter," the example of the text sets $\lambda = 0.01$):

$$p_1 = p_0 + \lambda s$$

This formula is a customary starting point for financial modeling of the market. See, e.g., Admati & Pfleiderer, *A Theory of Intraday Patterns*; Albert S. Kyle, *Continuous Auctions and Insider Trading*, 53 ECONOMETRICA 1315 (1985). It is a fair approximation of "walking the book" because it captures in its simplicity the adverse effect that traders expect to have on prices without sacrificing realism. The empirical proof that trades move prices as a function of their size is compelling. See Jerry Hausman, Andrew Lo & Craig MacKinlay, *An Ordered Probit Analysis of Transaction Stock Prices*, 31 J. FIN. ECON. 319, 357 (1993) ("[T]rading a larger quantity [of stock] always yields a larger price impact."). For an empirical work using a closely related function with relative success, see Roger D. Huang & Hans R. Stoll, *Market Microstructure and Stock Return Predictions*, 7 REV. FIN. STUDIES 179 (1994).

8 The trader seeks to maximize profits g from the single trade. The trader's gain per share is the distance between true value (v = $100 in our example) and the price that the trade will produce. The trader determines the size of the trade to maximize profits. In the example's setting, the profits are the product of the resulting price p_1 minus $100 multiplied by the size s of the trade. Profits can be expressed mathematically as

$$g = (v - p_1)s$$

or after substituting from note 7 the function for p_1,

$$g = (v - p_0)s - \lambda s$$

The perfectly competitive informed trader will now maximize profits g by taking their first derivative with respect to size s and equating the derivative to zero:

In this case, the information during trade 1 is exclusive to only one trader. The first competitive trade is then trade 2. The fact that the single informed trader does not trade corresponds to the prohibition of insider trading. Another optimizing competitive trader makes trade 3, which would consist of a purchase of 500 shares and would push price up another \$5 to \$115.

By contrast, if insider trading is allowed, the informed trader who does not face competition, the insider, can trade repeatedly on the same information and knows it. In this case, the insider's advantage allows exactly two trades. Because the insider wants to preserve profits for a second trade, the first trade would not be as large as that of the competitive trader. In the first trade, the insider is aware of the additional possible profits from the second trade. The first trade will establish the price before the second trade: the smaller the first trade, the more profitable is the second trade. The possibility of trading twice means that the insider's first trade will be smaller than 1,000 shares and will, of course, result in a smaller correction of prices. In the second trade, since it will be the last, the insider will follow the competitive strategy.[9] By correcting prices less, the insider preserves profits for the next trade.

$$\frac{dg}{ds} = (v - p_0) - 2\lambda s = 0 \Leftrightarrow s = \frac{v - p_0}{2\lambda}$$

Therefore, $s = -20/0.02 = -1{,}000$ shares. This is a maximum because the second derivative is negative. If the trader sells 995 or 1,005 shares, too few or too many, profits decline. Selling 995 shares brings price to \$110.05, gain per share to \$10.05, and profits to \$999.75. Selling 1,005 shares brings price to \$109.95, gain per share to \$9.95, and profits to \$999.75 again.

9 We already know that the insider's strategy that will determine trade size s_2 in the second trade will be

$$s_2 = (v - p_1)/2\lambda$$

and that after the second trade, price p_2 will be

$$p_2 = p_1 + (v - p_2)/2$$

The total profit g_T that the insider is trying to maximize is the sum of the profits from both trades:

$$\begin{aligned} g_T &= (v - p_1)s_1 + (v - p_2)s_2 \\ &= (v - p_1)s_1 + [v - p_1 - (v - p_1)/2](v - p_1)/2\lambda \end{aligned}$$

After substituting the formula for p_1 and simplifying, profits become

$$g_T = (v - p_0 - \lambda s_1)s_1 + \frac{(v - p_0 - \lambda s_1)^2}{\lambda^2}$$

Take the first derivative with respect to s_1, equate it to 0, and solve for s_1 (which will, again, be a maximum):

$$\begin{aligned} \frac{dg_T}{ds_1} &= (v - p_0 - 3\lambda s_1)/2 = 0 \\ s_1 &= (v - p_0)/3\lambda = -20/0.3 = -666.667 \end{aligned}$$

The result is that the insider will maximize profits by selling 666.667 shares in both the first and second trades.

This lighter "strategic trading"[10] does not correct prices as much as trading under competition and produces greater informed profits. The two insider trades correct price less than the two competitive trades but take a larger profit for the informed trader.[11]

A graphical illustration of this situation shows the effect of regulation. If the monopolist informed trader is barred from trading, there will be no informed trade at time 1, but trades 2 and 3 will be competitive. The important difference between the competitive and noncompetitive trading regards the total profits of the informed trader. In every trade, the profits are the difference of the price from true value multiplied by the size of the trade. In a three-dimensional graph (time, trade size, and price being the axes), this is the product of the price error multiplied by trade size.

Figure 18.1 allows a visual comparison of the profits of informed traders in the stylized case where an informed insider has an advantage of one trade in a world with three total trades. The time axis represents the trades in time. The price axis represents the gain compared to true value, which is at the origin; the origin of the axes corresponds to a price of $100 and gain of zero. The gain decreases as price decreases and approaches true value. For example, the first informed trade at a price of about $113.33 corresponds to the largest of the gains at over $13. Information is exclusive during trade 1. The narrower, lighter rectangles represent

10 In the complexity of actual securities exchanges, strategic trading would involve placing small orders that are hidden in the order flow, thus breaking a large order into many small ones, or placing limit orders in the middle of the spread so as not to move prices all the way to the market maker's bid or ask. A "limit order" (as opposed to a "market order") is an offer to trade at a given price. Placing a limit order within the market maker's bid-ask spread would involve, for example, offering to sell 200 shares of IBM at $100 if the market maker offers to buy at $99 (bid) and to sell at $100¼ (ask). If there are buyers of IBM on the market, the limit order is "filled," and the seller avoids selling at the bid. The opposite, an aggressive trading strategy, would involve placing large orders to be filled at the market price, accepting that the price will move as far as the market will require to absorb the large trade, to the trader's disadvantage. Strategic trading can be conceptualized as "slow" or "passive" trading, in contrast to the "aggressive" trading of traders who face time pressure to complete their trades.

11 A table captures the price, trade size, profits per trade, and total profits:

Scenario	Price	Size	Profit per trade	Running total
No prohibition	$113.33	−666.67	$8,888.89	No prohibition
	$106.67	−666.67	$4,444.44	$13,333.30
	$103.33	−166.67	$555.56	$13,888.90
Prohibition	$110.00	−1,000.00	$10,000.00	Prohibition
	$105.00	−500.00	$2,500.00	$12,500.00

The insider takes a profit of $13,333 from two trades. This scenario allows a third informed trade, which happens under competitive conditions. The total profit of informed traders from three trades is $13,888.90. If insider trading is prohibited, the two informed trades produce a smaller profit of $12,500.

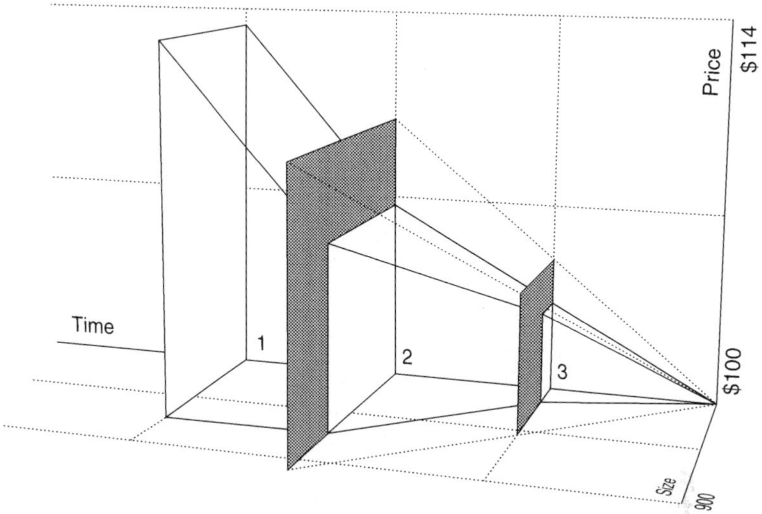

FIGURE 18.1 A simple comparison with insider trading allowed and prohibited.

the trading of the insider, who trades at trades 1 and 2 on the same information. Notice that trades 1 and 2 have the same size, 667 shares; the insider is not forced to trade intensively in the first trade due to lack of competition. The wider, darker rectangles are the result of a prohibition on trading by the exclusive holder of information, a ban on insider trading. In this regime, no informed trading occurs during trade 1, and trading begins on a competitive footing from trade 2. Competition forces a faster approach of price to true value because traders are induced to take full advantage of each trade separately. The point of this example is that the prohibition of exclusive informed trading reduces the profits of informed trading.

Moving to an example of greater complexity, the correction of prices will occur by the forces of trading. Also, information will not make an immediate transition from exclusive to public. Instead, information will spread from one to four informed traders, according to the different advantages traders have in obtaining it. This more complex example also allows us to observe the difference in the speed of price correction – efficiency – under the two regimes.

The trader with the greatest advantage, the insider, reaches the information first. Knowing that a second trader will not uncover the information for a while, the first trader engages in strategic trading as the sole holder of the information. Traders optimize using some estimate of the probability of trading again, which in the case of the sole informed trader is near 100%. At some point, three more traders become informed. Each trader expects to make one-quarter of the future informed transactions and also expects more competitors to join. The competition results in larger trades and a faster approach of price to true value.

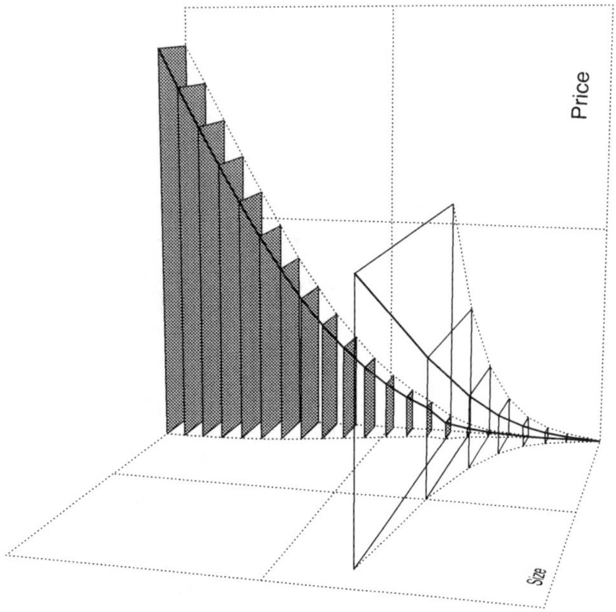

FIGURE 18.2 Insider trading prohibition comparison over many trades.

Figure 18.2 follows the pattern of Figure 18.1 to illustrate the effect of a prohibition with the realism of enough trades for price to correct by trading forces. The Appendix explains the example and the derivation of the optimal trades fully. The lone insider has an advantage of 15 trades.[12]

From the fifteenth trade forward, four informed traders compete for each trade. If insider trading is prohibited, no informed trading occurs during the first trades. Again, the focus is on total informed profits. If insider trading is unrestrained, the total informed profits are over 21% greater.

The second issue, besides profits, is speed of price correction. Competitive trading corrects prices fast, whereas the insider's strategic trading delays the correction of prices.[13] Therefore, the prohibition has little cost in terms of price correction: With

[12] The Appendix explains this fully.

[13] The notion that insiders will trade strategically has been modeled. See, e.g., Jean-Jaques Laffont & Eric S. Maskin, *The Efficient Market Hypothesis and Insider Trading on the Stock Market*, 98 *J. Pol. Econ.* 70 (1990) (presenting a model under which trading by insiders does not influence prices sufficiently to render prices fully efficient because insiders behave strategically so as to minimize the amount by which they affect market prices); Leonard J. Mirman & Larry Samuelson, *Information and Equilibrium with Inside Traders*, 99 *Econ. J.* 152 (Suppl. 1989) (presenting a model concluding that insiders will trade less than if the market were unable to decode their information, with further citations on the effect of large inside traders on prices). In contrast to the analysis in this chapter, however, these economic models neither address the definition of insider trading nor show how insider trading regulation may reduce the adverse selection problem that uninformed traders face.

or without the prohibition, price becomes correct at almost the same time even though the prohibition delays greatly the onset of informed trading.

The figure also shows that prices correct completely long before the end of the example's trading time. The graph shows only the first two-thirds of trading, yet price has reached value.

This example illustrates that prohibiting trading to a group of traders that can trade strategically costs little in terms of market efficiency, but greatly reduces the profits of informed traders. Reduced profits for informed traders reduce the adverse selection transaction cost that burdens uninformed traders.

ii. Relaxing the Assumption of Constant Uninformed Trading

In the preceding analysis, uninformed trading was constant. Because, however, the prohibition against insider trading reduces the adverse selection transaction cost, more uninformed trading should result and thus greater liquidity, leading to more informed profits. The possibility exists that informed trading profits increase more than proportionately, returning the adverse selection transaction cost to its preprohibition level and making the prohibition pointless. As it happens, however, the increased liquidity actually has a beneficial feedback effect.

The increased liquidity reduces the cost of both informed and uninformed trading. The cheaper trading drives both groups to trade more. For the informed trader, however, liquidity is more than a reduction of cost. Because their trades move price less, their trading is also more profitable. But this increased profitability attracts more informed traders, and the resulting competition erodes informed trading profits so that they increase less than proportionately, as finance theory and evidence confirm.

The theoretical support for the feedback effect comes from an unexpected direction. Exploring the phenomenon that trading volume tended to cluster in certain periods of the day, Admati and Pfleiderer explain this clustering with a model that has received empirical support.[14] According to their argument, the clustering is to the advantage of uninformed traders because it increases liquidity and reduces the per-uninformed-trade profits of informed traders (i.e., it reduces the quasi-transaction cost burdening uninformed traders). The feedback benefit seen in the clustering of trading volume is the same that accrues to uninformed traders from the prohibition of insider trading: more competitive informed trading benefits uninformed trading.

Nothing argues against generalizing the conclusion of Admati and Pfleiderer to changes in overall trading volume (instead of changes in trading volume within a day). By contrast, their mathematical model, although designed to simulate

[14] See note 16.

trading during the day, is based on a sequence of auctions and resembles more day-to -day trading than trading within each day.

iii. Extrapolating from the Assumed Pricing Mechanism

The above model of the insiders' optimization rests, as does much of the microstructure literature, on the equation that produces a new price from the old depending on the size of an order. While this is an acceptable simplification for the purpose of theoretical analysis, actual stock markets have additional complexities. One is that market makers quote a bid-ask spread rather than a pricing equation. Prices change as trades exhaust the quantities asked or bid for, the depth at the ask or bid. A second discrepancy, very important for insider trading analysis, is that traders can place orders that may not execute immediately, namely, limit orders.

A "limit order" is an order to trade at a specified price or better. A limit order to purchase designates a willingness to buy at the specified price or lower and one to sell at the specified price or higher. The opportunity cost of limit orders becomes apparent when price moves in the direction that would benefit the trader but bypasses the limit order. For example, a trader places an order to buy at $10 or better when the bid-ask spread is at $9.95 by $10.05. Then the next few trades are purchases at $10.05 and higher, pushing the price up. The limit order does not execute because no seller appeared in time for the $10 bid of the limit order. A market order placed at the same time would have produced a gain.

Limit orders also produce gains. The gain becomes apparent when a trader seeking to trade immediately in the opposite direction from the limit order places a market order. In the same example, if a seller places a market order (to immediately sell at the current best price), it will match the limit order. With a market order, the trader would have bought at $10.05, but with the limit order, the trader managed to buy at $10.

In sum, placing a limit order means accepting the risk of missing anticipated gain but receiving the benefit of extracting a small premium from someone who seeks to trade immediately. Notice, also, that limit orders compete with market makers and reduce the price pressure on market makers. When a trader places a limit order to buy at $10 and another places a limit order to sell at $10.03, the market maker of our example will not trade and will not have the imbalance of inventory pushing for a change of price (nor will the market maker have the profit from the additional trades).

The analysis of competitive informed trading is not distorted by having used a price equation instead of trying to model the reality of bid-ask spreads and limit orders. Competitive traders cannot afford the delay and risk of limit orders or small orders that do not exhaust the depth at the bid or ask. The opposite is true for monopolistic informed trading. The absence of competition allows insiders to have little effect on price by placing limit orders or small orders that do not exhaust the depth at the bid or the ask, as the evidence shows.[15] The formal analysis, however, assumes that even insiders would push price toward correction. The reality is that insiders need not place market orders and tend not to push price toward correction. Thus the compromise (between a delay in price accuracy in exchange for a reduction in informed profits) that insider trading regulation involves is understated by the formal analysis. The actual compromise is much more in favor of regulation because insiders produce trivial movement of price toward its accurate level.

iv. Empirical Validation

The model of Admati and Pfleiderer is intuitive and has received empirical support.[16] The preceding analysis supporting the prohibition of insider trading is also fully consistent with the evidence. The most vivid support for the benefit of insider trading comes from international comparisons. Different jurisdictions adopt and enforce their insider trading laws at different times. This has enabled researchers to observe how the law changes prices, liquidity, and volatility. The evidence consistently shows an increase in liquidity, as the analysis here predicts.[17] The evidence also shows greater volatility. This is also consistent

[15] See Bradford Cornell & Erik R. Sirri, *The Reaction of Investors and Stock Prices to Insider Trading*, 47 J. FINANCE 1031 (1992) (examining a single period of insider trading activity in Campbell Taggart; insider trades occurred after smaller adverse price moves than those of outsiders, i.e., insiders faced smaller execution costs than outsiders, and insiders were able to use limit orders); Lisa K. Meulbroek, *An Empirical Analysis of Illegal Insider Trading*, 47 J. FINANCE 1661 (1992) (examining a series of insider trading instances and finding that insider trading caused corrections of one-third of their postannouncement correction).

[16] See Michael Barclay, Robert Litzenberger & Jerold Warner, *Private Information, Trading Volume, and Stock-Return Variances*, 3 REV. FIN. STUD. 233 (1990). This work offers an empirical verification of the Admati and Pfleiderer model. The study involved a comparison of weekends when the Tokyo Stock Exchange was open on Saturdays with weekends when it was closed. The alternative hypothesis to the Admati and Pfleiderer model, trading noise, was refuted both because the weekly variance did not increase in the longer weeks and because US stocks did not have increased variance if traded in Tokyo on weekends. The theory that both uninformed and informed traders will cluster in markets of great liquidity is upheld by the observation of the low volume and return variance that stocks listed in multiple exchanges have in their secondary exchanges. Volume is concentrated in the more liquid "parent" exchange, where the stock is principally traded. Informed trading also avoids the foreign exchanges with the result of slowing the adjustments of prices to new information, thereby lowering efficiency. Although these observations do not verify the process, i.e., that the decreased efficiency of foreign markets is due to reduced uninformed trading, they do correlate efficiency with volume and liquidity.

[17] Utpal Bhattacharya & Hazem Daouk, *The World Price of Insider Trading*, 57 J. FINANCE 75 (2002); Lisa N. Beny, *Do Insider Trading Laws Matter? Some Preliminary Comparative Evidence*, 7 AMER. L & ECON. REV. 144 (2002); cf. Nuno Fernandes & Miguel A. Ferreira, *Insider Trading Laws and Stock Price Informativeness*, 22 REV. FINANC. STUD. 1845 (2009) (enforcement of insider trading laws improves price informativeness in developed markets but less so in emerging markets).

with the analysis here, which indicates that prices approach true value with greater speed after the prohibition. The evidence does not show changes in values or price levels. Again, this is consistent with the analysis, in which the prohibition only has an indirect effect on price by merely making investing more appealing.

19

Concluding the Insider Trading Analysis

The economic explanation for the prohibition of insider trading followed a route quite separate from the line of reasoning behind the legal doctrine of the prohibition. While this is not an unusual tension between the economic justification of a rule and the legal reasoning behind it, here the divergence reveals room for improvement.

The doctrine relies on the notion of inappropriate use of information, through either a fiduciary breach or misappropriation. The economic justification of the prohibition, however, rests on the lack of competition between informed traders. The tension appears by considering a fiduciary breach that leads to informed trading that is competitive. Existing legal doctrine would sanction it, but it would not be socially harmful.[1] The improvement in the doctrine would be to allow actual competition as a defense. A defendant against an insider trading charge should be able to avoid liability by showing that the circumstances indicated that competition may well have existed during the insider's trading and that the insider traded in a competitive manner, that is, by placing a few large market orders over a brief period of time rather than several and mostly limit orders over a long period of time. The materiality element opens an interpretive avenue in this direction. Information on which trading would produce insider trading liability (under either the classical or the misappropriation theory) needs to be material. Information that is held by enough traders that they act competitively in trading on it should be considered immaterial as a matter of law. This interpretation would be an extension of the treatment of the fraud-on-the-market presumption of reliance discussed in Chapters 12 to 15. If a misrepresentation does not mislead the trading public, then the resumption of reliance fails, the statement lacks materiality, or it falls under the truth-on-the-market exception.[2] Possession

[1] *Newman*'s more stringent state of mind requirement that makes the prosecution of remote tippees more difficult may eventually be interpreted so as to function in parallel with this analysis. *United States v. Newman*, 773 F.3rd 438 (2d Cir. 2014), cert. denied 136 S.Ct. 242 (2015).

[2] As discussed in Chapters 12 to 15 and especially Chapter 14, the presumption of reliance fails if the market knows the truth, as *Basic* itself points out: "For example, if petitioners could show that the

of the inside information by traders who act competitively is analogous to revelation of the falsity of a misrepresentation. The insider's use of the information is not harmful, just as the false statement does not mislead the market. From the perspective of the older analysis of insider trading from the 1960s, if inside information produces competitive trading, then the older analysis applies. The prohibition merely delays the correction of prices without reducing the adverse selection transaction cost that burdens uninformed trading.

In sum, the prohibition of insider trading is a form of regulation of informed trading. It is justified as a reduction in the adverse selection transaction cost that burdens uninformed trading. This does not mean that a broader prohibition is necessarily desirable. Too broad a prohibition could chill informed trading and erode the accuracy of prices. The proper prohibition of insider trading ensures that uninformed traders enjoy trading at accurate prices without too high an adverse selection transaction cost.

By completing the insider trading analysis, the virtuous cycle of securities regulation is complete. The discussion of insider trading showed how the reduction of a transaction cost, the adverse selection cost that uninformed trading faces, increases liquidity and how that increase, by attracting competitive informed trading, produces more accurate prices. The earlier analyses on disclosure and deterrence showed how accurate prices function as reduced costs of trading for risk-averse traders by reducing the risk of trading at false prices. The virtuous cycle from lower cost of trading to liquidity, which begets accurate prices, which function as lower cost of trading, is complete.

'market makers' were privy to the truth . . . and thus that the market price would not have been affected by their misrepresentations," then the presumption of reliance would not apply, 485 US at 248. A statement of known falsity also does not influence the "total mix of information" and therefore lacks materiality per *TSC v. Northway*, 426 US 438 (1976).

PART V

The Virtuous Cycle of Liquid Markets, Accurate Prices, and Cheap Trading

20

The Virtuous Cycle

Four effects of securities regulation were the focus of this book: the focus on only passive investments (Chapters 2 to 8 on the definition of a security), extensive disclosure rules (Chapters 10 to 11), the intense deterrence of broad class actions (Chapters 12 to 15), and the understanding of the prohibition of insider trading as an enforcement of competition in informed trading (Chapters 16 to 19). The same laissez-faire-ist objection to regulation is raised in every one of those issues. Investors should and would protect themselves from the underlying dangers. While this objection was rebutted on each occasion, this chapter identifies the overarching commonality of these rebuttals. The justification of each one of these fundamental aspects of securities regulation lies in a feedback phenomenon – the "virtuous cycle."

A. THE CYCLE

The main effects of the law of securities regulation enhance the virtuous cycle from reduced transaction costs to greater liquidity of the securities markets and accuracy of the markets' pricing function. Earlier this book stressed the feedback effect between accurate prices, reduced transaction costs, and liquidity. Concluding, let us collect and review all these effects.

Turn first to the economic forces that promote the virtuous cycle of liquid markets that leads to accurate prices, which, in turn, reduce transaction costs, which improve market liquidity. After their discussion and a graphical illustration, this chapter turns to the forces that the legal system produces. This categorization of the forces into economic and legal does not seek to classify their importance or magnitude. The purpose is merely to illustrate the virtuous cycle and the synergy of the rules of securities law with the market forces. The market's economic forces build Figure 20.1, and the forces that the legal system creates are shown in Figure 20.2.

The economic force leading from reduced transaction costs to greater liquidity is elementary. Reductions in transaction costs produce more trading of every color. Obviously, the informed and the irrational trade more because the cost of their activity drops. However, the lifecycle uninformed traders also trade more because the reduced cost of trading means that they can put funds that have a shorter investment horizon into the market. Greater trading activity translates into greater liquidity directly. As the flow of trading activity increases, trades of a given size diminish in importance and impact on prices.

The economic force leading from liquidity to accurate prices rests on the reality that liquidity attracts informed trading. Little liquidity means that trades move prices a lot. Informed traders dislike influencing prices because that reduces their profits. A very liquid market implies that trades have a small effect on prices. Informed trades can place larger trades and move price less to their disadvantage. This translates into greater profits for informed traders, which attracts more informed trading. The increased informed trading increases the competitiveness of informed trading. Traders cannot wait or temporize and need to take full advantage of their information through aggressive trading. Competitive trading results in fast price corrections. Thus the more competitive informed trading leads to prices that are more accurate. More competitive informed trading also leads to a reduction in aggregate informed profits per uninformed trade. This is a reduction of the transaction cost of uninformed trading.

Accurate pricing reduces transaction costs because of aversion to risk. Traders dislike the risk that they may be trading at false prices. This applies to both informed traders and lifecycle uninformed traders. As confidence in the accuracy of market prices increases, the reluctance to trade diminishes.

Figure 20.1 illustrates the economic forces forming the vicious cycle. Liquidity attracts informed trading, leading to price accuracy, which reduces aversion to

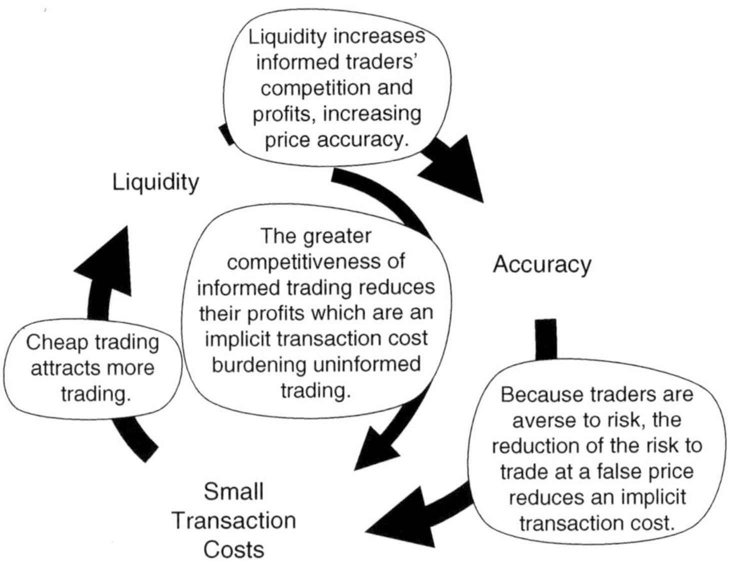

FIGURE 20.1 Economic forces forming the virtuous cycle.

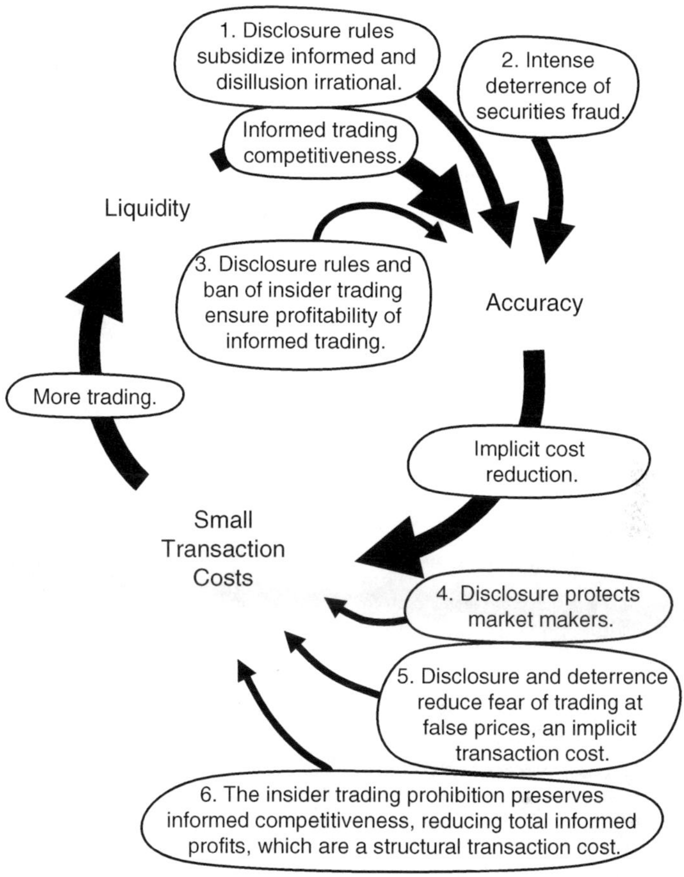

FIGURE 20.2 Legal forces enhancing the virtuous cycle.

trading, a transaction cost. More competitiveness of informed trading also leads directly to lower transaction costs for uninformed trading. The cheaper trading increases trading activity, which increases liquidity.

Next, Figure 20.2 illustrates the forces that the legal system produces and that are synergistic with the virtuous cycle. These are six.

The disclosure rules that Chapters 10 and 11 discussed subsidize informed trading and dispel some irrational trading. The increased likelihood that rational informed traders dominate the market is an increase in the accuracy of prices. This appears as force 1 in the figure.

The intense deterrence of securities fraud of Chapters 12 to 15 strengthens the incentive to provide accurate information to market participants, increasing the accuracy of prices. This appears as force 2.

Disclosure rules and the ban on insider trading also ensure that informed trading is profitable, ensuring the existence of a strong class of informed traders.

The resulting competitive and aggressive informed trading leads to price accuracy. This appears as force 3.

Disclosure rules also protect market makers. Market makers, because they stand ready to buy or sell opposite anyone, may enter into losing trades with traders who are better informed. Disclosure rules level the playing field by making information about firms readily accessible to everyone, including market makers. This protection of market makers translates as a smaller bid-ask spread, which is a reduction of a transaction cost. This appears as force 4.

Disclosure rules and the existence of strong deterrence against false statements also have a feedback effect. Traders are more confident that prices are accurate, which encourages them to trade. In other words, the confidence in the deterrence of securities fraud reduces the functional transaction cost of aversion to trading that traders have because they are risk averse, as further discussed in Chapter 10 (see also note 22 in Chapter 13). This appears as force 5.

Finally, the prohibition of insider trading, as Chapters 16 to 19 explained, is a regulation of informed trading. The ban on insider trading ensures that those who trade on new information face competition. The competition and associated aggressive trading reduce the aggregate informed profits. For uninformed traders, the reduction in informed profits operates as a reduction of a transaction cost. This appears as force 6.

The premises of the virtuous cycle of liquidity, accuracy, and cheap trading resolve some paradoxes that had troubled financial economics. For example, scholars considered perfectly accurate prices to lead to the cessation of trading, the "efficiency paradox," because they only focused on informed trading.[1] The recognition that uninformed trading is a very significant component of market activity and that noise trading does occur eliminates the paradox.

The virtuous cycle is central to the quality of the regulation of securities markets. If regulation produces an imbalance, the quality of the market suffers. Too much noise trading would produce pricing that would be too uncertain and volatile for both uninformed and informed traders. Too much uninformed trading would tend to also randomize prices, too much informed trading would produce very accurate prices, but in both these latter cases the adverse selection transaction cost that uninformed traders would bear would be large.

B. LIQUIDITY AS A PUBLIC GOOD

The virtuous cycle is also the answer to the free-market objection to regulation. In the eyes of the inflexible free-market proponent, private parties would perfectly foresee the ills that regulation seeks to prevent and would make the least costly

[1] See Sanford J. Grossman & Joseph E. Stiglitz, *On the Impossibility of Informationally Efficient Markets*, 70 AM. ECON. REV. 393 (1980).

arrangements to avoid those ills. The inflexibility and distorted incentives that regulation creates would never arise.

The attack of free-market idealists against securities regulation rests on the idea that firms or exchanges would pursue all the benefits of the virtuous cycle. Then private initiative would arrange to address the issues covered by securities regulation. Because those arrangements would not be governmental, they would have the flexibility imposed by competition and would fully allow innovation. However, even though an inflexible free-market objection always favors deregulation, the diffuse benefits of liquidity justify securities regulation.

Each part of this book has justified a different facet of securities regulation against this free-market objection. This chapter gives a unified answer. Neither corporations nor stock exchanges have adequate incentives to produce the level of market liquidity that will encourage maximal entrepreneurship, innovation, and competition.

Securities regulation favors shorter holding periods, whereas corporations would choose policies that favor the median holding period. This phenomenon may be most pronounced in disclosure rules but is also present in insider trading and the deterrence of fraud. The prohibition of insider trading reduces a cost of uninformed trading, inducing trading and liquidity. Fraud deterrence, similarly, increases the accuracy of prices, encouraging trading and liquidity. In every case, the law benefits frequent traders at some cost to all shareholders.

Disclosure rules illustrate the same dynamic even more vividly. Disclosure is costly, and the benefit it conveys – accurate stock prices – is mostly realized in trading. Frequent traders benefit from accurate prices and favor more disclosure. Long-term holders benefit from reduced expenditure and favor less disclosure. The regulatory regime forces an outcome in favor of frequent traders because the liquidity they produce is socially valuable.

The free-market objection has such monumental obstacles to overcome that it is not credible. In order to choose the policy of frequent disclosure, firms, exchanges, or investors must internalize the benefits from the economic growth that the well-regulated, very liquid stock market produces when it fosters entrepreneurship. None of these do or ever have. Corporations and exchanges do not internalize this benefit because to a large extent it accrues to others. Part of the benefit that liquid markets produce is the facilitation of financing for future enterprises – potential competitors to the listed firms and perhaps to the exchanges themselves. Thus the argument that firms or exchanges will create good disclosure policies is implausible. Neither is it plausible that investors will let their diffuse interests in economic growth outweigh their concrete interests as shareholders of specific corporations.

Because liquidity makes the stock market more attractive to investors, a large part of the attractiveness of the market accrues to the benefit of future corporations, ones that will reap the benefits of liquidity when they go public. Listed corporations have little incentive to pave the way for upstarts. Although exchanges have an incentive to encourage future listings because they represent future fees and profits, this interest pales compared to society's interest in entrepreneurial innovation and competition. Even if exchanges demonstrated a willingness to promote liquidity in the face of corporations' opposition, which they never have, the rules they would pass would induce less liquidity than is desired. In other words, only securities legislation can approach the ideal level of liquidity.

Indeed, even if in a perfect world investors might make decisions obviating the need for good securities regulation, in actuality, the evidence shows that regulation increases welfare. The imposition of disclosure obligations by the 1933 and 1934 Securities Acts and their expansion in the 1960s increased valuations.[2] Similarly, the evidence from international comparisons is that jurisdictions that impose insider trading liability realize gains in liquidity.[3]

To weave together the last strands of the seamless web, return to the boundary of securities law – the definition of a security (discussed in detail in Chapters 2 to 8). The understanding of the liquidity function of securities regulation circles back to the boundary as a substantive, functional issue. In discerning liquidity as an overarching function of securities regulation, consider *Santa Fe v. Green*.[4] The Supreme Court refused to extend the protection of federal securities laws to plaintiffs who had alternative protection under state corporate law. Both in *Santa Fe* and the definition of a security, at issue is the boundary that distinguishes federal securities regulation from state corporate law.[5] According to the analysis in this book, securities regulation has a specific ultimate goal: the liquidity of securities markets. The boundary between securities and corporate law is not arbitrary. Securities law's consistent promotion of liquidity distinguishes it clearly from corporate law's protection of the various corporate stakeholders.[6]

[2] See note 13 in Chapter 13. [3] See notes 15 and 17 in Chapter 18.

[4] 430 US 462 (1977). See also *CTS Corp. v. Dynamics Corp. of America*, 481 US 69, 82 (1987) ("[N]o principle of corporation law is more firmly established than a State's authority to regulate domestic corporations, including the authority to define the voting rights of shareholders."); *Schreiber v. Burlington Northern, Inc.*, 472 US 1 (1985) (Tender offer antifraud provision § 14(e) is only violated by misstatement, not misconduct.).

[5] The problematic distinction of state corporate law from federal securities law was brought forth mostly with the state antitakeover statutes of the 1980s. States sought to restrain tender offers for their corporations. One of the issues on which the cases were decided was whether tender offers were corporate control events or transactions in securities. See, generally, *Edgar v. MITE Corp.*, 457 US 624 (1982) (invalidating an Illinois antitakeover statute); *CTS Corp. v. Dynamics Corp. of America*, 481 US 69, 82 (1987) (reversing the lower courts and upholding an Indiana antitakeover statute); *People v. Boyer*, 48 Cal. 3d 247 (1989).

[6] Corporate law focuses on the conflicts between corporate control and ownership, pitting management and controlling shareholders against minority shareholders. Appraisal rights, fiduciary duties, and derivative and class actions are typical examples of the vehicles that try to protect the minority owners from the controllers while preserving the functionality of the corporation. See, e.g., Nicholas L. Georgakopoulos, *Meinhard v. Salmon and the Economics of Honor*, 1999 COLUM. BUS. L. REV. 137.

21

Closing Note: Financial Crises and Securities Law

A book about securities law jurisprudence cannot stay silent regarding financial crises, especially given the experience with the crisis of 2008. Through history, more frequent companions of markets are financial crises rather than good securities law. Granted, securities law would be desirable even if it only functioned well at normal times (assuming that it did not aggravate crises). Law that averts crises would be even better. How does securities law protect against financial crises, and how can this protection improve?

This chapter introduces financial crises, uses as an illustration the boom and bust cycle around the 2008 financial crisis, surveys securities regulation for its protective features, and proposes improvements.

The years since 2008 have produced much work about the financial crisis that started at the end of 2007 (the "2008 crisis") and brought about the Great Recession: a steady stream of articles[1] and books,[2] a congressional investigation committee

[1] A Westlaw search on July 13, 2013, produced 208 articles about the financial crisis (database "jlr"; the search identifies articles with "crisis" in the title and reference to the crisis under its three alternative appellations: search string "'2008 crisis' 'great recession' '(crisis /3 2007) & ti(crisis)'"; excluding the requirement of "crisis" in the title produced 1915 articles referring to it). Some notable ones include, e.g., David A. Skeel, Jr., *Institutional Choice in an Economic Crisis*, 2013 WIS. L. REV. 629–47; Morgan Ricks, *A Regulatory Design for Monetary Stability*, 65 VAND. L. REV. 1289–1358 (2012); Jonathan C. Lipson, *Epic Fail: An Institutional Analysis of Financial Distress*, University of Wisconsin Law School Legal Studies Research Paper Series, Paper No. 1201, 2012, available at ssrn.com /abstract=2117430.

[2] Extraordinary are the books of the protagonists, the Fed Chair and the Secretary of Treasury: Ben S. Bernanke, THE FEDERAL RESERVE AND THE FINANCIAL CRISIS (Princeton University Press, 2013); HENRY PAULSON, ON THE BRINK (2010). The academic, World Bank, and central banker insight appears in Raghuram G. Rajan, *FAULT LINES* (HarperCollins 2012) (the author is a professor at the University of Chicago, was the chief economist at the World Bank, and the chair of India's central bank). See also Alan Blinder, AFTER THE MUSIC STOPPED: THE FINANCIAL CRISIS, THE RESPONSE, AND THE WORK AHEAD (2013). Many journalists with an intimate understanding of the financial markets who reported on the crisis as it unfolded have also produced vivid accounts, David Wessel, *IN FED WE TRUST* (Crown, Random House 2009); Andrew Ross Sorkin, TOO BIG TO FAIL: THE INSIDE STORY OF HOW WALL STREET AND WASHINGTON FOUGHT TO SAVE THE FINANCIAL SYSTEM – AND THEMSELVES (2009); Gretchen Morgenson and Joshua Rosner, *RECKLESS ENDANGERMENT* (Times Books, Henry Holt, New York, 2011). The financial

report,[3] and a massive legislative response, the Dodd-Frank Act.[4] From the perspective of securities regulation, this crisis had the unusual feature that the investors whose errors contributed most to the euphoria that led to the crisis were sophisticated institutions, not the retail, unsophisticated investors that conventionally need protection.

This chapter has two purposes. First, it offers a mostly rational (i.e., traders merely and realistically fall somewhat short of the ideal of perfect rationality rather than exhibiting the systematic errors of bounded rationality) account of euphorias that lead to crises, with the 2008 crisis as an illustration. Producing a rational account of crises is more disquieting, and more accurate, than theories of mass delusions. The rational account is more disquieting because we cannot expect foresight or caution to protect from such crises and more accurate because none of the extremely sophisticated regulators and businesspeople in positions of power did forecast the crisis.[5] Reality validated the quip that predicting is difficult, particularly about the future.[6]

understanding and vivid narration of Michael Lewis make his THE BIG SHORT: INSIDE THE DOOMSDAY MACHINE (W.W. Norton, New York, 2010) one more interesting read. Leading economists held a conference on the crisis, and their contributions, which are much less radical than, e.g., Morgan Ricks's, note 1, form the chapters of THE SQUAM LAKE REPORT: FIXING THE FINANCIAL SYSTEM (2010). The brilliance of Judge Posner is once again evident in his recounting of the crisis, A FAILURE OF CAPITALISM: THE CRISIS OF '08 AND THE DESCENT INTO DEPRESSION (2009), and his subsequent THE CRISIS OF CAPITALIST DEMOCRACY (2010). A slightly more distant and self-doubting examination of the crisis is WHAT CAUSED THE FINANCIAL CRISIS (Jeffrey Friedman ed., 2011). Most of these and several more are reviewed and found lacking consensus in Andrew W. Lo, *Reading about the Financial Crisis: A 21-Book Review*, 50 *J. ECON. LIT.* 151 (2012). Three popular claims seem false, however: that the development of institutions that were "too big to fail" induced irresponsible borrowing, that SEC rule changes induced irresponsible borrowing (because the leverage of investment bank had been at the same level since the 1990s), and that senior executive compensation induced excessive risk-taking (because CEOs lost enormous amounts due to the crisis). An important comparison of responses internationally and strong criticism of Dodd-Frank comes from Hal S. Scott, CONNECTEDNESS AND CONTAGION: PROTECTING THE FINANCIAL SYSTEM FROM PANICS (2016).

3 Financial Crisis Inquiry Commission, THE FINANCIAL CRISIS INQUIRY REPORT (2011), available at www.gpo.gov/fdsys/pkg/GPO-FCIC/pdf/GPO-FCIC.pdf.

4 Dodd-Frank Wall Street Reform and Consumer Protection Act, Pub. L. No. 111-203, 124 Stat, 1376 (codified in scattered sections of USC).

5 Of all the extremely sophisticated regulators and businesspeople populating the financial markets, the few who forecasted the crisis were not in positions of power. Indeed, Michael Lewis's book, THE BIG SHORT: INSIDE THE DOOMSDAY MACHINE (2011), is a recounting of the difficulties faced by a handful of hedge fund managers who had made trades assuming that mortgage-backed securities were overvalued. As the bubble kept growing and produced losses, their investors complained and tried to abandon their funds.

6 In the United States, this quip is usually credited to Yogi Berra, the philosophizing catcher for the New York Yankees in the mid-twentieth century, but Europeans give credit to Neils Bohr, the well-known Danish physicist. See EUROPE WITHOUT ILLUSIONS: THE PAUL-HENRI SPAAK LECTURES, 1994–1999 (Andrew Moravcsik ed. 2005), at 125 (mentioning the disagreement over the source); Madison Guy, *Bohr Leads Berra, But Yogi Closing the Gap*, LETTER FROM HERE (December 2, 2006), available at www.peterpatau.com/2006/12/bohr-leads-berra-but-yogi-closing-gap.html (discussing the debate).

Second, this chapter looks for anticrisis features in the law of securities regulation. The backbone of securities regulation was created in the 1930s as a reaction to the crash that led to the Great Depression. Surveying securities regulation reveals some surviving anticrisis features but also warns that a slow-building bubble such as the one that led to this crisis may be impossible to address in a flexible legal system because it subverts the very flexibility on which the legal system relies for remaining up to date.[7] The timeframe of the buildup to the 2008 crisis indicates that even if the antieuphoria features of the law had the highest resistance to change that our legal system can provide, constitutional protection, they still could have succumbed to the pressures that built the bubble.[8]

Section A explores the issue of contagion infecting the real sector after a rational euphoria and crash in the financial sector, and Section B shows how the Great Recession is an illustration of such a contagion. Sections C and D turn to the ramifications for the legal system, assessing the legislative, administrative, and case-law environment of securities law; explore the small room for improvement; but conclude that trusting the legal system in the short run to prevent rational euphorias is futile. In the long term, a desirable change would be to enshrine constitutionally a specialized legislative branch with heightened independence that would have exclusive authority on financial legislation.

A. THE TRANSMISSION OF FINANCIAL CRISES TO THE REAL SECTOR

Euphorias and panics are the one constant companion of financial markets despite modernization, scientific inroads into finance, and technological improvements in the communication and processing of financial information and the structure of markets. The cycle has persisted from late medieval times (e.g., tulip mania) through the 2005–6 mortgage-backed securities bubble and the Great Recession that

[7] As technology, tastes, and socioeconomic conditions change, law needs to change to continue serving society. Inflexible legal systems are not viable in the long term. The Anglo-American common-law systems, as we can infer from the age of their institutions, seem to be especially adaptable, as confirms theory and evidence. Examples of the theoretical work are Nicholas L. Georgakopoulos, *Predictability and Legal Evolution*, 17 INT'L REV. L.& ECON. 475 (1997); Steven Shavell, *Risk Aversion and the Optimality of Attenuated Legal Change*, American Law and Economics Association Annual Meeting (May 17, 2013). Examples of the empirical work are the pieces that constitute the law and finance literature, e.g., La Porta, Lopez-de-Silanes, Shleifer, & Vishny, *Law and Finance*, 106 J. POL. ECON. 1113 (1998); collectively reviewed in Nicholas L. Georgakopoulos, *Statistics of Legal Infrastructures: A Review of the Law and Finance Literature*, 8 AMER. L. & ECON. REV. 62 (2006). An important addition to that literature observes that the resources that each legal system provides to its securities regulator has strong explanatory power for the vitality of its stock market; see Howell E. Jackson and Mark J. Roe, *Public and Private Enforcement of Securities Laws: Resource-Based Evidence*, 93 J. FIN. ECON. 207–38 (2009).

[8] See below.

followed it.[9] For panics to arise, euphorias must precede them, and euphorias seem to be an unavoidable component of the psychology of human interaction, especially in capital markets.

Euphorias need not be entirely irrational. Possibly the only error may be the inaccurate prediction of when a new technology stops contributing significantly to economic growth, that is, when the implementation of a new technology is effectively complete. The seed is an innovation that truly increases productivity. As businesses reap the gains, they show unusual growth. Because adoption of the new technology is gradual, the unusually high growth also appears to be persistent. Adoption of the new technology may reach saturation at some point, and growth will return to its normal level. Even investors who realize that the growth is temporary cannot tell beforehand when it will stop, that is, when the new technology will reach its saturation point.

The result of high growth with an unknown end date influences the pricing of the goods that will form the bubble, usually stocks. Estimates for future economic performance include an assumption of continued growth at the high rate. Applying this estimation to the valuation process produces escalating price increases that continue past the point in time when the new technology reaches saturation and economic growth returns to the normal level. Stock prices continue rising when the economy slows, forming a pricing bubble.

Economists have studied bubbles and crises. From a theoretical perspective, the hurdle to bubbles is that they would produce an opportunity for trading profits. For example, if prices tend to rise every January (as they did[10]), then traders would know to buy at the end of December. This trading would eliminate the unprincipled price change (although the January effect may persist, arguably for behavioral reasons[11]). However, economists have devised mechanisms that produce bubbles (overvaluations) by relying only on pricing information (whereas the month is not) that would not give rise to trading profits (whereas the January effect would).[12] Those are called "intrinsic bubbles." The "rational euphoria" posited here is distinguishable from economists' theories of "intrinsic bubbles" or "rational bubbles." For example, a theory of intrinsic bubbles can rest on the change in dividends, as that of Froot

9 Charles P. Kindleberger and Robert Z. Aliber, MANIAS, PANICS AND CRASHES: A HISTORY OF FINANCIAL CRISES (6th ed. 2011); Charles Mackay, EXTRAORDINARY POPULAR DELUSIONS AND THE MADNESS OF CROWDS (1841).

10 Michael S. Rozeff & William R. Kinney, *Capital Market Seasonality: The Case of Stock Returns*, 3 J. FIN. ECON. 379 (1976) (identifying the January effect); Marc R. Reinganum, *The Anomalous Stock Market Behavior of Small Firms in January*, 12 J. FIN. ECON. 89 (1983); Richard Roll, *Vas ist das? The Turn of the Year Effect and the Return Premia of Small Firms*, 9 J. PORTFOLIO MGMT. 18 (1983).

11 See, e.g., Richard Thaler, *Anomalies: The January Effect*, 1 J. ECON. PERSP. 197 (Summer 1987); Mark Haug & Mark Hirschey, *The January Effect*, 62 FIN. ANALYSTS J. 78, September–October 2006.

12 Kenneth A. Froot & Maurice Obstfeld, *Intrinsic Bubbles: The Case of Stock Prices*, 81 AM. ECON. REV. 1189 (1991).

and Obstfeld. Rational speculators cannot profit from the overvaluation despite the fact that they know proper valuation should rest on actual earnings alone.

The rational euphoria presented here has some similarities to the intrinsic bubble literature but also differences. The similarities of rational euphorias with intrinsic bubbles lie in the overvaluation and in the usual correspondence of new technologies with increases in earnings and dividends. The differences are that intrinsic bubbles assume false valuations, valuations based on erroneous concepts of what drives value. Rational euphorias, however, allow perfectly proper valuation while merely allowing inaccurate foresight about the end of the impact of a new technology on growth. This makes rational euphorias more plausible. Rational euphorias, however, do not seek to preclude the possibility of profitable trading. This does not reduce the plausibility of rational euphorias because of the impossibility of predicting the end of the impact of a new technology on economic growth.

Returning to the mechanism of the rational euphoria, the point is that when the impact of the new technology on industry reaches its saturation point, the acceleration of economic growth ceases. The return to normal growth rates defies the optimistic projections, investors recognize the error of the lofty valuations, and the euphoria collapses. All those caught having borrowed or having lent based on euphoric valuations wake up with a jolt: the borrowers unable to repay and the lenders unable to collect. If the overvaluation was large and widespread, then this malady hits a vast number of businesses and families.

The financial sector is the one most sensitive to this predicament. Financial firms need to collect from failed firms of the real sector, but they are not unique in this. Firms of the real sector also have trouble collecting their bills. The two aggravating factors are that financial firms extend credit as a matter of course and that they have significant borrowing. They provide investment services, meaning that their customers invest through them, to a significant extent as depositors but also as lenders in different guises, such as direct lenders or bond investors. As the euphoria recedes and the financial crisis begins, the widespread financial difficulties are already widely known or anticipated, but unknown is which financial firms have the most exposure to losses. As soon as investors identify the most exposed, they withdraw their (uninsured) deposits and stop lending to the endangered financial firms. The failure of these firms is virtually unavoidable.

In normal economic times, the economic system can easily withstand the failure of a few firms, real or financial. Some failures are even part of the natural casualties of innovation through creative destruction.[13] When a large bubble collapses, however, the number and size of the failed financial firms may be so large that a majority of the financial institutions in an economy may be at risk. In such a case, the danger

[13] The "gale of creative destruction" from competition as the engine of economic growth was identified by Joseph Schumpeter, Can Capitalism Survive? 24 (1978).

arises that the financial collapse may infect the real economy and become a recession or depression.

The businesses of the real sector of the economy depend on the financial system to fund their expenses because their cash fluctuates. When the financial sector experiences a massive shock, financial firms that were lenders (or funders through equity) need to hoard their cash to make up for their losses and do not make loans (or provide equity funding). The result is a "credit crunch" – the borrowing difficulty that a financial crisis produces. A real business that finds itself short of cash is likely unable to find a lender, even if it is sound and would be able to borrow in normal times. Therefore, even healthy businesses may default on their obligations as a result of the crisis and close. Businesses that can pay their expenses still protect themselves from the risky environment by shrinking and reducing their expenses: their purchases from other businesses, their employment rolls, and the wages they pay. These closures and reduced spending begin the vicious cycle of the recession, leading to further reductions in expenses and even less spending.

B. THE 2008 CRISIS AS AN ILLUSTRATION

The Great Recession illustrates this sequence of events. Numerous books and a congressionally authorized commission investigation report agree on the details.[14] Unlike the preceding account of a largely rational euphoria and panic, several authors have treated the bubble that led to the 2008 crisis as a mass delusion.[15] Seeing euphorias and panics as products of rationality should be even more disquieting than attributing them to mass delusions. We cannot expect even wise regulators and hardnosed businesspeople to protect the economy or themselves from such euphorias. A caveat and a ray of hope arise from the story of this crisis, however. Regulators and businesspeople might not have been able to avert the euphoria, but they did mitigate the effect of the crisis, at least in the United States.[16]

[14] See notes 2 and 3.

[15] See, e.g., Robert J. Shiller, The Subprime Solution: How Today's Global Financial Crisis Happened, and What to Do about It 4 (2008) ("The view that the ultimate cause of the global financial crisis is the psychology of the real estate bubble . . . has certainly been expressed before."); see also generally Michael Lewis, The Big Short (W.W. Norton 2010); Gretchen Morgenson & Joshua Rosner, Reckless Endangerment: How Outsized Ambition, Greed, and Corruption Led to Economic Armageddon (2011).

[16] However, Europe has suffered much more. See, generally, Barry Eichengreen, Hall of Mirrors: The Great Depression, The Great Recession, and the Uses-and Misuses-of History (Oxford University Press 2015); Nicholas L. Georgakopoulos, *Lessons from Greco-Multilateralism for Creditors*, 28 Conn. J. Int'l L. 21 (2012); Nicholas L. Georgakopoulos, *PIRG Doldrums: Exit via Overrecapitalization*, 37 Eur. J.L. & Econ. doi 10.1007/s100657-014-9447-y (2014).

i. An Innovation: Improved Securitization

An innovation that fueled the bubble preceding the Great Recession was an improved type of securitization. "Securitization" is the aggregation of obligations that makes them safer as assets than obligations of single firms.[17] The aggregation of obligations creates a diversified group of obligors and reduces the credit risk of the aggregation. The probability that all obligors would fail together is ordinarily minuscule. Leading into the crisis, securitizations would become even safer in various ways, including having an outside guarantee.[18]

Securitization started by aggregating assets of real businesses. For example, the receivables of numerous businesses would be aggregated – securitized – into a fund, shares of which institutional investors would purchase without requiring as great an interest rate or return as they would if they were lending to the individual businesses. The businesses are able to obtain cheaper financing than they would by pledging their receivables as a single borrower. From this perspective, securitization is a true improvement in the business environment because it reduces the cost of capital.

The seed of the trouble was the expansion of securitization to the claims of home mortgage lenders. The claims on homeowners' mortgage payments were securitized into "mortgage-backed securities" and the very similar "collateralized debt obligations."

Other design details sought to further reduce risk. For example, mortgage-backed securities were divided into tranches (slices), with the riskiest tranche assigned to suffer the first losses from any defaults, leaving the safest tranche extremely safe.[19] Their designers made them even safer by adding the guarantee (as a credit default swap) of a large financial institution, all too often AIG. To further increase their appeal, credit rating agencies would rate the resulting securities as extremely safe (AAA). Furthermore, mortgage-backed securities paid a slightly greater interest than other similarly rated securities. This made them very appealing, especially to banks, because they had regulatory reasons to hold securities rated so safe.[20]

[17] See, e.g., Frank S. Alexander, *Mortgage Prepayment: The Trial of Common Sense*, 72 CORNELL L. REV. 288, 329 (1987) ("In 1970 the federal government took the lead in the 'securitization' of mortgages by issuing, through the Government National Mortgage Association (GNMA), the first publicly traded mortgage-backed security."); Christine A. Pavel, SECURITIZATION: THE ANALYSIS AND DEVELOPMENT OF THE LOAN-BASED/ASSET-BACKED SECURITIES MARKETS (1989).

[18] The guarantee usually took the form of a credit default swap. FCIC Report 50 ("AIG [accumulated] a One-Half Trillion Position in Credit Risk").

[19] See Lewis, THE BIG SHORT (describing this structure with detail and unusual clarity).

[20] Thus the reliance of bank regulation on credit ratings has been considered a contributing factor to the crisis. FCIC Report (at xvii: "major firms and investors blindly relied on credit rating agencies"; at xxv: "regulatory capital standards were hinged on them").

ii. The Euphoria

Mortgage lending reached a high of well over four times its level in the 1990s.[21] The flow of money pushed local lenders to make more loans and borrowers to buy more housing than they could otherwise afford, pushing housing prices ever higher, justifying refinancings, buying houses for resale (known as "flipping"), and more lending.[22]

Not only did the government fail to stop the euphoria, it stoked the fire. Politicians of all stripes urged Fannie Mae and Freddie Mac, the quasi-governmental entities that standardized and helped aggregate mortgage loans, to loosen their standards so that more borrowers could share the American dream of home ownership.[23] Some lone regulators tried to stem the tide to no avail.[24] Congress protected credit default swaps, the guarantees that backed securitized home mortgages, from the jurisdiction of regulators who worried.[25]

The arrival of the innovation of securitization to the home mortgage market was initially very desirable because it reduced borrowing cost and increased the amount of capital available for borrowing. At some point, however, a securitization fever took over the banking and housing markets. Instead of serving them, mortgage-backed securities were driving them, meaning that instead of housing demand and pricing being driven by incomes, they started being driven by lenders' demand for mortgage loans. This changed the source of risk for real estate and for many financial institutions. When nonfinancial demand for real estate drove price, then aggregating real estate from many different metropolitan areas provided true diversification; each area had different industries and incomes, was exposed to different natural disasters, and generally had independent sources

21 Mortgages went from an annual rate of about $1 trillion in the 1990s to a high of over $4.5 trillion in 2003. See 2011 MORTGAGE MARKET STATISTICAL ANNUAL, vol. 2, pp. 3–6; Michael Simkovic, *Competition and Crisis in Mortgage Securitization*, 88 IND. L.J. 213, 220 fig. 2 (2013).

22 See *FCIC Report*, pp. 157 et seq.

23 Both the Clinton and Bush administrations with bipartisan support pursued initiatives to facilitate home ownership. See, generally, Alexander S. Bonander, *Note: Fannie Mae, Freddie Mac, and Due-Diligence Failures: Should Comparative Responsibility Be Imposed on a Government-Sponsored Entity's Claims Brought under Sections 11(A) and 12(A)(2) of the Securities Act of 1933?*, 98 IOWA L. REV. 835, 845 (2013) (with further citations); David Skeel, *Making Sense of the New Financial Deal*, 5 LIBERTY U. L. REV. 181, 182 (2011).

24 *Concept Release Concerning Over-the-Counter Derivatives Market*, CFTC Release No. 4142-98, May 7, 1998; Rick Schmitt, *Prophet and Loss – Brooksley Born Warned that Unchecked Trading in the Credit Market Could Lead to Disaster*, STANFORD NEWS, March 2009. See FCIC Report 15-21 (recounting ignored warnings).

25 Ariel Meyerstein, *Transnational Private Financial Regulation and Sustainable Development: An Empirical Assessment of the Implementation of the Equator Principles*, 45 N.Y.U. J. INT'L L. & POL. 487 n. 1 (2013) (Credit default swaps were protected by the Commodity Futures Modernization Act of 2000, H.R. 5660, 106th Cong. [2d. Sess. 2000], enacted as part of the Consolidated Appropriations Act of 2001, Pub. L. No. 106-554, App. E, 114 Stat. 2763 [2000]); Lindsey, Richard R., Testimony of Richard R. Lindsey, Director, Division of Market Regulation, Securities and Exchange Commission, July 24, 1998.

of risk. When the price of real estate became driven by financial demand for mortgage-backed securities, all real estate was exposed to a single risk: the popularity of the new securitization. Thus the risk-reducing effect of diversification designed into mortgage-backed securities disappeared due to their dominance. While securitization seeks to protect against the failure of borrowers, the success of securitization made the failure of borrowers so likely that at the depth of the crisis in 2008, these triple-A-rated mortgage-backed securities became unmarketable and took the label "toxic assets."

iii. Crash! They All Fall Down

The party was fun while it lasted, generating an enormous boom for mortgage brokers[26] and delighting borrowers.[27] However, housing prices relate to the incomes that buyers use to service their debt. While the prices of homes were skyrocketing, incomes were not. The euphoria was unsustainable. Eventually, housing prices started falling.[28] Suddenly the folly of mortgage lending on the expectation of perpetual increases in housing prices became apparent. The borrowers could not be expected to repay; they did not have the necessary income, and their houses no longer had the value to secure the loans. The insurer, AIG, could not cover the large fraction of the US residential loan market that it had guaranteed. Thus the banks found themselves with assets – their securitized claims – that had lost their value. As a result, banks violated their capital requirements or even became insolvent.

By September 2008, what had started as the March failure of Bear Stearns had expanded to infect and knock out Lehman Brothers, Merrill Lynch, AIG, Wachovia, Washington Mutual, Fannie Mae, and Freddy Mac. Citigroup was teetering. Money-market fund investors were on a full run, withdrawing $300 billion from (nongovernment) money-market funds.[29] Lending was frozen: the nonfinancial commercial paper market (which has money-market funds as important participants) had shrunk from about $840 billion to about $560 billion (approximately 33%), as Figure 21.1 illustrates, and bank lending shrunk by 47%.[30] Borrowing was so dysfunctional that debtors as credible as General Electric had to receive financing

26 FCIC Report 13 ("more than 200,000 new mortgage brokers"). 27 *Id.* at 13–14.

28 *Id.* at 17 (by March 2007 housing prices had been declining for a year).

29 Lawrence D. W. Schmidt, Allan G. Timmermann, & Russ Wermers, *Runs on Money Market Mutual Funds*, January 2013, available at http://papers.ssrn.com/sol3/papers.cfm?abstract_id=1784445 (noting withdrawals from money-market funds that did not invest only in government obligations of $300 billion; as the total assets of the non-government money-market funds was about $1.9 trillion, *id.*, table 4; the withdrawals constituted almost 16%). See also note 70 below.

30 Victoria Ivashina & David S. Scharfstein, *Bank Lending during the Financial Crisis of 2008* (July 30, 2009), EFA 2009 Bergen Meetings Paper, available at SSRN: http://ssrn.com/abstract=1297337 (accessed February 15, 2017).

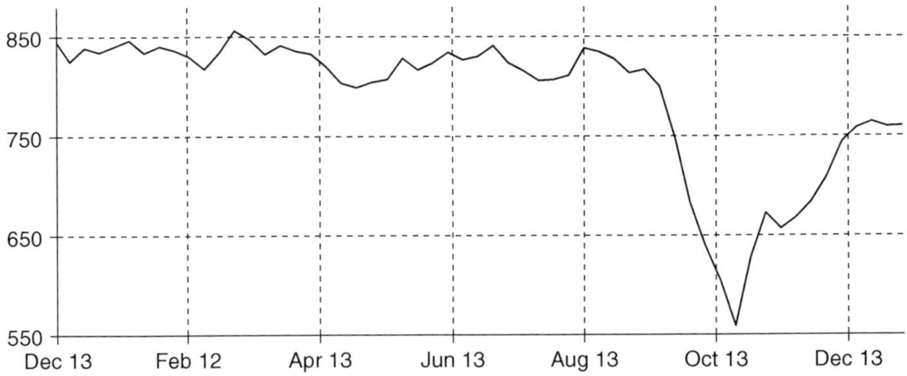

FIGURE 21.1 Outstanding commercial paper from December 2007 to December 2008, nonfinancial, seasonally adjusted, all maturities, weekly data, in billions of US dollars, showing the October 13 date of the meeting. (*Source:* www.federalreserve.gov/data download/.)

from Warren Buffet's Berkshire Hathaway at high interest rates, as did Goldman Sachs.[31] The difficulty that real businesses had in borrowing was the first symptom: the financial crisis had infected the real sector.

iv. The Danger to the Real Sector

The failure of financial firms, painful as it is, is vastly less disruptive than the failure of real firms. Simplified, a financial firm consists of its professionals, its clerical personnel, the premises (usually leased), the computer systems, its capital, and its debtors and creditors. Consider the fate of those on its failure. The pace of change in the information technology (IT) industry limits the value of the computer systems and, therefore, the waste from idling them. The failure of a financial firm means merely that its employees, the landlords who lease space to it, its debtors, and its creditors have to find new matches: new employers, new tenants, new lenders, and new borrowers. The extraordinary mobility of modern capital makes the last two moves, of lenders and borrowers, virtually costless. Employees and landlords may miss several months of compensation, which involves some pain, but the nonclerical employees tend to be skilled, clerical employees can obtain other employment, and the premises tend to easily accommodate

[31] Tom Petruno, *Buffett's Berkshire Hathaway Invests $5 Billion in Goldman Sachs*, BALTIMORE SUN, September 24, 2008, available at http://articles.baltimoresun.com/2008-09-24/news/0809230187_1_buffett-billion-in-goldman-goldman-sachs (accessed February 15, 2017); Steve Lohr, *Buffett's Bet on G.E.: Almost as Good as a Bailout*, N.Y. TIMES, October 1, 2008, available at www.nytimes.com/2008/10/02/business/02electric.html?_r=0 (accessed February 15, 2017).

alternative uses. In the language of industrial organization, this means that compared with real firms, financial firms have fairly little firm-specific financial and human capital. Compared with real firms, financial firms' physical plants are not especially customized, and their employees are capable of being productive in other businesses with little retraining.

Compare this with the consequences of the failure of real firms. If Chrysler or General Motors, for example, were to close, then four consequences would ensue, and their closing would tend to be much graver than that following the failure of a financial business. First, massive factories and other production facilities would remain idle. Finding new users for them, given the specialized structures, would be unlikely. The repurposing of these structures would be a major undertaking. Second, vast numbers of workers with firm-specific skills would be unemployed and difficult to reemploy. Third, numerous suppliers and retailers would find their major, if not only, customer or producer gone, and fourth, governmental units, from national to local, would find their tax revenues shattered and their obligations explicit, such as those for social services and retirement guarantees, as well as implicit, such as those for assisting in the retraining of the unemployed or the repurposing of the idled real estate, sharply higher. In contrast to financial firms, some real businesses have vast amounts of firm-specific human, physical, and financial capital that would dissipate with their closure.

This does not mean that real firms should not be allowed to fail. Failures are necessary adjuncts of the creative destruction of economic competition and innovation.[32] If the economy and the financial sector are in normal conditions, letting real businesses that cannot cover their costs fail is necessary to move their resources to more productive uses and let the obsolete businesses disappear.

However, a credit crunch may cause creditworthy real businesses to fail due to temporary cash shortages. Businesses that have valuable assets but no cash could have survived if they could borrow and pay their obligations, but the credit crunch impedes borrowing.[33] Not only does letting them fail aggravate the crisis, but also the large cost of their failure may not be necessary. A business may be unable to meet its expenses only temporarily due to the crisis. After the crisis, the business may be able to survive indefinitely or, if it is indeed obsolete, may go through an orderly restructuring.

If a financial crisis starts infecting the real sector, businesses start failing due to the crisis rather than their inefficiency. Failing to buttress those businesses allows the financial crisis to expand to the real sector with catastrophic consequences.

32 Schumpeter, Can Capitalism Survive?

33 The credit crunch also reduces the potential buyers for such businesses' assets. Therefore, the credit crunch also harms the squeezed businesses' capacity to convert assets to cash. They can neither borrow nor sell.

v. Emergency Resuscitation

The chairman of the Federal Reserve in 2008 was Ben Bernanke, a Princeton economics professor and scholar of the Great Depression.[34] Along with Treasury Secretary Henry Paulson, former head of Goldman Sachs, he was determined not to let the financial crisis spread to the real sector. The Fed used long-forgotten emergency authority for the first time.[35] Aided by the firepower that Congress eventually gave it through the Troubled Asset Relief Program (TARP)[36] – after voting it down led to an 8.8% point drop in the Standard & Poor's (S&P) 500 Index[37] – Bernanke and Paulson staved off disaster with several measures that included (1) helping real businesses borrow through the commercial paper market, (2) guaranteeing most obligations of most financial institutions, and (3) injecting massive funding into banks so that (a) nobody could fear that they would fail and (b) banks had to start funding businesses in order to cover the cost of the new capital.[38] The massive injection of new funds and the guarantees to banks started at a meeting with the chiefs of all the big banks on October 13, 2008. Figure 21.1 shows how the commercial paper market contracted in September 2008 and how it started recovering in mid-October.

The freeze on lending validates Paulson's claim that the crisis could have developed into a depression with unemployment rates eclipsing those of the Great Depression.[39] The aggressive investment in the economy by the government

[34] See, e.g., Ben S. Bernanke, Essays on the Great Depression (2004).

[35] Ben S. Bernanke, The Federal Reserve and the Financial Crisis at 78 (2013); Richard A. Posner, The Crisis of Capitalist Democracy at 65 (2010).

[36] 12 USC §§ 5211–41 (Suppl. V 2011).

[37] See, e.g., *Defiant House Rejects Huge Bailout; Stocks Plunge; Next Step Is Uncertain*, N.Y. Times p. A1, September 29, 2008, available at www.nytimes.com/2008/9/30/business/30cong.html (accessed February 15, 2017); historical S&P 500 values from finance.google.com. While the contingent capital idea is laudable, it has yet to be implemented and tested in a real crisis. Moreover, it applies only to entities designated as banks. Thus it would fail to stem a panic such as that of 2008. That was triggered by the failure of investment banks (Bear Stearns and Lehman) and produced runs on money-market funds. The contingent capital proposal in Dodd-Frank touches neither.

[38] See Ben Bernanke, The Federal Reserve and the Financial Crisis 78 (2013) ("The Fed provided cash or short term lending to [brokerage houses] ... Commercial paper borrowers received assistance, as did money market funds ... [T]he Fed created some new liquidity programs to help get [the asset backed securities market] started again, which we were successful in doing."); Nicholas L. Georgakopoulos, *PIRG Doldrums*, 37 Eur. J.L. & Econ. doi 10.1007/s10657-014-9447-y (2014).

[39] Henry M. Paulson, Jr., Five Years Later: on the Brink – The New Prologue: A Look Back Five Years Later on What Happened, Why It Did, and Could It Happen Again? 40 (Hachette Digital, 2013) ("Unemployment levels that topped out at 10 percent ... could easily have risen to 25 percent."); N. Gregory Mankiw, Macroeconomics and the Financial System 537 (2011) (quoting Paulson saying, "There was a time when the credit markets had essentially frozen and when blue chip industrial companies were having trouble raising money. I knew then we were on the brink ... We easily could have had unemployment of 25 percent.").

made the crisis into merely a long recession that produced no more than 10% unemployment.[40]

The global economic system was lucky that Bernanke and Paulson were able to douse the crisis despite initial congressional opposition. Clearly, relying on emergency revival techniques is not a sound approach to financial regulation. Financial crises are dangerous, and they remain equally or more dangerous despite the passage of additional regulation.[41] Rather than prevent future bubbles or crises, the regulatory reaction actually reduced the Fed's discretionary powers to resuscitate the economy.[42] Coming back to the regulation of securities markets, the question becomes: what can the design of securities law do to prevent euphorias (and thus panics)? Economists have proposed various other measures, from more and contingent capital for banks (which would convert debt to equity during a crisis to ensure adequate capitalization[43]) to the anachronistic notion of returning to the gold standard (which is procyclical and hinders growth[44]). These remedies, however, are beyond the scope of this chapter. To approach the question of how securities regulation can alleviate euphorias and panics, let us first assess the statutes, the Securities and Exchange Commission (SEC) rules, and the courts' interpretation.

[40] Seasonally adjusted unemployment hit a high of 10% in October 2009, and the raw high was 10.6% in January 2010, Bureau of Labor Statistics, www.bls.gov/webapps/legacy/cpsatab1.htm.

[41] Dodd-Frank Wall Street Reform and Consumer Protection Act, Pub. L. No. 111-203, 124 Stat, 1376 (codified in scattered sections of USC).

[42] Dodd-Frank Act §1101; see also David Skeel, THE NEW FINANCIAL DEAL: UNDERSTANDING THE DODD-FRANK ACT AND ITS (UNINTENDED) CONSEQUENCES 136 (2011) (discussing restrictions).

[43] See Financial Stability Oversight Council, Report to Congress on Study of a Contingent Capital Requirement for Certain Nonbank Financial Companies and Bank Holding Companies, July 2012, available at www.treasury.gov/initiatives/fsoc/studies-reports/Documents/Co%20co%20study[2].pdf (accessed February 15, 2017). Anat Admati and Matin Hellwig argue for a direct return to banks with much less leverage; Anat Admati & Martin Hellwig, THE BANKERS' NEW CLOTHES: WHAT IS WRONG WITH BANKING AND WHAT TO DO ABOUT IT (2014).

[44] Some have argued in favor of a return to the gold standard with the argument that the more fixed supply of gold compared to fiat currencies would tend to reduce the intensity of euphorias and the economic expansion they cause; see, e.g., David Boaz, *Time to Think about the Gold Standard?*, CATO AT LIBERTY, March 12, 2009, available at www.cato.org/blog/time-think-about-gold-standard (accessed February 15, 2017). The gold standard, however, aggravates economic cycles. During the euphoria, people tend to accept others' obligations and do not insist on specie payment, enabling inflation that can easily be greater than well-regulated fiat money. During the contractions, not only do most actors insist on specie payment, but the government also does not have the leeway to foster economic growth. Accordingly, theory and evidence oppose a return to the gold standard; see, e.g., Paul Krugman, *The Gold Bug Variations*, SLATE NOV. 23 1996, available at www.slate.com/articles/business/the_dismal_science/1996/11/the_gold_bug_variations.html (accessed February 15, 2017). For example, the six-year period from 1837 to 1843 saw deflation of −33%. The five-year period from 1843 to 1847 saw inflation of 11%. See Robert C. Sahr, INFLATION CONVERSION FACTORS FROM YEAR 1774 TO ESTIMATED 2026 at 2 (2016) (reporting the deflator of the Bureau of Labor Statistics in 1982 dollars going from 0.096 in 1837 to 0.074 in 1843, a 33% drop and going from 0.074 in 1843 to 0.082 in 1847, an 11% increase), http://liberalarts.oregonstate.edu/sites/liberalarts.oregonstate.edu/files/polisci/faculty-research/sahr/inflation-conversion/pdf/infcf17742016.pdf (archived at) https://perma.cc/7A3F-42TP) (accessed February 15, 2017).

C. THE EFFECTIVE ANTIEUPHORIA COMPONENTS

This section addresses what performed well in the securities law legal system. The securities statutes, the rules thereunder, and the courts' securities law jurisprudence do not bear responsibility for the euphoria that led to the Great Recession. While their antieuphoric effect may have been secondary and minor, they were certainly not procyclical.

i. Statutes

The principal effects of the securities laws are the structure and delay that they impose on the public issuance of securities and the voluminous disclosure they require in both public and private sales, that is, offerings. Whatever other beneficial consequences this structure and delay have, they may also have a minor antieuphoria aspect. The process and the delay do not allow opportunistic rushing to market in reaction to short-term stimuli. The disclosure that securities laws mandate, however, has a more salient effect – although neither their sole nor necessarily central one – in averting euphorias: the extensive disclosure of risk factors, namely, everything that can turn to the disadvantage of the issuer and the holder of the security. Granted, the exact quantification of the risk factors' sobering effect is elusive, and some may dismiss the disclosure of risk factors as legal niceties that buyers in practice ignore. As the euphoria builds up, the attention to cautionary statements tends to shrink. However, even if exuberant buyers ignore the disclosed risk factors, the potential liability[45] probably continues to somewhat deter excessively optimistic statements.

ii. SEC Rules

Two groups of SEC rules have some antieuphoria effect (discussed in the following paragraphs). Then the focus shifts to borrowing limits. The simple improvement of adjusting the lending limits of margin rules could strengthen their antieuphoria effect.

The SEC rules primarily follow the mild antieuphoric pattern imposed by the registration process by carrying it over to private offerings. Private offerings are exempt from SEC registration, but the rules that allow private offerings condition them on a disclosure equivalent to that of the registration statement.[46] The result is not only the disclosure of the accounting statements and business description of the issuer but also the inclusion (in issuers' private placement memoranda) of cautionary language akin

45 The regime that the securities laws establish imposes liability on issuers for misstatements or omissions and an obligation to disclose. Thus, whereas sellers of real goods may stay silent, sellers of financial goods must disclose. The result is that issuers disclose the risk factors that can adversely influence the future performance of the securities being issued.

46 See 17 CFR § 230.502 (2012); see also *id.* § (3) (requiring disclosure in private offerings commensurate to registration statement).

to that required in the registration statement. Thus the private placement rules replicate the regulation process's deterrence of excessively optimistic statements.

A different set of rules also deters overly optimistic statements. Nine of the general rules under the 1933 Act contain various "safe harbors," rules that preclude liability if the issuer complies with their requirements.[47] Brokerage houses discuss securities trading. This conflicts with the restrictions that the registration process (Section 5) of the 1933 Act places on the dissemination of information. This set of nine rules addresses this conflict. Brokerage houses ordinarily (1) may advise their clients about what stocks to buy; (2) they may issue newsletters discussing various trends, industries, or specific equity, debt, or convertible securities; and (c) they enable their clients to trade securities. According to Section 5, however, these actions are potential violations of its prohibitions against offers, prospectuses, and sales. These nine rules preserve the intent of Section 5 by reducing the communications of brokers in ways that tend to curb puffery. For example, Rule 139 allows brokerage houses that are involved in issuances to continue covering the issuer in the brokerage house's newsletters that report about the issuer's industry, provided that they place no emphasis on the issuer.[48] Without this rule, the newsletters could be construed as offers and as prospectuses and would violate Section 5.

iii. Antieuphoric Borrowing Limits

Securities and banking regulators control various limits on borrowing by banks, by securities firms, and by individual investors.[49] Those limits aim at safety, especially during a crisis. The fact that these limits are static, despite our knowledge about euphorias and panics, should be remarkable. Without going into the details of each one of those regulatory environments, all should depend on whether the stock market is euphoric, reducing borrowing in euphoric environments and increasing borrowing in recessions. This would directly reduce the dangers of a crash because investors and financial institutions would become safer, but it would also, indirectly, combat the euphoria by reducing the funds available to the market.

Hinging borrowing limits on the stock market's euphoria is easier said than done, of course. The very premise of free markets, the rationality of individuals and institutions, suggests that euphorias should be difficult to recognize because they should appear rational, as indeed they do. For such borrowing limits to operate

[47] Numbered from Rules 134 to 136; although this seems to indicate three rules, the sequence includes rules numbered with appended letters.

[48] 17 CFR § 230.139(2) ("(iii) The research report includes similar information with respect to a substantial number of issuers in the issuer's industry ... (iv) The analysis regarding the issuer or its securities is given no materially greater space or prominence.").

[49] See Roberta S. Karmel, *The Future of the Securities and Exchange Commission as a Market Regulator*, 78 U. CIN. L. REV. 501, 534 et seq. (2009) (discussing the regulatory history of margin rules and capital requirements).

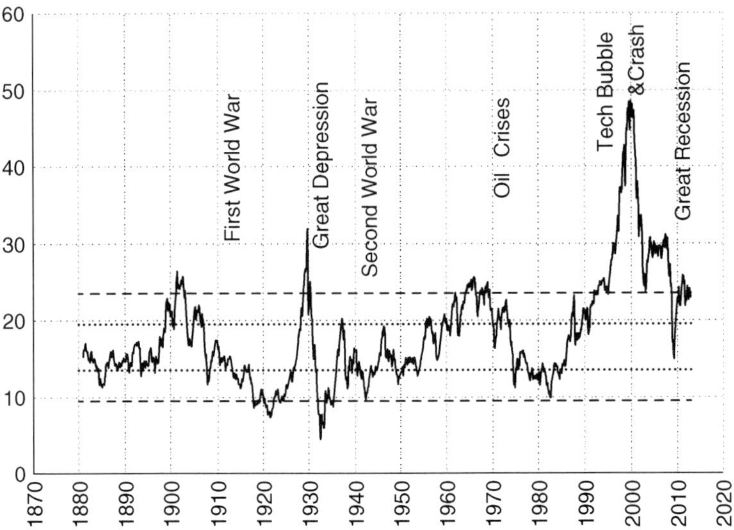

FIGURE 21.2 P/E10 and possible boundaries for margin lending. The boundaries illustrated are 9.5, 13.5, 19.5, and 23.5. The average P/E10 is about 16.5 (~SD 6.5), and the boundaries are in increments of three above and below that.

objectively, an immediate and unambiguous metric is necessary for regulators and investors to know the borrowing limit that will apply.

Unambiguous, immediately visible market-wide metrics of price level do exist. For example, the price-to-earnings (P/E) ratio based on the ratio of the S&P 500 Index to the average of its earnings of the last 10 years, the 10-year trailing-average earnings (P/E10, to which Professor Shiller brings attention), could be an appropriate metric.[50] Figure 21.2 shows the evolution of P/E10 from 1880 to 2010.[51] Its long-run average is close to 16.5 with a standard deviation of approximately 6.5. Values above 23.5 and below 9.5 are quite rare, whereas values above 19.5 and below 13.5 are merely unusual. Using these hurdles can improve borrowing limits.

Margin borrowing and capital adequacy, for example, can operate using four ratios, four limits on borrowing. Each limit would have a different level of permissiveness and would apply depending on the range of values that PE10 takes.

From Figure 21.2 we can see when this example would have produced the narrowest borrowing and the most ample. The rule would have reduced borrowing to the minimum, for example, before the 1929 market crash that was followed by the Great Depression but it would have increased borrowing to the maximum at the depths of the Depression. Such a rule would also have reduced borrowing to

50 See Shiller, *Margin Calls: Should the Fed Step In?*, WALL STREET JOURNAL, April 10, 2000, p. A46; Robert J. Shiller, IRRATIONAL EXUBERANCE 2 (2d ed. 2005).

51 Data available at www.econ.yale.edu/~shiller/data.htm (accessed February 15, 2017).

the minimum before the tech bubble of the late 1990s and before the Great Recession.

Granted, P/E10 is not above criticism. A drawback is that in the case of a revolutionary technology that increases productivity gradually over a long time, P/E10 could rationally stay very high (as it has since the onset of Internet businesses in the mid-1990s, which could be such a technology), producing potentially erroneously restricted credit. If a better yardstick than P/E10 or better defined thresholds and adjustments to borrowing appear, then those should apply. The point is that allowing the borrowing limits to vary dampens euphorias and rekindles market activity in panics.

iv. Court Interpretation

The courts, in their interpretation of securities law, have maintained their antieuphoria aspect. The major interpretive function of the courts is the shaping of the law of securities fraud. The securities acts and the rules that the SEC and the Commodity Futures Trading Commission (CFTC) have promulgated consistently but vaguely prohibit fraud. The courts, with occasional interjections of guidance from the US Supreme Court, have given substance to this vague prohibition. As we have seen throughout this book, in principle, the courts have borrowed the basic concepts from common-law deceit to create a cause of action against fraud. The adaptation is mindful of the differences between the financial markets of securities fraud and the real markets of deceit.

One of the principal deviations of securities fraud from common-law deceit regards reliance. In deceit, reliance acts as a test of causation. Recipients of misrepresentations only have a claim that misrepresentation was the cause of their actions; they have no claim for results of their independent decisions.[52] The recipients of a misrepresentation need to show that the misrepresentation induced their actions effectively under a "reasonable person" standard.[53]

Securities fraud accepts a rebuttable presumption of reliance. The fraud-on-the-market presumption of reliance presumes the reliance of those who traded securities at prices influenced by misrepresentations.[54]

The presumption of reliance enables class actions. Without the presumption, a large fraction of the traders would not be able to show any reliance because their trades were not motivated by information but by decisions to save or consume. Traders who do act on information may be able to show that they relied on the false

[52] See chapters 13-15; see also, generally, Nicholas L. Georgakopoulos, *Frauds, Markets, and Fraud-on-the-Market: The Tortured Transition of Justifiable Reliance from Common Law Deceit to Securities Fraud*, 49 MIAMI L. REV. 671–730 passim (1995).

[53] *See* RESTATEMENT (SECOND) OF TORTS, Deceit sections 525 et seq.

[54] See *Basic, Inc. v. Levinson*, 485 US 224 (1988); see, generally, Nicholas L. Georgakopoulos, *Frauds, Markets, and Fraud-on-the-Market: The Tortured Transition of Justifiable Reliance from Common Law Deceit to Securities Fraud*, at 671–730.

statements directly, and some traders may be able to show indirect, perhaps, reliance. However, since each claimant would have to show reliance, individual questions could well predominate over the common ones, defeating class-action certification. The presumption of reliance ensures that a class action is possible and increases the number of claimants. Furthermore, without the class action, most plaintiffs would not consider individual litigation to be justified. Thus, facilitating class actions and increasing the number of claimants results in more frequent prosecution and greater damages claims.

In other words, the fraud-on-the-market presumption of reliance increases the probability and magnitude of securities fraud liability. As a result, the deterrence of securities fraud is much more intense than the deterrence of common-law deceit.

The intensity of deterrence is an ally in the prevention of bubbles. Consider the two recent bubbles, that of the Internet revolution in the late 1990s (the "dot-com bubble") and the "mortgage-backed security bubble." Neither has produced significant reports of egregiously optimistic statements by corporations benefiting from the bubbles. Rather, when visible statements against the formation of a bubble appeared, as in Greenspan's "irrational exuberance"[55] or Warren Buffett's calling derivatives "financial weapons of mass destruction,"[56] the only attacks came by the press rather than corporate America. Perhaps the intense deterrence of securities fraud performed appropriately or even admirably.

While up to the early 1980s the jurisprudence of securities fraud tended to expand liability, thereafter interpretation tends to restrict it. Thus we see a temporary narrowing of insider trading liability with *Chiarella*,[57] a limit on the obligation to update past statements with *Polaroid*,[58] a somewhat narrow statement of the state of mind requirement in *Ernst and Ernst*,[59] a strict approach to implied private rights of action in several cases,[60] and the elimination of liability for aiding and abetting in *Central Bank of Denver*.[61]

Leaving aside aiding and abetting for closer scrutiny, these interpretations had no relation to the euphoria leading to the 2008 crash. Insider trading was not a contributing factor. The lack of an obligation to update was similarly not involved. Moreover, Congress had created a safe harbor clarifying and expanding the lack of

55 Alan Greenspan, *Remarks at the Annual Dinner and Francis Boyer Lecture of the American Enterprise Institute for Public Policy Research: The Challenge of Central Banking in a Democratic Society* (December 5, 1996), available at www.federalreserve.gov/boarddocs/speeches/1996/19961205.htm (accessed February 15, 2017).

56 Letter from Warren E. Buffett, Chairman of the Board, Berkshire Hathaway Inc., to Shareholders of Berkshire Hathaway, Inc. 15 (February 21, 2003), available at www.berkshirehathaway.com/letters/2002pdf.pdf.

57 *Chiarella v. United States*, 445 US 222 (1982).

58 *Backman v. Polaroid Corp.*, 910 F.2d 10 (1st Cir. 1990).

59 *Ernst & Ernst v. Hochfelder*, 425 US 185, 201 (1976).

60 With, e.g., *S.I.P.C. v Barbour*, 421 U.S. 412 (1975); and *Transamerica Mortg. Advisors, Inc. (TAMA) v. Lewis*, 444 US 11 (1979).

61 *Central Bank of Denver, N.A. v. First Interstate Bank of Denver, N.A.*, 511 US 164, 114 S.Ct. 1439 (1994).

an obligation to update even forward-looking statements.[62] Nor was the euphoria noticeably stoked by misrepresentations that could have been deterred by a more expansive interpretation of the state of mind or of private rights of action beyond securities fraud.

Aiding and abetting liability appears to have had the capacity for some deterrence of the creation of the bubble. The appearance stems from the success that intermediaries had in selling mortgage-backed securities. The borrowers ended up often unable to repay, and the lenders were hammered by the drop in value of the collateral. Yet the intermediaries who created these instruments had some profits, albeit temporary. The intermediaries may well have been more reluctant to issue them if they were subject to aiding and abetting liability.

Even this concern, however, does not withstand scrutiny as a major contributing factor to the euphoria. Even with aiding and abetting liability, securities fraud liability would not be easy to impose on intermediaries. Litigation has revealed that the disclosures at the issuance of these securities did include cautionary language about their sensitivity to concurrent drops of real estate prices in many metropolitan areas.[63] Thus liability for misrepresentation could not arise. Liability for aiding and abetting is, consequently, also very difficult to imagine. The buyers of mortgage-backed securities knew the danger of a real estate drop and accepted that risk.

In sum, the survey of the interpretation of securities fraud jurisprudence does not reveal mistakes that aggravate euphorias or bubbles. The extension of the scope of liability through the fraud-on-the-market presumption of reliance probably has an antieuphoric role, complementing the expansive disclosure that the SEC has established. The only potentially questionable interpretation appears to be that limiting aiding and abetting liability. Nevertheless, the 2008 crisis did not reveal it to have particular importance.

Thus the securities statutes, the rules thereunder, and the courts' securities law jurisprudence do not bear responsibility for the euphoria that led to the Great Recession. The legislative and political establishments, however, do not fare nearly as well, as the next section shows.

D. THE LEAD CULPRIT AND PROPOSED COUNTERMEASURES

The preceding overview of securities regulation did not reveal significant imperfections that may have contributed to the euphoria leading to the financial crisis.

[62] Section 21E, the safe harbor for forward-looking statements, was written into the 1934 Act as part of the Private Securities Litigation Reform Act of 1995, Pub. L. No. 104-67, 109 Stat. 737, 753–5 (codified at 15 USC § 78u-5 [2006]).

[63] Indeed, even the toxic securities that led to the crash had adequate disclosure; see Steven M. Davidoff, *Reading the Fine Print in Abacus and Other Soured Deals*, N.Y. TIMES (November 2, 2012), available at http://dealbook.nytimes.com/2012/11/02/reading-the-fine-print-in-abacus-and-other-soured-deals/ (accessed February 15, 2017). See also discussion in Chapter 6, note 41 and accompanying text.

The borrowing rules have room for improvement, but they do not bear the blame. The main nonregulatory causes of the crash, the governmental support of home mortgage lending and the fever to issue mortgage-backed securities, were not direct results of any single regulatory failure. It is still unclear what measures may have mitigated the bubble. The Financial Crisis Inquiry Commission (FCIC) Report and commentators have pointed to the reliance of bank regulation on rating agencies and their regulation,[64] to the end of the separation of investment banks from commercial banks with the Gramm-Leach-Bliley Act,[65] to the insufficient protection of mortgage borrowers,[66] to the blocking of the FDIC's attempt to regulate credit default swaps and the insulation of credit default swaps from the regulatory authority of the SEC, the CFTC, and state insurance commissioners,[67] and to relaxation of the lending standards led by political pressure by Fannie Mae and Freddie Mac.[68] Yet each one of these alleged errors could neither cause the euphoria nor would its repair have prevented it. Even the separation of investment banks from commercial banks can be exonerated by pointing out, first, that the several financial crises that occurred during their separation[69] show that the separation did not eliminate crises and, second, that the crash of the dot-com crisis occurred after the end of the separation without creating a significant depression danger.[70] The separation of commercial from investment banking was not – and perhaps no longer is – related to the transformation of financial crises into credit crunches. In the 2008 crisis, that transformation happened through money-market funds.

64 See note 20.

65 FCIC Report 55; see also, e.g., Michael Simkovic, *Competition and Crisis in Mortgage Securitization*, 88 IND. L.J. 213, 256 (2013).

66 See, generally, e.g., Nestor M. Davidson, *New Formalism in the Aftermath of the Housing Crisis*, 93 B.U. L. REV. 389, 396 (2013).

67 See note 25. 68 See note 23.

69 The National Bureau of Economic Research (NBER) lists 13 recessions after the Great Depression. The Great Recession reduced production (GDP) by 5.1%. Greater or comparable reductions came from the recessions of 1937–8 (−18.2%), 1945 (−12.7%), 1953 (−2.6%), 1958 (−3.7%), 1973–5 (−3.2%), and 1981–2 (−2.7%). Although associated with smaller recessions, one should also consider important financial crises such as the savings and loan crisis of the early 1990s (GDP reduction of 1.4%) and the crash of the tech bubble in the early 2000s (−0.3%). National Bureau of Economic Research, *US Business Cycle Expansions and Contractions*, available at www.nber.org/cycles/cyclesmain.html.

70 The collapse of the tech bubble (dot-com bubble) is illustrative of the key role of lending institutions in the contagion into the real sector. The contagion at the collapse of the mortgage-backed securities bubble occurred when a run occurred on the money-market funds, which had taken a central role in business lending. The collapse of the tech bubble neither produced a run on any financial institution nor otherwise constrained lending to businesses. The lesson from the juxtaposition of the two crises is that money-market funds made Glass-Stagall's separation of banking less important but that measures to prevent runs on money-market funds and to prevent them from having investments that are exposed to financial crises should be at the center of our regulatory attention; however, that has not happened. See N. Gregory Mankiw, MACROECONOMICS AND THE FINANCIAL SYSTEM 549 fig. 19-2 (2011 Worth Publishers, New York); and Schmidt, Timmerman and Wermers, *Runs on Money Market Mutual Funds*, 203 (noting that depositors withdrew $300 billion from prime money-market funds in mid-September 2008 after the Lehman bankruptcy).

While each piece of regulatory relaxation may neither have caused nor could its reversal have averted the crisis, their aggregation reveals two problems. First, the absence of a financial crisis with a strong potential to influence the real sector since the Great Depression allowed the gradual relaxation of regulatory safeguards that slightly increased the probability of a financial crisis. Second, the successful efforts of financial entrepreneurs to circumvent regulation lend a futility to legislative solutions. Again, the 2008 crisis illustrates this.

The 2008 crisis underlines what the Great Depression had already taught: that the path by which a financial crisis infects the real sector is through the financial institutions that provide short-term lending to businesses. Before the Great Depression and until the 1970s, those institutions were the banks. In the 2008 crisis, they were the money-market funds. The regulation of commercial banks, the Federal Deposit Insurance Corporation (FDIC) guarantee of their deposits, and the extraordinary capacity of the FDIC to take over a failing bank and maintain its liquidity all intended to insulate real lending from the panic of financial crises. Money-market funds do not have similar safeguards and experienced a run that led to the credit freeze of September 2008.[71] Despite that several banks were still solvent, businesses could still not borrow because banks were no longer equipped to so lend; short-term borrowing had moved away from banks and was done by money-market funds, mostly though the commercial paper market.

The SEC has only forced the money-market funds that have institutional investors to move to a fluctuating value.[72] Arguably, other regulators, especially the Financial Stability Oversight Council (FSOC), may further regulate money-market funds.[73] Regulating money-market funds does not solve the larger problem, however. Depositors moved to mutual funds from banks because the safety and the regulatory expenses of banks made them uncompetitive. Money-market funds were able to take a little more risk and have smaller expenses so as to offer a slightly higher interest rate to depositors. Regulating money-market funds will only offer a short-term solution. In the long term, nothing prevents a repeat: the development of yet another alternative vehicle for savings that would again offer slightly greater returns at slightly greater risk. Neither banks nor regulated money-market funds would be able to compete with the new alternative. Depositors would gradually move. The financial power of the new alternative would attract real sector businesses to borrow from it instead of borrowing from banks or money-market funds. Eventually, the cycle would close, with the new alternative being in a position to transmit a financial crisis to the real sector.

71 *Id.*; also see Figure 21.1 and accompanying text.

72 See SEC, *Money Market Fund Reform*, Release No. 33-9616, October 14, 2014 (requiring institutional money market funds "to sell and redeem shares based on the current market-based value of the securities in their underlying portfolios").

73 But see Eric D. Roiter, *Should Money Market Funds Be Designated as "SIFIs"?*, 31 *REV. BANKING & FIN. L.* 749 (2012) (arguing that the FSOC should not designate money-market funds as systemically important financial institutions).

In sum, the defects of regulation leading into the 2008 financial crisis were numerous but small. The human errors, however, were legion. Disquietingly, one of the main weaknesses of the regulatory regime is its flexibility, not so much of the courts or regulators but that of legislators. Legislators, by constitutional design, are responsive to popular opinion and responded to the popular exuberance. Establishing any legal regime at the aftermath of a crisis is pointless if it will be dismantled or circumvented when the euphoria takes hold.

The observation of the importance of legislative drift raises three issues that the following subsections engage. First, since crises continue to produce legislative reactions, an assessment of the recent ones is warranted. Second, an assessment is necessary of the means to reduce legislative discretion and avoid the legislative weakening during euphorias. This bifurcates into two explorations: one of the effectiveness of constitutional protection and one of the plausibility of redirecting financial legislative authority.

i. Unproductive Legislative Reactions

The futility of using law to avert euphorias understates the true problem. Not only is the legislature willing to weaken protections at the time of euphorias, but the legislature also reacts to crises with poorly guided laws. This is especially apparent in regulatory responses to the last few financial crises. The Great Recession brought the Dodd-Frank Act of 2010, and the collapse of the dot-com bubble that took down Enron and WorldCom brought the Sarbanes-Oxley Act of 2002. Any support they have received from the academy or practice has been scattered.[74] Instead, strong has been their condemnation.[75] Sarbanes-Oxley has been cogently accused of increasing the personal risk to being a senior executive and reducing the ability of young companies to make initial public offerings (IPOs).[76] Dodd-Frank is mocked for being longer than the Scriptures[77] and pointless. Consider the change to the emergency powers of the Federal Reserve that Dodd-Frank brought. In the 2008 crisis, the Fed was able to use its emergency powers to effectively guarantee the entire financial system and forcibly over-capitalize banks.[78] Instead of thanking the Fed for averting another Great

[74] See, e.g., Peter C. Kostant, *From Lapdog to Watchdog: Sarbanes-Oxley Section 307 and a New Role for Corporate Lawyers*, 52 N.Y.L. SCH. L. REV. 535 (2007–8).

[75] See, e.g., Roberta Romano, *The Sarbanes-Oxley Act and the Making of Quack Corporate Governance*, 114 YALE L.J. 1521–1604 (2005).

[76] *Id.*

[77] See William Brodsky, *The Multi-Purpose JD: How My Law Degree Helped Me in My Career in My Business*, University of Chicago Podcast, www.law.uchicago.edu/audio/by/title/william_brodsky_the_multi-purpose_jd_how_my_law_degree_helped_me_in_my_career_in_business. Strictly speaking, the Dodd-Frank Act is only longer than the New Testament, which at 181,253 words is a bit more than half the 354,668 words of the Dodd-Frank Act.

[78] See note 38.

Depression that could have produced over 25% unemployment,[79] the legislature sought to control its apparently excessive power to "bail out" banks. The result is a prohibition against the Fed providing emergency financing to any institution that has not been declared systemically important by a new body, the Financial Stability Oversight Council.[80] The new regime is, at best, pointless but, at worst, catastrophic.

The new regime is catastrophic if it operates according to its superficial reading because it would prevent the actions that saved the economy from chaos in 2008. At calm times, very few institutions have the capacity to topple the financial system by failing. Thus only those very few institutions are systemically important. From this perspective, very few of the big institutions that the Fed backed during the crisis could receive support – the rest would not have been declared systemically important. In a replay of 2008 under this regime, the Fed would have been able to do much less than it did. The credit freeze that followed the failure of Lehman may not have thawed and a major depression may not have been averted.

The optimistic replay of the 2008 crisis under the Dodd-Frank regime would consider that the Financial Stability Oversight Council (FSOC) would be actively involved and recognize that, as panic grips the markets, more institutions become systemically important. Under the most optimistic version of this replay, the FSOC would have declared as systemically important all the institutions that the Fed actually helped in the 2008 crisis – including all banks, all money-market funds, and all businesses that borrow at the commercial paper market.[81] Then Dodd-Frank would have had no delaying effect. A difference exists, however. Instead of a single collective body having the capacity to save the economy in a crisis (which used to be the Fed), Dodd-Frank produces two collective bodies that both need to act with wisdom and foresight to contain a crisis. The danger that their opinions would diverge in a true crisis may be small, in part, because some overlap of the FSOC membership with the (offices of the) protagonists who saved the economy in 2008 exists[82] and, in part, for the same reason that would have persuaded a single collective body, like the Fed alone, to agree to act: a truly severe crisis may be necessary and sufficient to align political opponents. However, the danger of disagreement exists, and we have no reason to believe that would help the economy exit a crisis.

79 Quoted in N. Gregory Mankiw, Macroeconomics and the Financial System 537 (2011).

80 Dodd-Frank Act § 111 ("Financial Stability Oversight Council established"). The criticism here of Dodd-Frank is parallel to that by Hal S. Scott, Connectedness and Contagion: Protecting the Financial System from Panics (2016).

81 See note 38.

82 The FSOC has 10 voting members; Dodd-Frank Act § 111. The Treasury Secretary is a member and chairs it. The chair of the Fed and that of the FDIC are also members. Thus Paulson, Bernanke, and Bair would have participated in the FSOC if Dodd-Frank was already in effect in 2008. However, Tim Geithner, chief of the New York Federal Reserve Bank, was also involved and would not be included in the FSOC unless he were the independent member of it.

The verdict on the FSOC will have to await a true crisis rather than a hypothetical reenactment. Its present evaluation can only speculate along the lines of political economy. The critical issues are if and when aggressive resuscitation of the economy will occur. Four possibilities exist. The possibility that the FSOC never decides to allow aggressive resuscitation of the economy by the Fed is the pessimistic alternative. Otherwise, if the FSOC were to swing in favor of aggressive resuscitation of the economy at the same time that the Fed would have swung, then the addition of the FSOC in the decision sequence is pointless. If the FSOC swung in favor of aggressive resuscitation before the Fed, that would have no effect. Because Fed action is necessary for resuscitation, the Fed will only take aggressive action when it swings in favor of aggressive action.[83] Finally, if the FSOC swings in favor of aggressive resuscitation later than the Fed does, then the Dodd-Frank Act will have merely delayed resuscitation.

Consider the principal positions that have appeared in the press about the Fed's reaction to the crisis. Some factions claim that bailing out financial institutions that were complicit in causing the crisis was wrong. Presumably those factions would favor the pessimistic scenario of the FSOC never allowing aggressive action, which would lead to a disastrous repeat of the Great Depression. Most other factions seem to agree that the Fed acted too late.[84] For them, the Dodd-Frank dynamic of never accelerating action but possibly delaying or negating it is a step in the wrong direction. The cynical way to restate this is that the politicians with Dodd-Frank punished the Fed and the economy for a financial crisis for which the politicians are the most culpable party.

To the Dodd-Frank Act's evaluation juxtapose the passage of the JOBS Act at its heels.[85] Rather than strengthen securities regulation to protect investors, the JOBS Act weakens it. The JOBS Act exempts from the 1933 Act's registration requirements and the securities laws' tight control of advertisement offerings by corporations with sales up to $1 billion, provided that the sales are to accredited investors.[86] While in

[83] The members of the FSOC besides the Treasury Secretary, the chairman of the Fed, and the head of the FDIC are the chairs of the SEC, the CFTC, the National Credit Union Administration Board, the director of the Federal Housing Finance Agency, the Comptroller of the Currency, the director of the Consumer Financial Protection Bureau, and an independent member. Arguably, they may tend to have less of an overview of the economic system and would tend to be less likely than the Fed to pursue early action.

[84] Arthur E. Wilmarth, Jr., *The Dodd-Frank Act's Expansion of State Authority to Protect Consumers of Financial Services*, 36 J. CORP. L. 893, 899 & n. 36 (2011); Patricia A. McCoy, Andrey D. Pavlov, & Susan M. Wachter, *Systemic Risk through Securitization: The Result of Deregulation and Regulatory Failure*, 41 CONN. L. REV. 1327, 1347 (2009); see also Sudeep Reddy, *Currents: Fed Faces Grilling on Consumer-Protection Lapses*, WALL ST. J., December 2, 2009, at A22 (reporting that "many lawmakers and consumer advocates" viewed the Fed's reactions as "too little too late").

[85] Jumpstart Our Business Startups Act of 2012, Pub. L. No. 112-106, § 501, 126 Stat. 306, 325 [hereinafter JOBS Act].

[86] The JOBS Act expands the private offering exemption unambiguously by giving statutory authority to the exemption for small offerings (by adding to Section 4 of the 1933 Act: "Offers and sales exempt

other respects the JOBS Act correctly seeks to alleviate the burden of Sarbanes-Oxley on small business, the effect of the advertisement exemption is that if Bernie Madoff ran an operating company, like WorldCom, he could advertise to accredited investors and sell an unlimited amount of equity securities to not more than 1,999 of them without ever having to be audited.[87]

In hindsight, politicians bear the lion's share of the blame for the crisis: directly for promoting mortgage financing, indirectly for the legal lenience that enabled its risk, and for further aggravating the regulatory system in its wake. This is not the result of any wrongdoing, sacrifice to special interests, or some defect of election finance but the natural consequence of the design of the political system that makes the legislature responsive to popular opinion. It should be no surprise that Congress acts in a procyclical manner; Congress by design is sensitive to the concerns of the electorate, especially the House of Representatives, which is on a two-year election cycle. Congress will not interrupt a euphoria[88] or spend at the

under [Rule 506 on small offerings] shall not be deemed public offerings ... as a result of general advertising or general solicitation") as long as the issuer takes reasonable steps to ensure that purchasers are accredited investors. While a superficial reading of Rule 506 would indicate that the maximum number of offerees is 35, Rule 501(e)(1)(iv) excludes accredited investors from that count.

87 The JOBS Act also increases to 2,000 the number of shareholders that triggers an obligation to comply with the securities laws' reporting requirements; the JOBS Act also increases the assets required to $10 million from $1 million. The JOBS Act achieves this by amending Section 12(g)(1)(A) of the 1934 Act.

88 Indeed, the political reaction to Greenspan's prescient warning about the dot-com bubble was negative. See, e.g., Richard W. Stevenson, *Republican Senate Chief Questions the Fed*, N.Y. Times, December 8, 1996 (quoting Senator and Republican Majority Leader Trent Lott being "a little bit nervous about the degree of independence" of the Fed in reaction to Greenspan's "irrational exuberance" speech on December 5, 1996; see note 55), available at www.nytimes.com/1996/12/09/business/republican-senate-chief-questions-the-fed.html (accessed February 15, 2017).

However, President Bill Clinton's reaction to a request to comment on the Fed's concerns explicitly agrees with the thesis of this chapter that politicians' "job" is to deal exclusively with the real sector (ergo, leaving the financial sector to independent specialists). The language is worth an extensive quote:

> *I don't comment on the Fed's decisions* ... I'll tell you an interesting story. When the market fell in '87, by blind accident, when the market closed, the then wealthiest man in America, Sam Walton, was sitting in my office in Little Rock in the Governor's office. Just by pure coincidence. He was there on business. He came to see me, and we were sitting there at 4 o'clock in the afternoon, or whenever it was, when the market closed in New York, so he called, and I said, "Sam, how much money did you lose today?" He said, "A billion dollars on paper." I said, "What do you think about it?" He said, "I think tomorrow I'm going to get in my airplane and fly to a little town in Tennessee where they're opening a new Wal-Mart, and if the pick-ups and the cars show up and people get out and buy goods, America's all right. This is a Main Street economy." ... *My job is to keep the underlying fundamentals sound* so that tomorrow in all those little towns across America, people can get up and go to work and go [to] the store and buy something.

Excerpts from the President's News Conference at the White House, N.Y. Times, December 14, 1996, available at www.nytimes.com/1996/12/14/us/excerpts-from-the-president-s-news-conference-at-the-white-house.html?pagewanted=all (accessed February 15, 2017) (emphasis added).

bleakest time to end a crisis (as its initial rejection of TARP shows). The chief lesson of the 2008 financial crisis ought to be that politicians should not tamper with finance.

The obvious avenue for a movement in the direction of restricting political meddling with finance is to elevate the authority necessary for changing financial regulation. Two avenues present different prospects for reducing Congress's procyclical tendency.

ii. Futility of Constitutional Protection

Addressing the issue that politicians should not tamper with finance requires a constitutional rearrangement. The more obvious change would be to enshrine financial regulation in the constitutional text, requiring a constitutional amendment to change financial regulation. That is explored here. Section D.iii will explore the more plausible but radical alternative of reallocating legislative authority over finance.

Giving antieuphoria rules constitutional authority would impede and delay their repeal. For example, if all financial regulation until 1970 had constitutional authority, money-market funds would still have arisen,[89] but Congress could not have repealed Glass-Steagall's separation of commercial and investment banking with the Gramm-Leach-Bliley Act in 1999,[90] and Congress would not have been able to remove from the CFTC the authority to regulate credit default swaps in 2000.[91] Thus constitutional authority of financial regulation could have had some positive effect.

However, two drawbacks appear. First, merely giving constitutional authority to existing financial regulation would not prevent further legislative interference in finance. It would not have prevented Sarbanes-Oxley, and it would not have prevented the promotion of home borrowing. Since the promotion of home borrowing was the principal culprit for the euphoria, it is doubtful that the crisis would have been averted. Moreover, continuing the hypothetical of constitutional authority, it would not have prevented Dodd-Frank either. Moreover, Congress would still need to act in the depth of the crisis by approving TARP, which Congress almost failed to do. The first drawback of constitutional authority is that it does not prevent further legislative errors.

89 The first money-market fund was founded in 1972. See *Gartenberg v. Merrill Lynch Asset Mgmt., Inc.*, 694 F.2d 923 (2d Cir. 1982); SEC, Valuation of Debt Instruments and Computation of Current Price per Share by Certain Open-End Investment Companies, Release No. Ic-13380 (July 11, 1983) (Money-market funds may maintain constant value provided they invest in high-quality short-term obligations.). Thomas W. Andrews, *Termination of Section 36(B) Actions by Mutual Fund Directors: Are the Watchdogs Still the Shareholders' Best Friends?*, 50 Fordham L. Rev. 720 (1982) ("[A]n industry comprising 54 funds with assets of $6.8 billion in 1978 [in 1982] encompasses 162 funds managing assets totaling $186.8 billion.") (footnotes omitted).

90 Gramm-Leach-Bliley Act of 1999, Pub. L. No. 106-102, 113 Stat. 1338 (codified at 15 USC §§ 6801 6809).

91 See note 25.

The second drawback of constitutional authority is that it may well be repealed. In the context of the 2008 crisis, the timeframe of the relaxation of regulation spanned from the early 1970s, when money-market funds took hold, to the 2002–4 encouragement toward Fannie Mae lending. Given this 30-year time span and persistent relaxation of rules, even constitutional protection could have been repealed. Various rules have been given constitutional authority only to be later denuded of it, the chief example being Prohibition and its repeal.

Constitutional authority thus would not eliminate further legislative interference and therefore may have been insufficient to avert the crisis and other legislative mistakes. Moreover, even if we were to consider constitutional protection the appropriate change, the slow buildup of the euphoria shows that the euphoria could produce the constitutional countermeasure of a repealing amendment. Furthermore, constitutional-level protection would have no effect on technological change; it would have not prevented the development of money-market funds. For effective protection against euphorias and legislative mismanagement of finance, a more dramatic change is necessary, one that will avoid Congress's procyclical tendencies, demonstrated in the 2008 crisis: Congress built the crisis up by jumping on the home financing bandwagon, then showed fear to spend to reverse it, and hurried to overregulate in its wake.

iii. Exploring Redirecting Financial Legislative Authority

The preceding assessment of the legislative reaction as procyclical and wasteful and the pointlessness of constitutional protection seems bleak. The current constitutional structure does not and will not produce safety against euphorias and crises. The satisfactory performance of the courts and the Federal Reserve, however, suggest that branches with more independence may react better. Although true immunity to euphorias is unattainable, any movement toward greater capacity for countercyclical action would be an improvement. Thus the long-term desirable change is toward a constitutional reallocation of legislative authority over finance away from Congress and toward a body with financial expertise and true independence.

The Secretary of the Treasury does not have any independence but performed admirably in the crisis. This may be an accident due to the specific person. According to his book, Paulson requested some independence at the time of his appointment, the president accepted, and apparently respected that commitment.[92] However, the Secretary of the Treasury could have greater

[92] See Paulson, ON THE BRINK, end of chaps. 2 and 3 (listing the "asks" of Paulson: "In addition to being the administration's primary economic adviser and spokesman ... to replace political appointees, and bring in [his] own team, and to have access to the president on a par with the secretaries of Defense and State ... to chair the economic policy lunch held at the White House.").

independence, implicitly or by design. For example, the Secretary of the Treasury could achieve this independence if removal required a specific supermajority vote of the Senate.

The unlikely ideal, essentially, would be a major constitutional amendment creating a new legislative branch, a branch that would have exclusive authority over financial regulation and would not be subject to the short-term interests of legislatures that are elected with the current frequency – the two-year term of representatives.[93] If the new branch were to be elected directly, its members' terms should well exceed those of senators and should be more staggered.[94] If it were to have appointed members, their terms should be very long, making it effectively a cross between the Federal Reserve and the federal courts. The Federal Reserve has the expertise and some independence, but its independence is limited and it has no constitutionally exclusive authority. The federal courts have complete independence. Although the courts do not have the financial expertise, their performance was unimpeachable.

More realistic would be a tacit reallocation of authority, akin to a "constitutional moment."[95] Precedent exists: Congress has respected the authority of the Federal Reserve over monetary policy despite that nothing in the Constitution requires that. Similarly, Congress could continue the practice that the Dodd-Frank Act arguably

93 This proposal is very different from the various proposals for balanced-budget amendments (BBAs). Under most such proposals, neither the Federal Reserve nor Congress would have been able to take the forceful measures to stem the panic that they took; see note 38 and the accompanying text. The objective is to preserve the ability for fiscally expansionist policies for ending and exiting from crises but to prevent the lenience that leads to euphorias and the unwise reactions to crises. By contrast, most BBA proposals would bring a procyclical result because the ample tax receipts of boom years would enable more government spending and the reduced tax receipts of recessions would restrict spending, further aggravating them. A recent call for a BBA came from R. Glenn Hubbard & Tim Kane, *Republicans and Democrats Both Miscalculated*, N.Y. TIMES, August 11, 2013, available at www.nytimes.com/2013/08/12/opinion/republicans-and-democrats-both-miscalculated.html (accessed February 15, 2017) (trying to overcome this procyclical tendency by averaging the tax receipts of the last five years, which would have allowed neither TARP nor any other expansionary measures). See also Shane Nichols, *A Balanced Budget Amendment Fit for the Constitution: The Elimination of Partisanship and Substantive Provisions*, 46 J. MARSHALL L. REV. 583, 584 & nn. 6 and 7 (2013) (containing citations to the political history of BBAs and academic commentary).

94 Members of the SEC, FDIC, and CFTC, which have five members each and five-year terms, are staggered by year so that one-fifth is appointed each time. The Senate, with six-year terms and biannual elections, is effectively staggered in thirds. As the number of staggered fractions increases, the independence of the body also increases because a smaller fraction can be replaced in each election. For example, if a body were staggered in two halves, half its members would be strongly influenced by popular opinion. A body with financial authority should be staggered in sixths so that only one-sixth of its members would be directly influenced by the current mood.

95 See, generally, Daniel Taylor Young, *Note: How Do You Measure a Constitutional Moment? Using Algorithmic Topic Modeling to Evaluate Bruce Ackerman's Theory of Constitutional Change*, 122 YALE L.J. 1990 et seq. (2013) (explaining Bruce Ackerman's theory of constitutional moments).

sets of not making rules in the financial arena directly but instead delegating their creation to the various agencies. Such a practice, along with the extension of the terms of the members of the agencies and some increased independence for the Secretary of the Treasury, could result in an effectively full delegation of financial legislative authority to bodies that would be independent enough to act countercyclically.

Large as this change may appear, similar major constitutional changes have occurred in the financial (and even more in the nonfinancial) area. Consider from the perspective of the early nineteenth century the problem that gold coinage is procyclical, tending to aggravate economic swings.[96] A strict constitutional interpretation would not authorize the printing of paper currency nor the elimination of its convertibility to gold.[97] A proposal to switch to a paper currency without the possibility of conversion to gold would have seemed absurd, but it is now the norm. The removal of financial authority from the legislature has the same nature of seeming unattainable but, being sensible, may similarly materialize almost unexpectedly.

E. CONCLUSION: SECURITIES LAW IN THE SOMBER UNAVOIDABILITY OF EUPHORIAS

Financial markets are a great gift to productivity. This gift, however, comes with the occasional euphorias that lead to financial crises with potentially devastating consequences. Technological innovations that are absorbed gradually and leave unpredictable the end of their boost to productivity create a predisposition toward a bubble. The 2008 crisis could be an example of such a rational bubble. The financial crisis could have crippled the economic system if it spilled into the real sector, but was abated by the forceful actions of the Fed, the Treasury, and the FDIC. In 2008, the world financial system had the good luck that their radically aggressive measures averted the transmission of the financial crisis to the real sector. As large and terrifying as the crisis was, it revealed no major gap in

[96] See, e.g., Richard Sylla, *Political Economy of Supplying Money to a Growing Economy: Monetary Regimes and the Search for an Anchor to Stabilize the Value of Money*, 11 THEORETICAL INQUIRIES IN LAW 1 at 7 (2010) (discussing how deflations in a gold standard are exacerbated by an additional incentive to hoard gold, how the opposite is true during inflation, with citations to historical evidence). For example, the six-year period from 1837 to 1843 saw deflation of −33%. The five-year period from 1843 to 1847 saw inflation of 11%. See Robert C. Sahr, *Inflation Conversion Factors from Year 1774 to Estimated 2026* at 2 (2016) (reporting the deflator of the Bureau of Labor Statistics in 1982 dollars going from 0.096 in 1837 to 0.074 in 1843, a 33% drop, and from 1843–7 going from 0.074 to 0.082, an 11% increase), available at http://liberalarts.oregonstate.edu/sites/liberalarts.oregonstate.edu/files/polisci/faculty-research/sahr/inflation-conversion/pdf/infcf17742016.pdf (archived at https://perma.cc/7A3F-42TP, accessed February 15, 2017). See also note 44.

[97] See, generally, Gerard N. Magliocca, *The Gold Clause Cases and Constitutional Necessity*, 64 FLA. L. REV. 1243 (2012).

financial regulation. To the extent that any regulatory culprits appear, they are a series of small changes, a gradual legislative relaxation of regulation that is part of the cycle of optimism that forms the euphoria.[98] The only countermeasure to legislative procyclicality is to move financial legislative authority to a body that is better insulated from political pressure so as to have the independence for the countercyclical approach that public finance requires. Even this would be no panacea: experts with independence *can* be infected by euphorias.

[98] Other research draws attention to the cycle of underregulation before crises and overregulation after them. The point made here is distinguishable in showing that the underregulation that accompanies a slow-building euphoria can negate most antieuphoria features of securities law. The research on the cycle of under- and overregulation proposes delayed implementation of relaxations and tightenings of the law, but when the issue is a slowly building euphoria, then any delay may not be sufficient. See, e.g., Larry E. Ribstein, *Bubble Laws*, 40 HOUS. L. REV. 77–97 (2003); Roberta Romano, *The Sarbanes-Oxley Act and the Making of Quack Corporate Governance*, 114 YALE L.J. 1521–1604 (2005). Accepting that the recent legislative interventions, Dodd-Frank and the JOBS Act, have been wasteful suggests that delayed implementation is inferior to the proposal here of moving legislative authority to a more independent body that may never have enacted those.

APPENDIX

Informed Trading Optimization and Proof

This Appendix first describes the example that produced Figure 18.2, assuming that informed traders have determined how to maximize their profits. Then the second section establishes the solution for the informed traders' optimization over any number of trades.

A. EXAMPLE OF INFORMED TRADING OVER MANY TRADES

The example has three main components: (1) the trading, (2) the estimate of future competition, and (3) the actual spread of information. Informed traders trade in sequence using their optimization process, as described in Section B of this Appendix.

Informed traders estimate the probability with which competitors will get the information and take future trades so that the optimizing trader does not trade. In the example, the insider estimates the probability of trading in every jth subsequent trade at $p_j = 1 - [(j-1)/n]^2$, where j is the number of the trade and n is the number of trades, in the example, 31. More traders, however, enter when the insider still expects to be able to trade alone with 80% probability, at trade 15. Thereafter, three more traders enter, and all four know this. Therefore, each has a 25% probability of making any subsequent trade.

Price before informed trading starts at p_0 = \$10, whereas the information shows that value is v = \$5. The liquidity of the market is such that it takes a trade of 1,000 shares to move price by \$1, making the liquidity parameter $\lambda = 0.001$.

The following tables show the optimal trades, the corresponding price differences, and the profit per trade under the two scenarios, one where insider trading is not prohibited and one where it is and, therefore, trading begins at trade 15.

Table A.1 shows the sequence of trades when insider trading is not prohibited. Trading starts as soon as the insider obtains the information, at trade 1. Although

TABLE A.1 *Trading Sequence with No Prohibition*

Trade	Size	Price diff.	Profit
1	444.9	$4.56	$2,026.57
2	444.1	$4.11	$1,825.58
3	440.8	$3.67	$1,617.81
4	433.6	$3.24	$1,403.49
5	421.4	$2.82	$1,186.39
6	403.4	$2.41	$973.00
7	379.5	$2.03	$771.21
8	349.9	$1.68	$588.71
9	315.8	$1.37	$431.52
10	278.4	$1.09	$302.94
11	239.5	$0.85	$203.27
12	200.9	$0.65	$130.13
13	164.2	$0.48	$79.38
14	130.6	$0.35	$46.10
15	134.8	$0.22	$29.39
16	83.3	$0.13	$11.23
17	51.5	$0.08	$4.29
18	31.8	$0.05	$1.64
19	19.7	$0.03	$0.63
20	12.2	$0.02	$0.24
21	7.5	$0.01	$0.09
22	4.6	$0.01	$0.03
23	2.9	$0.00	$0.01
24	1.8	$0.00	$0.01
25	1.1	$0.00	$0.00
26	0.7	$0.00	$0.00
27	0.4	$0.00	$0.00
28	0.3	$0.00	$0.00
29	0.2	$0.00	$0.00
30	0.1	$0.00	$0.00
31	0.1	$0.00	$0.00

a trading horizon of 31 trades is illustrated, by trade 23, prices have corrected below the 1-cent precision that is displayed. The total profits of all informed traders are $11,634.

Table A.2 shows the trading sequence when the insider does not trade, simulating a prohibition of insider trading. Informed trading begins at trade 15 much more aggressively, with a trade size more than four times that of the insider's first trades. Price corrects at trade 29. The total informed profits are $9,949 with the prohibition. As we saw earlier, without the prohibition, informed profits are more than 21% greater.

TABLE A.2 *Trading Sequence with No Insider Trading*

Trade	Size	Price diff.	Profit
15	1909.8	\$3.09	\$5,901.70
16	1180.3	\$1.91	\$2,254.25
17	729.5	\$1.18	\$861.04
18	450.9	\$0.73	\$328.89
19	278.6	\$0.45	\$125.62
20	172.2	\$0.28	\$47.98
21	106.4	\$0.17	\$18.33
22	65.8	\$0.11	\$7.00
23	40.7	\$0.07	\$2.67
24	25.1	\$0.04	\$1.02
25	15.5	\$0.03	\$0.39
26	9.6	\$0.02	\$0.15
27	6.0	\$0.01	\$0.06
28	3.7	\$0.01	\$0.02
29	2.3	\$0.00	\$0.01
30	1.5	\$0.00	\$0.00
31	1.0	\$0.00	\$0.00

While the primary point of the example is to illustrate the effect of the prohibition on profits, two additional points are worth noting. First, the trading horizon of the example – 31 trades – is long enough to allow complete correction of price by trading alone. This removes the concern that the end of trading drives the consequences of the model. Second, notice the moment when price corrects (for the purpose of the example, when price reaches within 1 cent of value). This happens at trade 23 with insider trading and at trade 29 when insider trading is prohibited. Price correction differs by only six trades, even though trading begins 15 trades later when insider trading is prohibited. The strategic trading of the insider preserves profits for the insider without correcting prices nearly as fast as competitive informed trading.

B. THE OPTIMAL TRADING STRATEGY

This section derives the optimal trading sequence and the general pattern of optimal trades. The optimal size of the ith trade when the number of possible trades is j follows the pattern

$$s_{i,j} = \frac{p_{i-1} - v}{\lambda} z_{i,j}$$

where

$$z_{i,j} = 1 - \frac{1}{2 + \sum_{n=i+1}^{j} \left[2q_n z_{n,j}(z_{n,j} - 1) \prod_{m=i+1}^{n-1} (z_{m,j} - 1)^2 \right]}$$

The proof is recursive, starting from the last trade. The ideal trade at the penultimate trade requires calculation of the optimal final trade. Assume that the informed trader knows that price correction will take five trades, at most, that is, $j = 5$. The fifth trade will occur based on the price that the fourth trade establishes p_4. Substitute $(p_i - v)$ with d_i. From the market maker's price schedule $p_i = p_{i-1} + \lambda s_i$, we can restate price as price differences from true value v, $v - p_i = (v - p_{i-1}) - \lambda s_i$. Substitute the difference of price from value d_i to simplify the price schedule to $d_i = d_{i-1} - \lambda s_i$.

From note 8 in Chapter 18, we know that the optimal last trade is

$$s = \frac{v - p_0}{2\lambda}$$

According to the above statement of the answer pattern, that should be equivalent to

$$s_5 = \frac{d_4}{\lambda} z_{5,5}$$

which matches the pattern because $z_{5,5} = 1 - ½ = ½$.

The ideal penultimate trade, s_4, following the same method explained in notes 8 et seq. in Chapter 18 and calling the probability of trading in the last trade q_5, is derived from the profits made in the penultimate trade, g_4, in view of the probability of also making the last trade, q_5. Thus the expected profits in the penultimate trade, g_4, are a sum, the immediate profits $d_4 s_4$ plus the expected profits from the final trade adjusted by the probability of making that trade $q_5 d_5 s_5$:

$$g_4 = d_4 s_4 + q_5 d_5 s_5$$

which, after substituting d_5 and s_5 and then d_4 becomes

$$g_4 = (d_3 - \lambda s_4)s_4 + \frac{q_5[d_3 - \lambda s_4 + (\lambda s_4 - d_3)/2](d_3 - \lambda s_4)}{2\lambda}$$

which, simplifies to

$$g_4 = \frac{(d_3 - \lambda s_4)[d_3 q_5 - (q_5 - 4)\lambda s_4]}{4\lambda}$$

The derivative of profits with respect to price simplifies to

$$\partial_{s_4} g_4 = \frac{(q_5 - 4)\lambda s_4 - (q_5 - 2)d_3}{2}$$

Equating to zero and solving for s_4 gives

$$s_4 = \frac{d_3(q_5 - 2)}{\lambda(q_5 - 4)}$$

which again matches the pattern because

$$z_{4,5} = 1 - \frac{1}{2 + 2q_5 z_5(z_5 - 1)} = \frac{q_5 - 2}{q_5 - 4}$$

Backing up to trade 3, the profits include those from the next two trades, adjusted by their probabilities, q_i:

$$g_3 = d_3 s_3 + q_4 d_4 s_4 + q_5 d_5 s_5$$

which, after the substitutions, simplifies to

$$g_3 = -\frac{(\lambda s_3 - d_2)\{d_2[q_5 - 2q_4(q_5 - 2)] + [q_5^2 - 9q_5 + 2q_4(q_5 - 2) + 16]\lambda s_3\}}{\lambda(q_5 - 4)^2}$$

The derivative of profits with respect to price simplifies to

$$\partial_{s_3} g_3 = \frac{(q_5 - 2)(4q_4 + q_5 - 8)d_2 - 2[q_5^2 - 9q_5 + 2q_4(q_5 - 2) + 16]\lambda s_3}{(q_5 - 4)^2}$$

Equating to zero and solving for s_3 gives

$$s_3 = \frac{d_2(q_5 - 2)(4q_5 + q_5 - 8)}{\lambda 2[q_5^2 - 9q_5 + 2q_4(q_5 - 2) + 16]}$$

which again matches the pattern because

$$\begin{aligned} z_{3,5} &= 1 - \frac{1}{2 + 2q_4 z_{4,5}(z_{4,5} - 1) + 2q_5 z_{5,5}(z_{5,5} - 1)(z_{4,5} - 1)^2} \\ &= \frac{(q_5 - 2)(4q_5 + q_5 - 8)}{2[q_5^2 - 9q_5 + 2q_4(q_5 - 2) + 16]} \end{aligned}$$

Backing up to trade 2, the profits include four trades, the current one and the next three, the latter weighed by their probabilities q_i:

$$g_2 = d_2 s_2 + q_3 d_3 s_3 + q_4 d_4 s_4 + q_5 d_5 s_5$$

which after the substitutions simplifies to

$$g_2 = \frac{(d_1 - \lambda s_2)[d_1(q_5 - 4)^2 A + \lambda s_2(B - C + D)]}{4\lambda[q_5^2 - 9q_5 + 2q_4(q_5 - 2) + 16]^2}$$

where

$$A = [q_3(4q_4 + q_5 - 8) - 2q_4](q_5 - 2) + q_5$$

$$B = 4q_5^4 - 73q_5^3 + 460q_5^2 - 1168q_5 + 16q_4^2(q_5 - 2)^2$$

$$C = q_3(q_5 - 4)^2(q_5 - 2)(4q_4 + q_5 - 8)$$

$$D = 2q_4(q_5 - 2)(144 - 80q_5 + 9q_5^2) + 1028$$

The derivative of profits with respect to trade size is

$$\partial_{s_2} g_2 = \frac{\lambda s_2(-B + C - D) - d_1 EF}{2[q_5^2 - 9q_5 + 2q_4(q_5 - 2) + 16]^2}$$

where B, C, and D are as above, and

$$E = (q_5 - 2)(4q_4 + q_5 - 8)$$

and

$$F = q_3(q_5 - 4)^2 - 2q_5^2 + 2q_4(q_5 - 2) + 17q_5 - 32$$

Equating to zero and solving for trade size gives

$$s_2 = \frac{d_1 EF}{\lambda(-B + C - D)}$$

which again matches the pattern because

$$z_{2,5} = \frac{EF}{-B + C - D}$$

The first trade also matches the pattern but is so lengthy that the demonstration here would be excessive.[1]

[1] My website, www.nicholasgeorgakopoulos.org, has a Mathematica file that makes this comparison and shows this example and that of the main text.

Authorities and Bibliography

STATUTES

RULES

SEC Rule 175, 17 CFR 230.175 89
SEC Rule 301, 17 CFR § 242.301 (2009) 12

CASES

Abel v. Potomac Ins. Co., 858 F.2d 1104 (5th Cir. 1988) 99
Argent Classic Convertible Arbitrage Fund L.P. v. Rite Aid Corp., 315 F.Supp.2d 666 (E.D. Pa. 2004) 105
Backman v. Polaroid, Inc., 910 F.2d 10 (1st Cir. en banc 1990) 67
Basic Inc. v. Levinson, 485 US 224 (1987) 99
Blackie v. Barrack, 524 F.2d 891 (9th Cir. 1975), cert. denied, 429 US 816 (1976) 99
Cady, Roberts & Co., 40 SEC 907 (1961) 115
Canfield v. Rapp & Son, Inc., 654 F.2d 459 (7th Cir. 1981) 44
Central Bank of Denver, N.A. v. First Interstate Bank of Denver, N.A., 511 US 164, 114 S.Ct. 1439 (1994) 166
Chandler v. Kew, Inc., 691 F.2d 443 (10th Cir. 1977) 44
Chiarella v. United States, 445 US 222 (1980) 122
Christy v. Cambron, 710 F.2d 669 (10th Cir. 1983) 44
Committee on Children's Television, Inc. v. General Foods Corp., 673 P.2d 660 (Cal. 1983) 102
CTS Corp. v. Dynamics Corp. of America, 481 US 69 (1987) 148
Dirks v. Securities and Exch. Comm'n, 463 US 646 (1983) 197.1, ... 94
Edgar v. MITE Corp., 457 US 624 (1982) 148
Ernst & Ernst v. Hochfelder, 425 US 185 (1976) 166
Finkel v. Docutel/Olivetti Corp., 817 F.2d 356 (5th Cir. 1987) 99
Fisk v. Superannuities, Inc., 927 F.Supp 718 (S.D.N.Y. 1996) 52
Frederiksen v. Poloway, 637 F.2d 1147 (7th Cir.), cert. denied, 451 US 1017, 101 S.Ct. 3006, 69 L.Ed.2d 389 (1981) 44
Freeman v. Laventhol & Horwath, 915 F.2d 193 (6th Cir. 1990) 87
Gartenberg v. Merrill Lynch Asset Mgmt., Inc., 694 F.2d 923 (2d Cir. 1982) 174
Gianukos v. Loeb Rhoades & Co., 822 F.2d 648 (7th Cir. 1987) 107
Gordon v. Sonar Capital Management LLC, 962 F.Supp.2d 525 (S.D.N.Y., 2013) 105
Gould v. Ruefenacht, 471 US 701 (1985) 22
Gustafson v. Alloyd Co., Inc., 513 US 561 (1995) 43
Hanon v. Dataproducts Corp., 976 F.2d 497 (9th Cir. 1992) 104
Herman & MacLean v. Huddleston, 459 US 375 (1983) 80
Huddleston v. Herman & MacLean, 640 F.2d 534 (5th Cir. 1981) 80
In re Apple Computer Sec. Litig., 886 F.2d 1109 (9th Cir. 1989), cert. denied sub nom. *Schneider v. Apple Computer, Inc.*, 496 US 943 (1990) 87
In re CMS Energy Sec. Litig., 236 FRD 338 (E.D. Mich. 2006) 106
In re Convergent Technologies Sec. Litig., 948 F.2d 507 (9th Cir. 1991) 104
In re Donald J. Trump Casino Sec. Litig., 7 F.3d 357 (3d Cir. 1993), cert. denied sub nom. *Gollomp v. Trump*, 114 S.Ct. 1219 (1994) 87
In re Initial Public Offerings Securities Litigation, 471 F.3rd 24 (2nd Cir. 2006) 104
In re Nat'l Century Fin. Enters., Inc., 504 F.Supp. 2d 287 (S.D. Ohio 2007) 52
International Bhd. of Teamsters, Chauffeurs, Warehousemen & Helpers of Am. v. Daniel, 439 US 551 (1979) 22
King v. Winkler, 673 F.2d 342 (11th Cir. 1982) 44
Landreth Timber Co. v. Landreth, 471 US 681 (1985) 22

BOOKS

Baumol, William J., & Alan S. Blinder, ECONOMICS: PRINCIPLES AND POLICY (12th ed. 2012) 88
Berle, Adolf, & Gardiner Means, THE MODERN CORPORATION & PRIVATE PROPERTY (New York, Harcourt, Brace & World, 1932) 64
Bernanke, Ben S., ESSAYS ON THE GREAT DEPRESSION (2004) 160
Bernanke, Ben S., THE FEDERAL RESERVE AND THE FINANCIAL CRISIS (Princeton University Press, 2013) 149
Blinder, Alan, AFTER THE MUSIC STOPPED: THE FINANCIAL CRISIS, THE RESPONSE, AND THE WORK AHEAD (2013) 149
Brandeis, Louis D., OTHER PEOPLE'S MONEY AND HOW BANKERS' USE IT (1914) ... 63
Brealey, Richard, & Stewart Myers, PRINCIPLES OF CORPORATE FINANCE (2nd ed. 1984) 35
Bromberg, Alan R., & Lewis D. Lowenfels, BROMBERG & LOWENFELS ON SECURITIES FRAUD AND COMMODITIES FRAUD 80
Clark, Robert C., CORPORATE LAW (1986) 97
CORBIN ON CONTRACTS 21
Easterbrook, Frank H., & Daniel R. Fischel, THE ECONOMIC STRUCTURE OF CORPORATE LAW (1991) 64
Eichengreen, Barry, HALL OF MIRRORS: THE GREAT DEPRESSION, THE GREAT RECESSION, AND THE USES-AND MISUSES-OF HISTORY (Oxford University Press, 2015) 154
FARNSWORTH ON CONTRACTS 22
Friedman, Jeffrey, ed., WHAT CAUSED THE FINANCIAL CRISIS (2011) 150
Galbraith, John Kenneth, THE GREAT CRASH OF 1929 (1997) 69
Georgakopoulos, Nicholas L., PRINCIPLES AND METHODS OF LAW AND ECONOMICS: BASIC TOOLS FOR NORMATIVE REASONING (2005) 14
Gerding, Erik F., LAW, BUBBLES, AND FINANCIAL REGULATION (London, Routledge, 2011) 68
Hazen, Thomas L., LAW OF SECURITIES REGULATION (6th ed. 2009) 54
Hirsch, Werner Z., LAW AND ECONOMICS: AN INTRODUCTORY ANALYSIS (1988) 64
Hull, John, OPTIONS, FUTURES, AND OTHER DERIVATIVE SECURITIES (7th ed. 2009) 71
Jugulum, Rajesh, & Philip Samuel, DESIGN FOR LEAN SIX SIGMA: A HOLISTIC APPROACH TO DESIGN AND INNOVATION (2008) 33
Keeton, W. Page, et al., PROSSER & KEETON ON THE LAW OF TORTS (5th ed. 1984) 97
Kindleberger, Charles P., & Robert Z. Aliber, MANIAS, PANICS AND CRASHES: A HISTORY OF FINANCIAL CRISES (6th ed., London, Palgrave Macmillan, 2011) 152
Landes, William, & Richard Posner, THE ECONOMIC STRUCTURE OF TORT LAW (1987) 96
Lewis, Michael, THE BIG SHORT: INSIDE THE DOOMSDAY MACHINE (New York, W.W. Norton, 2010) 150
Lorie, James H., et al., THE STOCK MARKET: THEORIES AND EVIDENCE (2nd ed. 1985) 98
Loss, Louis, FUNDAMENTALS OF SECURITIES REGULATION (2nd ed. 1988) 80
Mackay, Charles, EXTRAORDINARY POPULAR DELUSIONS AND THE MADNESS OF CROWDS (1841) 152
Mankiw, N. Gregory, MACROECONOMICS AND THE FINANCIAL SYSTEM (2011) 160
Manne, Henry B., INSIDER TRADING AND THE STOCK MARKET (1966) 116
Markham, Jerry W., A FINANCIAL HISTORY OF THE UNITED STATES (2002) 8
Moravcsik, Andrew, ed., EUROPE WITHOUT ILLUSIONS: THE PAUL-HENRI SPAAK LECTURES, 1994–1999 (2005) 150
Morgenson, Gretchen, & Joshua Rosner, RECKLESS ENDANGERMENT (2011) 149

Paulson, Henry M., Jr., Five Years Later: On the Brink – The New Prologue: A Look Back Five Years Later on What Happened, Why It Did, and Could It Happen Again? (Hachette Digital, 2013) ... 160
Paulson, Henry M., Jr., On the Brink (2010) ... 149
Pavel, Christine A., Securitization: The Analysis and Development of the Loan-Based/Asset-Backed Securities Markets (Chicago, Probus Publishing, 1989) ... 155
Perkins, Edwin J., Wall Street to Main Street: Charles Merrill and Middle-Class Investors (Cambridge University Press, 1999) ... 3
Pierce, Richard J., Jr., Administrative Law (2nd ed.) (2012) ... 12
Polinsky, A. Mitchell, An Introduction to Law and Economics (2011) ... 64
Posner, Richard A., A Failure of Capitalism: The Crisis of '08 and the Descent into Depression (2009) ... 150
Posner, Richard A., Economic Analysis of Law (8th ed. 2011) ... 64
Posner, Richard A., The Crisis of Capitalist Democracy (Harvard University Press, 2010) ... 150
Pysdek, Thomas, & Paul A. Keller, Six Sigma Handbook (3rd ed. 2009) ... 33
Rajan, Fault Lines (HarperCollins 2012) ... 149
Restatement (Second) of Contracts ... 22
Restatement (Second) of Torts ... 22
Samuelson, Paul A., & William D. Nordhaus, Economics 54 (19th ed. 2010) ... 88
Schumpeter, Joseph, Can Capitalism Survive? 24 (1978) ... 153
Schwartz, Robert A., Equity Markets in Action: The Fundamentals of Liquidity, Market Structure, and Trading (2004) ... 98
Scott, Hal S., Connectedness and Contagion: Protecting The Finacial System From Panics (2016) ... 150
Shavell, Steven, Economic Analysis of Accident Law (2007) ... 96
Shiller, Robert J., Irrational Exuberance (2000) ... 104
Shiller, Robert J., Irrational Exuberance (2nd ed. Broadway Books, 2005) ... 164
Shiller, Robert J., Market Volatility (1989) ... 104
Shiller, Robert J., The Subprime Solution: How Today's Global Financial Crisis Happened, and What to Do about It (Princeton University Press, 2008) ... 154
Sorkin, Andrew Ross, Too Big to Fail: The Inside Story of How Wall Street and Washington Fought to Save the Financial System – And Themselves (2009) ... 149
Standard & Poor's 500 Guide (2012) ... 35
The Squam Lake Report: Fixing the Financial System (Princeton University Press, 2010) ... 150
Wessel, David, In Fed We Trust (2009) ... 149
Williston on Contracts (4th ed. 1990) ... 4

ARTICLES

Admati, Anat R., & Paul Pfleiderer, *A Theory of Intraday Patterns: Volume and Price Variability*, 1 Rev. Fin. Stud. 3 (1988) ... 70
Akerlof, George A., *The Market for "Lemons": Quality Uncertainty and the Market Mechanism*, 84 Q.J. Econ. 488 (1970) ... 63

Alexander, Frank S., *Mortgage Prepayment: The Trial of Common Sense*, 72 CORNELL L. REV. 288 (1987) 155
Allen, Julia Lees, *Note, Derivatives Clearinghouses and Systemic Risk: A Bankruptcy and Dodd-Frank Analysis*, 64 STAN. L. REV. 1079 (2012) 7
Amihud, Yakov, & Haim Mendelson, *Asset Pricing and the Bid-Ask Spread*, 17 J. FIN. ECON. 223 (1986) 67
Andrews, Thomas W., *Termination of Section 36(B) Actions by Mutual Fund Directors: Are the Watchdogs Still the Shareholders' Best Friends?*, 50 FORDHAM L. REV. 720 (1982) 174
Arrow, Kenneth J., *The Theory of Risk Aversion*, reprinted in 3 COLLECTED PAPERS OF KENNETH ARROW 147 (1984) 92
Ausubel, Laurence M., *Insider Trading in a Rational Expectations Economy*, 80 AM. ECON. REV. 1022 (1990) 117
Bainbridge, Stephen M., *Securities Act Section 12(2) after the Gustafson Debacle*, 50 BUS. LAW. 1230 (1995) 50
Baird, Douglas G., & Edward R. Morrison, *Dodd-Frank for Bankruptcy Lawyers*, 19 AM. BANKR. INST. L. REV. 287 (2011) 7
Bancroft, Margaret A., *Responding to Gustafson: Company Registration and a New Negligence Standard*, 9 INSIGHTS, July 1995 50
Barclay, Michael J., Robert Litzenberger, & Jerold B. Warner, *Private Information, Trading Volume, and Stock-Return Variances*, 3 REV. FIN. STUD. 233 (1990) 72
Barnes, Brooks, & Michael Cieply, *Disney Swoops into Action, Buying Marvel for $4 Billion*, N.Y. TIMES, September 1, 2009, at B1 56
Bear, Larry A., & Rita Maldonado-Bear, *The Securities Industry and the Law*, 26 J. BANKING & FINANCE 1867–88 (2002) 10
Bebchuk, Lucian A., & Chaim Fershtman, *Insider Trading and the Managerial Choice among Risky Projects*, 29 J. FIN. & QUANTITATIVE ANALYSIS 1 (1994) 116
Benston, George J., *Required Disclosure and the Stock Market: An Evaluation of the Securities Exchange Act of 1934*, 63 AM. ECON. REV. 132 (1973) 92
Benston, George J., *The Costs and Benefits of Government-Required Disclosure: SEC and FTC Requirements*, in CORPORATIONS AT THE CROSSROADS: GOVERNANCE AND REFORM 37–69 (Debra A. DeMott ed., 1980) 92
Beny, Lisa N., *Do Insider Trading Laws Matter? Some Preliminary Comparative Evidence*, 7 AMER. L & ECON. REV. 144 (2002) 137
Bessrminder, Hendrik, *Issues in Assessing Trade Execution Costs*, 6 J. FIN. MARKETS. 233 (2003) 6
Bhattacharya, Utpal, & Hazem Daouk, *The World Price of Insider Trading*, 57 J. FINANCE 75–108 (2002) 137
Black, Bernard S., *Shareholder Passivity Reexamined*, 89 MICH. L. REV. 520 (1990) 64
Black, Fischer, *An Equilibrium Model of the Crash*, in NBER MACROECONOMICS ANNUAL 1988, at 269 (Stanley Fischer ed., 1988) 68
Bonander, Alexander S., *Note: Fannie Mae, Freddie Mac, and Due-Diligence Failures: Should Comparative Responsibility Be Imposed on a Government-Sponsored Entity's Claims Brought under Sections 11(A) and 12(A)(2) of the Securities Act of 1933?*, 98 IOWA L. REV. 835 (2013) 156
Brodsky, Edward, *Assessing the Impact of Corporate and Securities Litigation*, N.Y. L.J., March 13, 1996 50
Brown, Stephen J., & Jerold B. Warner, *Using Daily Stock Returns: The Case of Event Studies*, 14 J. FIN. ECON. 3 (1986) 100

Brudney, Victor, *Insiders, Outsiders, and Informational Advantages under the Federal Securities Laws*, 93 HARV. L. REV. 322 (1979) 118
Buckles, Brian W., *Liquidity Dynamics in Commercial Real Estate*, 14 J. REAL EST. PORTFOLIO MGMT. 307 (October 2008) 6
Carlton, Dennis W., & Daniel R. Fischel, *The Regulation of Insider Trading*, 35 STAN. L. REV. 857 (1983) 116
Carney, Michael J., *Signalling and Causation in Insider Trading*, 36 CATH. U. L. REV. 863 (1987) 116
Chang, Kun Young, *Multinational Enforcement of U.S. Securities Laws: The Need for the Clear and Restrained Scope of Extraterritorial Subject-Matter Jurisdiction*, 9 FORDHAM J. CORP. & FIN. L. 89 (2003) 54
Coffee, John C., Jr., *The Mandatory/Enabling Balance in Corporate Law: An Essay on the Judicial Role*, 89 COLUM. L. REV. 1618 (1989) 64
Cornell, Bradford, & Erik R. Sirri, *The Reaction of Investors and Stock Prices to Insider Trading*, 47 J. FINANCE 1031 (1992) 137
Cutler, David M., James M. Poterba, & Lawrence H. Summers, *Speculative Dynamics and the Role of Feedback Traders*, 80 AM. ECON. REV. 63 (1990) 68
Davidson, Nestor M., *New Formalism in the Aftermath of the Housing Crisis*, 93 B.U. L. REV. 389 (2013) 168
De Long, J. Bradford, & Andrei Shleifer, *The Bubble of 1929: Evidence from Closed-End Funds* (National Bureau of Economic Research Working Paper No. 3523, 1990) 68
De Long, J. Bradford, Andrei Shleifer, Lawrence H. Summers, & Robert J. Waldmann, *Noise Trader Risk in Financial Markets*, 98 J. POL. ECON. 703 (1990) 68
DeLong, J. Bradford, Andrei Shleifer, Lawrence Summers, & Robert Waldman, *Positive Feedback Investment Strategies and Destabilizing Rational Speculation*, 45 J. FINANCE 379 (1990) 68
Easterbrook, Frank H., *Insider Trading as an Agency Problem*, in PRINCIPALS AND AGENTS: THE STRUCTURE OF BUSINESS 81 (John W. Pratt & Richard J. Zeckhauser eds., 1985) 116
Easterbrook, Frank H., *Insider Trading, Secret Agents, Evidentiary Privileges, and the Production of Information*, 1981 S. CT. REV. 309 116
Eleswarapu, Venkat R., & Chandrasekar Krishnamurti, *Liquidity, Stock Returns and Ownership Structure: An Empirical Study of the BSE*, Federal Reserve Bank of St. Louis, IDEAS database, http://ideas.repec.org/p/wpa/wuwpfi/9507005.html, 1995 72
Fama, Eugene F., & Kenneth R. French, *The Capital Asset Pricing Model: Theory and Evidence*, 18 J. ECON. PERSP. 25–46 (2004) 41
Fama, Eugene F., *Efficient Capital Markets: A Review of Theory and Empirical Work*, 25 J. FINANCE 383 (1970) 98
Fama, Eugene F., *Efficient Capital Markets: II*, 46 J. FINANCE 1575 (1991) 98
Fernandes, Nuno, & Miguel A. Ferreira, *Insider Trading Laws and Stock Price Informativeness*, 22 REV. FINANC. STUD. 1845 (2009) 137
Fischel, Daniel R., & David J. Ross, *Should The Law Prohibit "Manipulation" in Financial Markets?*, 105 HARV. L. REV. 503 (1991) 80
Fischel, Daniel R., *Efficient Capital Markets, the Crash, and the Fraud on the Market Theory*, 74 CORNELL L. REV. 907 (1989) 80
Fischel, Daniel R., *Use of Modern Finance Theory in Securities Fraud Cases Involving Actively Traded Securities*, 38 BUS. LAW. 1 (1982) 109
Fishman, Michael J., & Kathleen M. Hagerty, *Disclosure Decisions by Firms and the Competition for Price Efficiency*, 44 J. FINANCE 633 (1989) 69

Froot, Kenneth A., & Maurice Obstfeld, *Intrinsic Bubbles: The Case of Stock Prices*, 81 AM. ECON. REV. 1189 (1991) 68
Gadinis, Stavros, *From Independence to Politics in Financial Regulation*, 101 CAL. L. REV. 327 (2013) 4
Gemmill, Gordon, & Dylan C. Thomas, *Noise Trading, Costly Arbitrage, and Asset Prices: Evidence from Closed End Funds*, 57 J. FINANCE 2571–94 (2002) 68
Georgakopoulos, Nicholas L., *Meinhard v. Salmon and the Economics of Honor*, 1999 COLUM. BUS. L. REV. 137 148
Georgakopoulos, Nicholas L., *Classical and Cross Insider Trading: Variations on the Theme of Rule 10b-5*, 28 AM. BUS. L.J. 109 (1990) 117
Georgakopoulos, Nicholas L., *Frauds, Markets, and Fraud-on-the-Market: The Tortured Transition of Justifiable Reliance from Common Law Deceit to Securities Fraud*, 49 MIAMI L. REV. 671–730 (1995) 165
Georgakopoulos, Nicholas L., *Insider Trading as a Transaction Cost: A Market Microstructure Justification and Optimization of Insider Trading Regulation*, 26 CONN. L. REV. 1 (1993) 115
Georgakopoulos, Nicholas L., *Why Should Disclosure Rules Subsidize Informed Traders?*, 16 INT. REV. L. & ECON. 417–31 (1996) xiii
Georgakopoulos, Nicholas L., *Lessons from Greco-Multilateralism for Creditors*, 28 CONN. J. INT'L L. 21 (2012) 154
Georgakopoulos, Nicholas L., *PIRG Doldrums: Exit via Overrecapitalization*, 37 EUR. J.L. & ECON. doi 10.1007/s100657-014-9447-y (2014) 154
Georgakopoulos, Nicholas L., *Predictability and Legal Evolution*, 17 INT'L REV. L. & ECON. 475 (1997) 151
Georgakopoulos, Nicholas L., *The Statistics of Legal Infrastructures*, 8 AMER. L. & ECON. REV. 62–78 (2006) 10
Gerding, Erik F., *Laws against Bubbles: An Experimental-Asset-Market Approach to Analyzing Financial Regulation*, 2007 WIS. L. REV. 977 68
Gilson, Ronald J., & Reinier Kraakman, *The Mechanisms of Market Efficiency*, 70 VA. L. REV. 549 (1984) 98
Glosten, Lawrence R., & Paul R. Milgrom, *Bid, Ask and Transaction Prices in a Specialist Market with Heterogeneously Informed Traders*, 14 J. FIN. ECON. 71 (1985) 127
Gordon, Jeffrey N., *The Mandatory Structure of Corporate Law*, 89 COLUM. L. REV. 1549 (1989) 64
Gould, John P., & Robert E. Verrecchia, *The Information Content of Specialist Pricing*, 93 J. POL. ECON. 66 (1985) 127
Greenstone, Michael, Paul Oyer, & Annette Vissing-Jorgensen, *Mandated Disclosure, Stock Returns, and the 1964 Securities Acts Amendments*, 2006 Q. J. ECON. 399 92
Grossman, Sanford J., & Joseph E. Stiglitz, *On the Impossibility of Informationally Efficient Markets*, 70 AM. ECON. REV. 393 (1980) 146
Grossman, Sanford J., *The Information Roles of Warranties and Private Disclosure about Product Quality*, 24 J.L. & ECON. 461 (1981) 65
Guinan, Natasha S., *Nearly A Decade Later: Revisiting Gustafson and the Status of Section 12(A)(2) Liability in the Courts – Creative Judicial Developments and a Proposal for Reform*, 72 FORDHAM L. REV. 1053 (2004) 49
Guttman, Egon, *Federal Regulation of Transfer Agents*, 34 AM. U. L. REV. 281 (1985) ... 90
Haddock, David D., & Jonathan R. Macey, *A Coasian Model of Insider Trading*, 80 NW. U. L. REV. 1449 (1986) 116

Haltiwanger, John, & Michael Waldman. *Rational Expectations and the Limits of Rationality: An Analysis of Heterogeneity*, 75 AM. ECON. REV. 326 (1985) 11

Harris, Lawrence, & Eitan Gurel, *Price and Volume Effects Associated with Changes in the S&P 500 List: New Evidence for the Existence of Price Pressures*, 41 *J.* FINANCE 815 (1986) 108

Haug, Mark, & Mark Hirschey, *The January Effect*, 62 FIN. ANALYSTS *J.* 78, September–October 2006 152

Ivashina, Victoria, & David S. Scharfstein, *Bank Lending during the Financial Crisis of 2008* (July 30, 2009), EFA 2009 Bergen Meetings Paper, available at SSRN: http://ssrn.com/abstract=1297337 (accessed February 15, 2017) 157

Jackson, Howell E., & Mark J. Roe, Public and Private Enforcement of Securities Laws: Resource-Based Evidence, 93 J . FIN. ECON. 207–38 (2009) 20, 151

Jain, Prem C., *The Effect on Stock Price of Inclusion in or Exclusion from the S&P 500*, FIN. ANALYSTS *J.*, January–February 1987 108

Janet E. Kerr, *Ralston Redux: Determining Which Section 3 Offerings Are Public under Section 12(2) after Gustafson*, 50 S.M.U. L. REV. 175 (1996–7) 50

Jarrell, Gregg A., *The Economic Effects of Federal Regulation of the Market for New Security Issues*, 24 *J.*L. & ECON. 613 (1981) 92

Jovanovic, Boyan, *Truthful Disclosure of Information*, 13 BELL *J.* ECON. 36 (1982) 65

Kahan, Marcel, *Securities Laws and the Social Costs of "Inaccurate" Stock Prices*, 41 DUKE L. *J.* 977 (1992) 69

Kandel, Eugene, & Leslie M. Marx, *NASDAQ Market Structure and Trade Patterns*, 45 *J.* FIN. ECON. 61 (1997) 9

Karmel, Roberta S., *The Future of the Securities and Exchange Commission as a Market Regulator*, 78 U. CIN. L. REL. 501 (2009) 163

Kaufman, Michael J., *Mending the Weathered Jurisdictional Fences in the Supreme Court's Securities Fraud Decisions*, 49 S.M.U. L. REV. 159 (1996) 50

Kostant, Peter C., *From Lapdog to Watchdog: Sarbanes-Oxley Section 307 and a New Role for Corporate Lawyers*, 52 N.Y.L. SCH. L. REV. 535 (2007–8) 170

Kostel, Mary E., *Note, A Public Choice Perspective on the Debate over Federal versus State Corporate Law*, 79 VA. L. REV. 2129 (1993) 64

Kyle, Albert S., *Continuous Auctions and Insider Trading*, 53 ECONOMETRICA 1315 (1985) 118

La Porta, Rafael, Florencio Lopez-de-Silanes, & Andrei Shleifer, *What Works in Securities Laws?*, 61 *J.* FINANCE 1–32 (2006) 92

La Porta, Rafael, Florencio Lopez-de-Silanes, Andrei Shleifer, & Robert W. Vishny. *Law and Finance*, 106 *J.* POL. ECON. 1113 (1998) 151

Laffont, Jean-Jaques, & Eric S. Maskin, *The Efficient Market Hypothesis and Insider Trading on the Stock Market*, 98 *J.* POL. ECON. 70 (1990) 134

Lambert, Thomas A., *Overvalued Equity and the Case for an Asymmetric Insider Trading Regime*, 41 WAKE FOREST L. REV. 1045 (2006) 116

Leland, Hayne E., *Insider Trading: Should it be Prohibited?*, 100 *J.* POL. ECON. 859 (1992) 117

Levitin, Adam J., & Tara Twomey, *Mortgage Servicing*, 28 YALE *J.* ON REG. 1 (2011) 2

Lintner, John, *The Valuation of Risk Assets and the Selection of Risky Investments in Stock Portfolios and Capital Budgets*, 47 REV. ECON. & STAT. 13 (1965) 14

Lipson, Jonathan C., *Epic Fail: An Institutional Analysis of Financial Distress*, UNIV. OF WIS. LAW SCH. LEGAL STUDIES RESEARCH PAPER SERIES, Paper No. 1201, 2012, available at ssrn.com/abstract=2117430 149

Lo, Andrew W., *Reading about the Financial Crisis: A 21-Book Review*, 50 J. ECON. LIT. 151 (2012) 150
Macey, Jonathan R., & David D. Haddock, *Shirking at the SEC: The Failure of the National Market System*, 1985 U. ILL. L. REV. 315 72
Macey, Jonathan R., & Geoffrey Miller, *Toward an Interest-Group Theory of Delaware Corporate Law*, 65 TEX. L. REV. 469 (1987) 72
Macey, Jonathan R., & Geoffrey P. Miller, *Good Finance, Bad Economics: An Analysis of the Fraud-on-the-Market Theory*, 42 STAN. L. REV. 1059 (1990) 80
Macey, Jonathan R., & Geoffrey P. Miller, *The Fraud-on-the-Market Theory Revisited*, 77 VA. L. REV. 1001 (1991) 80
Macey, Jonathan R., et al., *Lessons from Economics: Materiality, Reliance, and Extending the Reach of Basic v. Levinson*, 77 VA. L. REV. 1017 (1991) 80
Macey, Jonathan R., *The Myth of "Reregulation": The Interest Group Dynamics of Regulatory Change in the Financial Services Industry*, 45 WASH. & LEE L. REV. 1275 (1988) 72
Macey, Jonathan, *Getting the Word Out about Fraud: A Theoretical Analysis of Whistleblowing and Insider Trading*, 105 MICH. L. REV. 1899 (2007) 116
Magliocca, Gerard N., *The Gold Clause Cases and Constitutional Necessity*, 64 FLA. L. REV. 1243 (2012) 177
Mahoney, Paul G., *Precaution Costs and the Law of Fraud in Impersonal Markets*, 78 VA. L. REV. 623 (1992) 80
Mandelbrot, Benoit, *Forecasts of Future Prices, Unbiased Markets, and "Martingale" Models*, 39 J. BUSINESS 242 (1966) 98
Manne, Henry G., *Insider Trading: Hayek, Virtual Markets, and the Dog that Did Not Bark*, 31 IOWA J. CORP. L. 167 (2005) 116
Manove, Michael, *The Harm from Insider Trading and Informed Speculation*, 104 Q.J. ECON. 823 (1989) 117
Markowitz, Harry, *Portfolio Selection*, J. FINANCE. 77 (1952) 14
McChesney, Fred S., *Behavioral Economics: Old Wine in Irrelevant New Bottles?*, 21 SUP. CT. ECON. REV. 43 (2013) 69
McCoy, Patricia A., Andrey D. Pavlov, & Susan M. Wachter, *Systemic Risk through Securitization: The Result of Deregulation and Regulatory Failure*, 41 CONN. L. REV. 1327 (2009) 172
Mehra, Rajnish, & Edward C. Prescott, *The Equity Premium in Retrospect*, in 1 HANDBOOK OF THE ECONOMICS OF FINANCE 889 (George M. Constantinides et al. eds., 2003) 118
Mehra, Rajnish, & Edward C. Prescott, *The Equity Premium: A Puzzle*, 15 J. MONETARY ECON. 145 (1985) 118
Meulbroek, Lisa K., *An Empirical Analysis of Illegal Insider Trading*, 47 J. FINANCE 1661 (1992) 137
Meyerstein, Ariel, *Transnational Private Financial Regulation and Sustainable Development: An Empirical Assessment of the Implementation of the Equator Principles*, 45 N.Y.U. J. INT'L L. & POL. 487 (2013) 156
Milgrom, Paul R., *Good News and Bad News: Representation Theorems and Applications*, 12 BELL J. ECON. 380 (1981) 65
Mirer, Jeanne, & Marjorie Cohn, *Lost in the Debt Ceiling Debate: The Legal Duty to Create Jobs*, 68 NAT'L LAW. GUILD REV. 116 (2011) 15
Mirman, Leonard J., & Larry Samuelson, *Information and Equilibrium with Inside Traders*, 99 ECON. J. 152 (Suppl. 1989) 134
Nichols, Shane, *A Balanced Budget Amendment Fit for the Constitution: The Elimination of Partisanship and Substantive Provisions*, 46 J. MARSHALL L. REV. 583 (2013) 176

Pan, Eric J., *Understanding Financial Regulation*, 2012 UTAH L. REV. 1897 4
Posner, Richard A., *Law and the Theory of Finance: Some Intersections*, 54 GEO. WASH. L. REV. 159 (1986) 80
Prentice, Robert A., & Dain C. Donelson, *Insider Trading as a Signaling Device*, 47 AM. BUS. L.J. 1 (2010) 116
Reddy, Sudeep, *Currents: Fed Faces Grilling on Consumer-Protection Lapses*, WALL ST. J., December 2, 2009, at A22 172
Reinganum, Marc R., *The Anomalous Stock Market Behavior of Small Firms in January*, 12 J. FIN. ECON. 89 (1983) 152
Ribstein, Larry E., *Bubble Laws*, 40 HOUS. L. REV. 77–97 (2003) 178
Ricks, Morgan, *A Regulatory Design for Monetary Stability*, 65 VAND. L. REV. 1289–1358 (2012) 149
Robert J. Shiller, *Speculative Prices and Popular Models*, 4 J. ECON. PERSP. 55 (1990) 105
Robertson, David W., *Negligence Liability for Crimes and Intentional Torts Committed by Others*, 67 TUL. L. REV. 135 (1992) 96
Roiter, Eric D., *Should Money Market Funds Be Designated as "SIFIs"?*, 31 REV. BANKING & FIN. L. 749 (2012) 169
Roll, Richard, *Vas ist das? The Turn of the Year Effect and the Return Premia of Small Firms*, 9 J. PORTFOLIO MGMT. 18 (1983) 152
Romano, Roberta, *Answering the Wrong Question: The Tenuous Case for Mandatory Corporate Laws*, 89 COLUM. L. REV. 1599 (1989) 64
Romano, Roberta, *The Sarbanes-Oxley Act and the Making of Quack Corporate Governance*, 114 YALE L.J. 1521–1604 (2005) 170
Rosenberg, David, *Galactic Stupidity and the Business Judgment Rule*, 32 J. CORP. L. 301 (2006–7) 28
Rosenberg, David, *Supplying the Adverb: The Future of Corporate Risk-Taking and the Business Judgment Rule*, 6 BERKELEY BUS. L.J. 216 (2009) 28
Ross, Stephen A., *Disclosure Regulation in Financial Markets: Implications of Modern Finance Theory and Signaling Theory*, in ISSUES IN FINANCIAL REGULATION 177 (Franklin R. Edwards ed., 1979) 65
Rozeff, Michael S., & William R. Kinney, *Capital Market Seasonality: The Case of Stock Returns*, 3 J. FIN. ECON. 379 (1976) 152
Sale, Hillary A., *Disappearing without a Trace: Sections 11 and 12(2) of the '33 Act*, 75 WASH. L. REV. 429 (2000) 57
Samuelson, P. *Proof that Properly Anticipated Prices Fluctuate Randomly*, 6 INDUS. MGMT. REV. 41 (1965) 98
Schmidt, Lawrence D. W., Allan G. Timmermann, & Russ Wermers, *Runs on Money Market Mutual Funds*, January 2013, available at http://papers.ssrn.com/sol3/papers.cfm?abstract_id=1784445 157
Schmitt, Rick, *Prophet and Loss – Brooksley Born Warned that Unchecked Trading in the Credit Market Could Lead to Disaster*, STANFORD NEWS, March 2009 156
Schotland, Roy A., *Unsafe at Any Price: A Reply to Manne, Insider Trading and the Stock Market*, 53 VA. L. REV. 1425 (1967) 118
Scott, Kenneth E., *Insider Trading: Rule 10b-5, Disclosure and Corporate Privacy*, 9 J. LEGAL STUD. 801 (1980) 116
Seligman, Joel, *The Case for Federal Minimum Corporate Law Standards*, 49 Md. L. Rev. 947 (1990) 64
Seligman, Joel, *The Historical Need for a Mandatory Corporate Disclosure System*, 9 J. CORP. L. 1 (1983) 63

Sethi, Jasmin, *Another Role for Securities Regulation: Expanding Investor Opportunity*, 16 FORDHAM J. CORP. & FIN. L. 783 (2011) 12

Seyhun, H. Nejat, *Insiders' Profits, Costs of Trading, and Market Efficiency*, 16 J. FIN. ECON. 189 (1986) 128

Sharpe, William F., *Capital Asset Prices: A Theory of Market Equilibrium under Conditions of Risk*, 19 J. FINANCE 425 (1964) 14

Shavell, Steven, *An Analysis of Causation and the Scope of Liability in the Law of Torts*, 9 J. LEGAL STUD. 463 (1980) 96

Shavell, Steven, *Risk Aversion and the Optimality of Attenuated Legal Change*, American Law and Economics Association Annual Meeting (May 17, 2013) 151

Shiller, Robert J., *Market Volatility and Investor Behavior*, 80 AM. ECON. REV. 58 (1990) 105

Shleifer, Andrei, & Robert W. Vishny, *Equilibrium Short Horizons of Investors and Firms*, 80 AM. ECON. REV. 148 (1990) 62

Shleifer, Andrei, & Robert W. Vishny, *The Limits of Arbitrage*, 52 J. FINANCE 35 (1997) 68

Simkovic, Michael, *Competition and Crisis in Mortgage Securitization*, 88 IND. L.J. 213 (2013) 156

Simon, Carol J., *The Effect of the 1933 Securities Act on Investor Information and the Performance of New Issues*, 79 AM. ECON. REV. 295 (1989) 92

Skeel, David A., Jr., *Institutional Choice in an Economic Crisis*, 2013 WIS. L. REV. 629–47 149

Skeel, David A., Jr., *Making Sense of the New Financial Deal*, 5 LIBERTY U. L. REV. 181 (2011) 156

Smith, Ethan, & Lauren A.E. Schuker, *Disney Nabs Marvel Heroes – Company Bulks Up with $4 Billion Deal But Must Contend with Tangle of Licenses*, WALL ST. J., September 1, 2009, at A1 56

Stigler, *Public Regulation of the Securities Markets*, 37 J. BUSINESS 117 (1964) 92

Stout, Lynn A., *The Unimportance of Being Efficient: An Economic Analysis of Stock Market Pricing and Securities Regulation*, 87 MICH. L. REV. 613 (1988) 70

Sylla, Richard, *Political Economy of Supplying Money to a Growing Economy: Monetary Regimes and the Search for an Anchor to Stabilize the Value of Money*, 11 THEORETICAL INQUIRIES IN LAW 1 (2010) 177

Teoh, Siew Hong, & Chuan Yang Hwang, *Nondisclosure and Adverse Disclosure as Signals of Firm Value*, 4 REV. OF FIN. STUDIES 283 (1991) 66

Thaler, Richard, *Anomalies: The January Effect*, 1 J. ECON. PERSP. 197 (Summer 1987) 152

Tobin, James, *On the Efficiency of the Financial System*, LLOYDS BANK REV. 1 (July 1984) 67

Verrecchia, Robert E., *Discretionary Disclosure*, 5 J. ACCT. & ECON. 179 (1983) 65

Wang, William K.S., *Trading on Material Nonpublic Information on Impersonal Stock Markets: Who Is Harmed and Who Can Sue Whom under SEC Rule 10b-5?*, 54 S. CAL. L. REV. 1217 (1981) 119

Wilmarth, Arthur E., Jr., *The Dodd-Frank Act's Expansion of State Authority to Protect Consumers of Financial Services*, 36 J. CORP. L. 893 (2011) 172

Wolfson, Nicholas, *A Critique of Corporate Law*, 34 U. MIAMI L. REV. 959 (1980) 72

Young, Daniel Taylor, *Note: How Do You Measure a Constitutional Moment? Using Algorithmic Topic Modeling to Evaluate Bruce Ackerman's Theory of Constitutional Change*, 122 YALE L.J. 1990 (2013) 176

Zhang, Guochang, *Regulated Managerial Insider Trading as a Mechanism to Facilitate Shareholder Control*, 28 J. BUS. FIN. & ACCT. 35, 36 (2001) 116

WEB SOURCES

A Brief History of the Mutual Fund, INVESTOPEDIA, available at www.investopedia.com/articles/mutualfund/05/mfhistory.asp (accessed February 15, 2017) 3

Average Bid/Ask Spread, Vanguard, available at https://advisors.vanguard.com/VGApp/iip/site/advisor/investments/bidaskspread (accessed February 15, 2017) 6

Beattie, Andrew, *The Birth of Stock Exchanges*, INVESTOPEDIA, available at www.investopedia.com/articles/07/stock-exchange-history.asp (accessed February 15, 2017) 8

Boaz, David, *Time to Think about the Gold Standard?*, CATO AT LIBERTY, available at www.cato.org/blog/time-think-about-gold-standard (accessed February 15, 2017) 161

Brodsky, William, *The Multi-Purpose JD: How My Law Degree Helped Me in My Career in My Business*, University of Chicago Podcast, available at www.law.uchicago.edu/audio/by/title/william_brodsky_the_multi-purpose_jd_how_my_law_degree_helped_me_in_my_career_in_business 170

Buffett, Warren E., Chairman of the Board, Berkshire Hathaway, Inc., *Letter to Shareholders of Berkshire Hathaway Inc.* 15 (February 21, 2003), available at www.berkshirehathaway.com/letters/2002pdf.pdf 166

Bureau of Labor Statistics, *Unemployment Data*, available at www.bls.gov/webapps/legacy/cpsatab1.htm 161

Complaint, SEC v. Madoff, No. 08-10791, (S.D.N.Y. December 11, 2008), available at www.sec.gov/litigation/complaints/2008/comp-madoff121108.pdf (accessed February 15, 2014) 11

Davidoff, Steven M., *Reading the Fine Print in Abacus and Other Soured Deals*, N.Y. TIMES DEALB%K, November 2, 2012, available at http://dealbook.nytimes.com/2012/11/02/reading-the-fine-print-in-abacus-and-other-soured-deals/ (accessed February 15, 2017) 55

Defiant House Rejects Huge Bailout; Stocks Plunge; Next Step Is Uncertain, N.Y. TIMES, p. A1, September 29, 2008, available at www.nytimes.com/2008/9/30/business/30cong.html (accessed February 15, 2017) 160

Excerpts from the President's News Conference at the White House, N.Y. TIMES, December 14, 1996, available at www.nytimes.com/1996/12/14/us/excerpts-from-the-president-s-news-conference-at-the-white-house.html?pagewanted=all (accessed February 15, 2017) 173

Georgakopoulos, Nicholas L., *The Capital Asset Pricing Model*, available at www.cali.org/lesson/756 13

Georgakopoulos, Nicholas L., *Valuation: Basic Skills*, available at www.cali.org/lesson/755 13

Global Comparison of Annualized Value of Trading, NYSE FACTBOOK HISTORICAL STATISTICS, available at http://www.nyxdata.com/nysedata/asp/factbook/viewer_edition.asp?mode=table&key=2215&category=14 (archived at https://perma.cc/J92R-EWTJ; accessed February 15, 2017) 8

Greenspan, Alan, *Remarks at the Annual Dinner and Francis Boyer Lecture of the American Enterprise Institute for Public Policy Research: The Challenge of Central Banking in a Democratic Society* (December 5, 1996), available at www.federalreserve.gov/boarddocs/speeches/1996/19961205.htm (accessed February 15, 2017) 166

Guy, Madison, *Bohr Leads Berra, But Yogi Closing the Gap*, LETTER FROM HERE, December 2, 2006, available at www.peterpatau.com/2006/12/bohr-leads-berra-but-yogi-closing-gap.html 150

Hubbard, R. Glenn, & Tim Kane, *Republicans and Democrats Both Miscalculated*, N.Y. TIMES, August 11, 2013, available at www.nytimes.com/2013/08/12/opinion/republicans-and-democrats-both-miscalculated.html (accessed February 15, 2017) 176

Inspect that Used Car Before Buying! (2009), available at www.edmunds.com/car-buying/inspect-that-used-car-before-buying.html (accessed February 15, 2017) 93

Krugman, Paul, *The Gold Bug Variations*, Slate (November 23, 1996), available at www.slate.com/articles/business/the_dismal_science/1996/11/the_gold_bug_variations.html (accessed February 15, 2017) 161

Kuepper, Justin, *Day Trading Strategies for Beginners*, Investopedia (June 25, 2011), available at www.investopedia.com/articles/trading/06/daytradingretail.asp 7

Lohr, Steve, *Buffett's Bet on G.E.: Almost as Good as a Bailout*, N.Y. Times, October 1, 2008, available at www.nytimes.com/2008/10/02/business/02electric.html (accessed February 15, 2017) 158

National Bureau of Economic Research, *US Business Cycle Expansions and Contractions*, available at www.nber.org/cycles/cyclesmain.html 168

New York Stock Exchange, *Daily NYSE Group Volume in NYSE Listed*, available at www.nyxdata.com (archived at https://perma.cc/PYR3-DENJ) (accessed February 15, 2017) ... 7

Nobel Prize in Economics 1990 Press Release (October 16, 1990), available at www.nobelprize.org/nobel_prizes/economics/laureates/1990/press.html (accessed February 15, 2017) 29

Petruno, Tom, *Buffett's Berkshire Hathaway Invests $5 Billion in Goldman Sachs*, *Baltimore Sun*, September 24, 2008, available at http://articles.baltimoresun.com/2008-09-24/news/0809230187_1_buffett-billion-in-goldman-goldman-sachs (accessed February 15, 2017) 158

Protess, Ben, & Lauren D'Avolio, *Jury Rules for Mark Cuban in Setback for S.E.C.*, N.Y. Times Dealb%k, October 16, 2013, available at http://dealbook.nytimes.com/2013/10/16/mark-cuban-cleared-of-insider-trading/ (accessed February 15, 2017) 123

S&P Indices: S&P 500, available at www.us.spindices.com/indices/equity/sp-500 (accessed February 15, 2017) 35

Sahr, Robert C., *Inflation Conversion Factors from Year 1774 to Estimated 2026* (2016), available at http://liberalarts.oregonstate.edu/sites/liberalarts.oregonstate.edu/files/polisci/faculty-research/sahr/inflation-conversion/pdf/infcf17742016.pdf (archived at https://perma.cc/7A3F-42TP) 161

Shiller, Robert J., *PE10 Data*, available at www.econ.yale.edu/~shiller/data.htm (accessed February 15, 2017) 164

Stevenson, Richard W., *Republican Senate Chief Questions the Fed*, N.Y. Times, December 8, 1996, available at www.nytimes.com/1996/12/09/business/republican-senate-chief-questions-the-fed.html (accessed February 15, 2017) 173

Index

Printed in the United States
By Bookmasters